Sexual Offences

To my wife, Paula
and to our sons, Ethan and Amos

Sexual Offences

Jeffrey Lamb

Barrister, Westgate Chambers, Lewes

LexisNexis™ UK

Members of the LexisNexis Group worldwide

United Kingdom	LexisNexis UK, a Division of Reed Elsevier (UK) Ltd, Halsbury House, 35 Chancery Lane, LONDON, WC2A 1EL, and 4 Hill Street, EDINBURGH EH2 3JZ
Argentina	LexisNexis Argentina, BUENOS AIRES
Australia	LexisNexis Butterworths, CHATSWOOD, New South Wales
Austria	LexisNexis Verlag ARD Orac GmbH & Co KG, VIENNA
Canada	LexisNexis Butterworths, MARKHAM, Ontario
Chile	LexisNexis Chile Ltda, SANTIAGO DE CHILE
Czech Republic	Nakladatelství Orac sro, PRAGUE
France	Editions du Juris-Classeur SA, PARIS
Germany	LexisNexis Deutschland GmbH, FRANKFURT, MUNSTER
Hong Kong	LexisNexis Butterworths, HONG KONG
Hungary	HVG-Orac, BUDAPEST
India	LexisNexis Butterworths, NEW DELHI
Ireland	Butterworths (Ireland) Ltd, DUBLIN
Italy	Giuffrè Editore, MILAN
Malaysia	Malayan Law Journal Sdn Bhd, KUALA LUMPUR
New Zealand	LexisNexis Butterworths, WELLINGTON
Poland	Wydawnictwo Prawnicze LexisNexis, WARSAW
Singapore	LexisNexis Butterworths, SINGAPORE
South Africa	LexisNexis Butterworths, DURBAN
Switzerland	Stämpfli Verlag AG, BERNE
USA	LexisNexis, DAYTON, Ohio

A CIP Catalogue record for this book is available from the British Library.

ISBN 0 406 95819 X

Printed and bound in Great Britain by Thomson Litho Ltd, East Kilbride, Scotland

Visit LexisNexis UK at www.lexisnexis.co.uk

Justice cries aloud, but her voice can hardly be heard above the tumult of the passions

(Baron de Montesquieu)

Preface

I first thought about writing a book on sexual offences while preparing for a trial in which my client was charged with raping a 15-year-old boy, and also with indecently assaulting him. He was acquitted of the rape charge and claimed that the sexual activity between them was entirely consensual. It was at a time when the case of *B v DPP* had been heard in the Divisional Court and the House of Lords. However, the case of *R v K.* was regarded as representing the state of the law relating to indecent assault because in that case the Court of Appeal had dismissed the arguments of the House of Lords in *B v DPP*, saying that different issues were being considered. My client was forced to plead guilty to indecent assault because it was said to be the law then that no defence existed of a belief that the complainant was at least 16 years of age. His conviction was later inevitably overturned when the House of Lords corrected the Court of Appeal in *R v K* It was a time when defence counsel were confident that the House had clarified, and improved, the law in the rulings set out in *B v DPP* but where judges relied on *R v K* to rebut such arguments. Fortunately for all concerned, the issue is now crystal clear and such a defence does exist.

My researches brought it home to me that while there were one or two textbooks available, none of them were of sufficient brevity and focus to be of too much help. In addition, there were no such textbooks that had been published in the last five years or so. A great many pages were dedicated to, for example, the law pertaining to the non-existence of marital rape as an offence, which of course was changed by the House of Lords in *R v R*. In a nutshell, they were all woefully out of date. This book is a reaction to that situation. While writing it I have tried to have the criminal practitioner in mind and consider what it is that he or she will want, and perhaps more importantly, need. My aim has been to give enough information about each topic for a practitioner to be confident of the legal issues both for and against their client's position.

While I write this preface noises are coming from the government that they are intent on a package of reforms of sexual offences. As is often the case these seem to be yet another knee-jerk reaction in response to perceived problems that do not necessarily exist. Such proposed reforms have not been addressed in this book for two reasons. First, government proposals do not always mature into reality and secondly, with the minds of our politicians on somewhat more important issues, it may well be quite some time before the proposals do indeed reach fruition, if at all.

The book is separated into two asymmetric sections. The first section comprises an analysis of the substantive crimes that make up the full canon of sexual offences. The second section relates to subsidiary issues relating to evidential matters. Much of the second section relates to the government's intentions, as introduced by the Youth and Criminal Evidence Act 1999, of seeking to ensure that more criminal trials of alleged sexual offences take place. They have done this by, among other things, extending the number of witnesses who will now be competent to give evidence, both sworn and unsworn; by introducing – or in some cases expanding - the concept of 'special measures' to aid witnesses give evidence and by prohibiting the sexual history of complainants being adduced. The final chapter is concerned with the disclosure of information that may be important in a trial situation. While disclosure is always an important issue, it is usually significantly more so in an offence of a sexual nature due to the often major topic of why the allegation is made in the first place.

Whenever an issue of human rights and/or the European Convention raises its head, it is dealt with in the text. However, it should be said that, with regard to substantive offences, most have been on the statute books for so long that any such issues have been dealt with long in the past. With regard to the second section of the book, the issues tend to be, conversely, so new that any arguments against them have yet to be taken to the higher courts.

In writing the book I have discussed a number of the issues addressed with my colleagues in Chambers, and I would like to thank them all for the encouragement and assistance they have extended to me. I would also like to thank all of my clerks, in particular Nicole Whitmore and Jason Britcher, for allowing me time out of court so as to get on with the necessary research. Most of all I would like to thank my wife Paula for taking our boys, Ethan and Amos, out of my immediate grasp and for pressing me to get on with it.

Jeffrey Lamb
Westgate Chambers
Lewes
East Sussex

Contents

CHAPTER TWO

'Unnatural offences' 25

CHAPTER THREE

Offences involving children 49

CHAPTER FOUR

Offences involving 'defectives' and patients 83

Chapter seven

Procurement and abduction 157

Acronyms

C(S)A 1997	Crime (Sentences) Act 1997
CDA 1998	Crime and Disorder Act 1998
CJA 1967	Criminal Justice Act 1967
CJA 1972	Criminal Justice Act 1972
CJA 1982	Criminal Justice Act 1982
CJA 1988	Criminal Justice Act 1988
CJA 1991	Criminal Justice Act 1991
CJCSA 2000	Criminal Justice and Court Services Act 2000
CJPOA 1994	Criminal Justice and Public Order Act 1994
CLA 1922	Criminal Law Act 1922
CLA 1967	Criminal Law Act 1967
CLA 1977	Criminal Law Act 1977
CP(AW)A 1965	Criminal Procedure (Attendance of Witnesses) Act 1965
CPIA 1996	Criminal Procedure and Investigations Act 1996
CYPA 1933	Children and Young Persons Act 1933
FLRA 1969	Family Law Reform Act 1969
HRA 1998	Human Rights Act 1998
ICA 1960	Indecency with Children Act 1960
MA 1949	Marriage Act 1949
MCA 1980	Magistrates Courts Act 1980
MH(A)A 1982	Mental Health (Amendment) Act 1982

MHA 1959	Mental Health Act 1959
MHA 1983	Matrimonial Homes Act 1983
NZCA 1961	New Zealand Crimes Act 1961
OAPA 1861	Offences Against the Person Act 1861
PACE 1984	Police and Criminal Evidence Act 1984
PCA 1978	Protection of Children Act 1978
PCC(S)A 2000	Powers of Criminal Courts (Sentencing) Act 2000
SO(A)A 1976	Sexual Offences (Amendment) Act 1976
SO(A)A 1992	Sexual Offences (Amendment) Act 1992
SO(A)A 2000	Sexual Offences (Amendment) Act 2000
SO(CI)A 1996	Sexual Offences (Conspiracy and Incitement) Act 1996
SO(PM)A 1997	Sexual Offences (Protected Material) Act 1997
SOA 1956	Sexual Offences Act 1956
SOA 1959	Street Offences Act 1959
SOA 1967	Sexual Offences Act 1956
SOA 1985	Sexual Offences Act 1985
SOA 1993	Sexual Offences Act 1993
SOA 1997	Sex Offenders Act 1997
TA 1968	Theft Act 1968
TPCA 1847	Town and Police Clauses Act 1847
VA 1824	Vagrancy Act 1824
VFA 1952	Visiting Forces Act 1952
YJCEA 1999	Youth Justice and Criminal Evidence Act 1999

Table of statutes

Table of rules and regulations

Table of cases

PARA

Practice Direction (Crown Court: allocation of business)[2000] 1 All ER 380, [2000] 1 WLR 203, [2000] 1 Cr App Rep 345 ... 1.6, 2.13, 2.46, 2.60, 3.4, 3.29, 3.59, 3.74, 3.85, 3.97, 4.7, 4.26, 4.39, 4.50, 4.61, 5.7, 5.36, 5.53, 6.5, 6.65, 6.88, 7.6, 7.24, 7.37, 7.51, 7.64, 7.80, 8.29, 8.41, 8.51, 8.69, 8.86, 8.93, 9.5, 10.4, 10.37

R

R v A (No 2) [2001] UKHL 25 [2002] 1 AC 45, [2001] 3 All ER 1, [2001] 2 WLR 1546, [2001] 2 Cr App Rep 351, 165 JP 609 .... 11.37

R v AM [1998] 1 All ER 874, [1998] 1 WLR 363, [1998] 2 Cr App Rep 57, [1998] 1 FLR 900, [1998] Fam Law 314, CA 6.56

R v Adkins [2000] 2 All ER 185, CA 1.42, 1.45

R v Adragna (1994) 15 Cr App Rep (S) 693, CA 3.38

R v Allen (1910) 4 Cr App Rep 181, CCA 5.24

R v Ananthanarayanan [1994] 2 All ER 847, [1994] 1 WLR 788, 98 Cr App Rep 1, 157 JP 1081, [1994] Crim LR 675, CA 6.24

R v Angel [1968] 2 All ER 607n, [1968] 1 WLR 669, 52 Cr App Rep 280, [1968] Crim LR 342, 112 Sol Jo 310, CA 2.10

R v Ansell [1975] QB 215, [1974] 3 All ER 568, [1974] 3 WLR 430, 60 Cr App Rep 45, 138 JP 781, [1974] Crim LR 616, 118 Sol Jo 715, CA 8.75

R v Baillie-Smith (1976) 64 Cr App Rep 76, [1977] Crim LR 676, CA 5.21

R v Ball [1911] AC 47, 5 Cr App Rep 238, 80 LJKB 89, 22 Cox CC 364, 104 LT 47, CCA 5.23

R v Billam [1986] 1 All ER 985, [1986] 1 WLR 349, 82 Cr App Rep 347, 8 Cr App Rep (S) 48, [1986] Crim LR 347, 130 Sol Jo 167, [1986] LS Gaz R 870, CA .. 1.47

R v Blight (1903) 22 NZLR 837 .... 3.38

R v Boal [1992] QB 591, [1992] 3 All ER 177, [1992] 2 WLR 890, 95 Cr App Rep 272, [1992] ICR 495, [1992] IRLR 420, 156 JP 617, [1992] BCLC 872, [1992] 21 LS Gaz R 26, 136 Sol Jo LB 100, CA 10.8

R v Bolingbroke [2001] 1 Cr App Rep (S) 80, CA 10.29

R v Bourne (1952) 36 Cr App Rep 125, CCA 2.17, 2.42, 6.68

R v Bowden [2001] QB 88, [2000] 2 All ER 418, [2000] 2 WLR 1083, [2000] 1 Cr App Rep 438, [2000] 2 Cr App Rep (S) 26, [2000] Crim LR 381, [1999] 47 LS Gaz R 29, 144 Sol Jo LB 5, CA 10.19

R v Broadfoot [1976] 3 All ER 753, 64 Cr App Rep 71, 141 JP 40, [1977] Crim LR 690, CA 8.33

R v Brown (1889) 24 QBD 357, 54 JP 408, 59 LJMC 47, 16 Cox CC 715, 38 WR 95, 61 LT 594, CCR 2.39

R v Brown [1895] 1 QB 119, 59 JP 485, 64 LJMC 1, 18 Cox CC 81, 15 R 59, 43 WR 222, 39 Sol Jo 64, 72 LT 22, 11 TLR 54, CCR 4.56

R v Brown [1984] 3 All ER 1013, [1984] 1 WLR 1211, 80 Cr App Rep 36, [1984] Crim LR 627, 128 Sol Jo 736, [1984] LS Gaz R 2617, CA 8.35

R v Brown [1994] 1 AC 212, [1993] 2 All ER 75, [1993] 2 WLR 556, 97 Cr App Rep 44, 157 JP 337, [1993] Crim LR 583, [1993] NLJR 399, HL 6.34, 6.72

R v Burrows [1952] 1 All ER 58n, 35 Cr App Rep 180, 116 JP 47, 96 Sol Jo 122, [1952] 1 TLR 51, CCA 6.49

R v C [1992] Crim LR 642, CA 6.41

R v Camplin (1845) 9 JP 424, 743, 1 Car & Kir 746, 1 Den 89, 1 Cox CC 220, 5 LTOS 266, CCR 1.25, 1.29, 7.13

PARA

PARA

S

W

Chapter one

Rape

1.1 The Sexual Offences Act 1956, s 1(1) originally set out in bald terms that '[I]t is an offence for a man to rape a woman.' The situation with regard to the offence of rape has changed considerably since then and, following a number of amendments to the section, the position now is as follows:

> 1.(1) It is an offence for a man to rape a woman or another man.
>
> (2) A man commits rape if –
> (a) he has sexual intercourse with a person (whether vaginal or anal) who at the time of the intercourse does not consent to it; and
> (b) at the time he knows that the person does not consent to the intercourse or is reckless as to whether that person consents to it.
>
> (3) A man also commits rape if he induces a married woman to have sexual intercourse with him by impersonating her husband.
>
> (4) Subsection (2) applies for the purposes of any enactment.

1.2 One of the amending Acts that have been introduced since 1956 was the Sexual Offences (Amendment) Act 1976 which provided that 'a rape offence' constitutes

> any of the following, namely rape, attempted rape, aiding, abetting, counselling and procuring rape or attempted rape, incitement to commit rape, conspiracy to rape and burglary with intent to rape.[1]

1 See SO(A)A 1976, s 7(2).

1.3 It will be seen that, from the early statutory offence of rape as set out in the SOA 1956, the ambit and definition of the offence has grown considerably. The two most significant changes to the statutory regime are that the offence of rape can now be committed against both men and women, and that the sexual intercourse can be either vaginal or anal. These developments have come as a result of the changing social attitudes to the offence of rape and a greater appreciation of the true nature of the offence, as reflected in both the developing case law and Parliament's desire to follow public opinion on the matter. This latter point became especially pertinent following the House of Lords ruling in the case of *DPP v Morgan*[1] which created a significant furore in setting down the requisite test for a defendant's belief as to whether the complainant was consenting to sexual intercourse. A good example of this desire on the part of Parliament appears in the SO(A)A 1976, s 1(2). The essence of rape is that the complainant was not consenting to the act of sexual intercourse. Other than when the defendant claims that it was not him who had sexual intercourse with the complainant, this will be the primary issue for a jury to consider in deciding his guilt or innocence. SO(A)A 1976, s 1(2) reads as follows:

> It is hereby declared that if at a trial for a rape offence the jury has to consider whether a man believed that a woman or man was consenting to sexual intercourse, the presence or absence of reasonable grounds for such a belief is a matter to which the jury is to have regard, in conjunction with any other relevant matters, in considering whether he so believed.

1 [1976] AC 182, [1975] 1 All ER 8.

1.4 This is akin to saying that the jury must take into consideration everything that must be taken into consideration. It is an entirely unnecessary provision because the jury will be directed that they must, in deciding whether the defendant truly believed that the complainant was consenting, consider whether reasonable grounds for the belief existed at the time of the alleged offence[1]. In order to do that the jury must appraise all of the evidence in relation to the point, including, of course, any testimony from the defendant, if he gives evidence. In short, the provision merely sets out what is obvious common sense; just the kind of thing that juries are told in trials up and down the country every day, and not merely in trials of rape. As has been said by respected academics:

> It is unfortunate that a matter of common sense should be enacted at all, particularly that it should be enacted in relation to one offence. So long, however, as it is understood that sub-s (2) [to the SO(A)A 1976, s 1] is a public relations provision and does not enact a rule peculiar to rape, it is harmless[2].

1 See the section on mens rea for details of this aspect of the offence.

2 Smith & Hogan *Criminal Law* (8th ed) 468.

1.5 It is beyond the scope of this work to consider the philosophical and moral attitudes to the offence of rape. However, it should be constantly borne in mind that the development of the law pertaining to the offence of rape since the original enactment of the SOA1956 has been something of a weathervane as to the changing social attitudes towards, and revulsion of, violence, and particularly sexual violence. Having said that, it should also be understood that not every rape involves the infliction of physical violence upon the victim, but it undoubtedly does involve the violation of the complainant's person, both physically and psychologically.

General Issues

Mode of Trial

1.6 The offence of rape, together with that of attempted rape, is triable on indictment only[1]. Both offences are Class 2 offences and, as such, can be tried only by a High Court judge unless the case is released by or on the authority of a presiding judge for trial by a circuit judge[2].

1 See the SOA 1956, s 37(2) and Sch 2, para 1.

2 *Practice Direction (Crown Court: allocation of business) (No 3)* [2000] 1 All ER 380, [2000] 1 WLR 203.

Parties to the Offence

1.7 It has already been made clear that both men and women can be complainants in an allegation of rape. Only a man can be convicted of rape as a principal, however, because the SOA 1956, s 1 states that '[I]t is an offence for a man to rape ...'. A woman though, may be convicted as an aider and abettor[1]. This is so even where the principal – ie the alleged rapist - may be acquitted of the offence itself. This proposition is exemplified in the case of *Cogan and Leak*[2]. Mr Leak, with the intention of humiliating and hurting his wife, persuaded Mr Cogan to have sex with her while he watched. Mrs Leak was not a willing partner and did not consent to the act of sexual intercourse. Cogan's defence was that he always thought that she was consenting. Although the trial took place before the case of *Morgan*[3] came before the House of Lords, the appeal was heard after, and the Court quashed Cogan's conviction. Mr Leak's appeal was on the basis that he should not be found guilty of aiding and abetting Cogan if the latter had been acquitted of the full offence. The Court dismissed the appeal out of hand by stating that there was absolutely no doubt that Mrs Leak had been raped – Cogan had had sexual intercourse with her without her consent and it was only the state of the law at the time of his appeal that made him 'innocent' – and that Leak had aided and abetted that offence. In the words of Lawton LJ:

> In the language of the law the act of sexual intercourse without the wife's consent was the actus reus: it had been procured by Leak who had the appropriate mens rea, namely his intention that Cogan should have sexual intercourse with her without her consent. In our judgement it is irrelevant that the man whom Leak had procured to do the physical act himself did not intend to have sexual intercourse with the wife without her consent. Leak was using him as a means to procure a criminal purpose[4].

1 See, for example, *R v Ram* (1893) 17 Cox CC 609.

2 [1976] QB 217, [1975] 2 All ER 1059.

3 [1976] AC 182, [1975] 2 All ER 347, HL.

4 [1976] AC 182 at 1062b, HL.

1.8 The clear reasoning in *Cogan and Leak* as to the various and distinct roles of the principal and the aider and abettor illustrates that it matters not whether the latter is a man or a woman.

1.9 It was not an issue in *Cogan and Leak* that Mr Leak had non-consensual sex with his wife both before and after Cogan. This was because the two were married. As a result of the case of *R v R*[1], on the facts of the case Mr Leak today could be indicted with an offence of rape.

1 [1992] 1 AC 599, [1991] 4 All ER 481, HL.

1.10 Where more than one man is alleged to have raped a single victim on a single occasion, they should all be charged with one rape, rather than as a rapist or rapists, together with aiders and abettors. In *DPP v Merriman*[1], a case which involved the indictment of two brothers for an offence of wounding, Lord Diplock said the following:

> ... whenever two or more defendants are charged in the same count of an indictment with any offence which men can help one another to commit it is sufficient to support a conviction against any and each of them to prove *either* that he himself did a physical act which is an essential ingredient of the offence charged *or* that he helped another defendant to do such an act, *and*, that in doing the act or in helping the other defendant to do it, he himself had the necessary criminal intent (his emphasis)[2].

The effect of this direction is that where more than one man is accused of rape, the jury does not have to decide who committed the act of non-consensual sexual intercourse, but need only be satisfied that each of the accused played a criminal part in the act.

1 [1973] AC 584, [1972] 3 All ER 42, HL.

2 [1973] AC 584 at 607F, HL.

1.11 Until September 1993 there was a common law presumption that a boy under the age of 14 could not indulge in sexual intercourse, either vaginal or anal. This presumption was abolished by the SOA 1993, s 1. The effect of that provision is to allow the conviction of any male aged 10[1] or over for any sexual offence involving the penetration of the vagina or anus of the complainant by him.

1 The age at which any criminal liability arises: see Children and Young Persons Act 1933, s 50.

Complainant's Anonymity

1.12 The complainant in an allegation of rape is entitled to comprehensive anonymity[1]. The anonymity of the complainant stretches to cover the publication of any matter relating to him/her 'if it is likely to lead members of the public to identify that person as the person against whom the offence is alleged to have been committed'[2]. The anonymity in these provisions remains in place throughout the complainant's lifetime. The anonymity provisions can however be over-ridden by an application by the accused to the trial judge to direct that SO(A)A 1992, s 1 should not apply in relation to the complainant. Under the SO(A)A 1992, s 3(1), in order for such a direction to be made the judge must be satisfied of two things, namely that:

(a) the direction is required for the purpose of inducing persons who are likely to be needed as witnesses at the trial to come forward; and
(b) the conduct of the applicant's defence at the trial is likely to be substantially prejudiced if the direction is not given.

1 Sexual Offences (Amendment) Act 1992, ss 1 to 4. These provisions apply to a large number of sexual offences.

2 See SO(A) 1992, s 1(1).

1.13 The trial judge can also direct that the SO(A)A 1992, s 1 should not apply if he is satisfied that such anonymity 'imposes a substantial and unreasonable restriction upon the reporting of proceedings at the trial' and 'that it is in the public interest to remove or relax the restriction'[1].

1 See SO(A) 1992, s 3(2).

1.14 The SO(A)A 1992, ss1-4 overlap somewhat with the anonymity provisions in the SO(A)A 1976, s 4 which is concerned specifically with complainants in rape cases alone. The two Acts should be considered together.

Alternative Verdicts

1.15 If a jury are satisfied that all of the elements of the offence of rape are made out except that of penetration of the vagina or anus by the defendant then he can be convicted of attempted rape. Without such penetration being proved he cannot be found guilty of rape.

1.16 If the complainant is under 16 years of age and the jury find that sexual intercourse took place but the complainant consented to the act, it is open to them to find the defendant guilty of indecent assault. This is because by virtue of the SOA 1956, ss 15 and 16 children under the age of 16 cannot give their consent so as to prevent an assault being indecent[1]. In an allegation of rape there must be an indecent assault as the law is presently constituted[2]. For the law pertaining to indecent assaults, see Chapter 6.

1 See Chapter 6 and especially paragraphs 6.43 to 6.46.

2 See *R v Mochan* [1969] 1 WLR 1331, 54 Cr App Rep 5.

1.17 On a count of rape the defendant may also be convicted of procurement of a woman by threats[1], procurement of a woman by false pretences[2], or of administering drugs to obtain or facilitate intercourse[3]. The fact that these offences are alternatives to a charge of rape stems from the SOA 1956, s 37(4) and Sch 2. The details of these offences are addressed in Chapter 7.

1 SOA 1956, s 2.

2 SOA 1956, s 3.

3 SOA 1956, s 4.

Actus Reus

Sexual Intercourse

1.18 The offence of rape – whether vaginal or anal – cannot be proved unless it is first established that penetration by the penis occurred. The SOA 1956, s 44 states that:

> Where, on the trial of any offence under this Act, it is necessary to prove sexual intercourse (whether natural or unnatural), it

> shall not be necessary to prove the completion of the intercourse by the emission of seed, but the intercourse shall be deemed complete upon proof of penetration only.

1.19 Any amount of penetration is sufficient to satisfy the test for sexual intercourse having taken place. The word 'complete' in the last line of the provision makes it clear that the act of intercourse – and therefore the offence, so long as the requisite mens rea exists – occurs as soon as penetration has happened.

1.20 Rape is a continuing offence and so, even if penetration takes place at a time when the complainant consents, once he or she ceases to consent, and the defendant is aware of that fact, if he continues with the sexual intercourse, he is guilty of the offence. In *Kaitamaki v R*[1] the defendant was charged with breaking into a young woman's home and twice raping her. He admitted having sexual intercourse with her but contended that she was a willing participant. He did however accept that after they had commenced the sexual intercourse he became aware that she had ceased to consent. He was convicted of rape and appealed, ultimately, to the Privy Council. His counsel submitted that if a man penetrates a woman with her consent he cannot then become guilty of rape once he realises that she is no longer consenting. This was, in effect, saying that in those circumstances, continuing intercourse after consent has been withdrawn is not rape because for the purposes of the Act it is complete upon penetration, and as the initial penetration was done with consent, it was done legally. The case originated in New Zealand where the provision in question (the New Zealand Crimes Act 1961, s 127) is very similar to that of the SOA 1956, s 44. Lord Scarman gave the ruling that their Lordships agreed with the opinion of the Court of Appeal, saying

> ... the purpose of [the NZCA 1961,] s 127 was to remove any doubts as to the minimum conduct needed to prove the fact of sexual intercourse. 'Complete' is used in the statutory definition in the sense of having come into existence, but not in the sense of being at an end. Sexual intercourse is a continuing act which only ends with withdrawal[2].

1 [1985] AC 147, [1984] 2 All ER 435, PC.

2 [1985] AC 147 at 151H, PC.

Absence of Consent

1.21 Once the Crown have established that sexual intercourse took place, it must establish that the sexual intercourse occurred without the consent of the complainant. As has been said before, lack of consent is the absolute essence of the offence of rape. Consent can be a difficult concept to get across to a jury but the lack of it is an essential ingredient to the offence of rape. In terms of the actus reus of the offence it matters not why consent was not present, merely that it was not. So, for example, the obtaining of consent by deception or misrepresentation *as to the nature of the act or the identity of the agent only* negatives that consent and the actus reus is complete. It is not the law however that *any* kind of misrepresentation by the accused towards the complainant vitiates the consent given.

1.22 In *Linekar*[1] the complainant was a prostitute who had sex with the defendant on the understanding that he would pay her money after the act. They had sex and Linekar ran away without paying, apparently never intending to pay. The trial judge directed the jury that if consent to sexual intercourse was obtained by the defendant's fraud (because he never intended to pay), that consent was vitiated and he would be guilty of rape. He was convicted and appealed. The Court of Appeal ruled that the reality of the complainant's consent to the act of sexual intercourse was not affected in any way by the fraud perpetrated upon her. In essence, she agreed to have sex with Linekar, albeit on the basis that she would be paid by him. The fact that he never intended to pay her played no part in extinguishing her consent. It follows from this case that any promise whatsoever given by the man to the complainant as to what will or might happen after the sexual intercourse will not alter the fact that proper consent is given by the latter for sexual intercourse to take place and it will therefore not be rape.

1 [1995] QB 250, [1995] 2 Cr App Rep 49.

1.23 As was said in paragraph 1.21 above, it is a fraud as to the *nature of the act or identity of the agent* which may vitiate the complainant's consent. Dealing with the first clause of that passage (ie 'the nature of the act'), the complainant must be persuaded that the act of sexual intercourse is necessary for some reason other than the perpetrator's sexual desire and s/he therefore consented to the act, believing it was a necessary operation. As such, that may appear a strange notion in this day and age, and it is difficult to imagine a man or woman, or even a boy or girl, today being persuaded that sexual intercourse was necessary in order to cure a medical condition[1] or for a choirmaster to test a girl's breathing powers[2] or for any other fanciful reason. If they were so persuaded however, then any consent given to the actual act of sexual intercourse would be vitiated by the fraudulent behaviour of the defendant and he would be guilty of rape.

1 See *R v Case* (1850) 4 Cox CC 220 and *R v Flattery* (1877) 2 QBD 410.

2 See *R v Williams* [1923] 1 KB 340, 17 Cr App Rep 56, CCA.

1.24 So far as the issue as to the 'identity of the agent' is concerned, it is rape if the complainant consents to sexual intercourse, believing their partner is either her husband or his/her partner when they are not. This is because the complainant is consenting to sexual intercourse with someone other than the person s/he is with and therefore consent to sexual intercourse with their actual partner is not present. Parliament got itself into a terrible state when it passed the provision in the Criminal Justice and Public Order Act 1994 which created a new s 1(3) to the SOA 1956. Prior to the introduction of the CJPOA 1994 the Court of Appeal held, in the case of *Elbekkay*[1], that it was just as much an offence for a defendant to impersonate the partner of a woman, as it was to impersonate her husband. This made a great deal of sense in that the courts had been, over the years, attempting to equalise the situation as the statutory law changed, for example with regard to rape within marriage, anal rape joining vaginal rape as an offence, etc. It must follow from the reasoning in *Elbekkay* that inducing a man to have sexual intercourse, in the belief that the perpetrator is his partner must also constitute rape. After *Elbekkay*, however, the CJPOA 1994 appeared not to consider the point and the law appeared to revert back to a situation whereby it was only an offence to impersonate a woman's husband. It is unlikely that this was parliament's intention and, as was well put in *Smith and Hogan*:

> In practice, it is thought that the courts are likely to treat it as what it is – a governmental and parliamentary blunder – and carry on as if it did not exist[2].

1 [1995] Crim LR 163.

2 Smith & Hogan *Criminal Law* (8th edn) 469.

1.25 It is important to appreciate the distinction between a complainant who submits to sexual intercourse and one who consents to it. The former may be submitting to the act as a result of fear through threats either to herself or to a close family member. Similarly, it may not be the person who rapes him/her who makes the threats but simply takes advantage of the victim's fear. Submission to sexual intercourse is not the same thing as consenting to it and this distinction was recognised as far back as Victorian times when, in the case of *Camplin*,[1] the Court of Appeal acknowledged that the offence of rape constituted sexual intercourse with a woman (then) who did not consent and not merely having sex against her will.

1 (1845) 1 Den 89.

1.26 It is also right to remember that rape does not have to involve the use or threat of violence. Prior to the case of *Camplin* it seems to have been thought that the offence of rape had to involve the use or threat of violence towards the victim or the use of fraud. This resulted in judges directing juries that, if they were satisfied that the evidence showed the use or threat of violence, or fraud used by the defendant in obtaining consent, the sexual act must then have taken place 'against her will'. That is not now the law and all that the jury has to be satisfied of – so far as the actus reus is concerned – is that sexual intercourse took place and it took place without the complainant's consent.

1.27 If this aspect of the law of rape needed spelling out in detail, it got it in the case of *Olugboja*[1]. The defendant and his friend (Lawal) took two girls (Jayne and Karen) back to their home after being at a dance. On arriving at the home Olugboja went into the house but the two girls refused to do so. Lawal followed them in his car and, after making attempts to get them to return to the house, he raped Jayne. The three eventually returned to the house where Lawal took Karen into his bedroom leaving Olugboja and Jayne in the living room. The defendant told Jayne that he was going to have sex with her; Jayne told him that Lawal had 'had her' in the car and she asked to be left alone. She submitted to sexual intercourse with him and did not complain when he penetrated her. She did however struggle when she thought that he would ejaculate inside her and he desisted. His conviction for rape was upheld on the basis that the events leading up to the sexual intercourse would make the impact of them on her mind clear and it would have been evident that she was not consenting to the sex. In an attempt to clarify the situation so far as proving lack of consent is concerned, Dunn LJ said:

> ... in so far as the actus reus is concerned, the question now is simply: at the time of the sexual intercourse did the woman consent to it? It is not necessary for the prosecution to prove that what might otherwise appear to have been consent was in reality merely submission induced by force, fear or fraud, although one or more of these factors will no doubt be present in the majority of cases of rape[2].

1 [1982] QB 320, [1981] 3 All ER 443, CA.

2 [1981] 3 All ER 443 at 448f, CA.

1.28 It should be said however, with regard to *Olugboja*, that the Court did not clarify all aspects of the issue of consent, recognising that the concept could be difficult, but saying that it was a matter for the jury, taking into consideration all of the relevant circumstances they have heard about, and that they should be directed to concentrate on 'the state of mind of the complainant immediately before the act of sexual intercourse ... and her reaction to them showing their impact on her mind'[1].

1 [1981] 3 All ER 443 at 449a, CA.

1.29 It will be seen then that consent might be said to be a 'positive act' on the part of the complainant. This is put in those terms because there have been a number of cases before the Court of Appeal that attempted to introduce the notion that if the complainant did not actively display a lack of consent, then rape is not made out. Examples of such cases are where the complainant is so affected by drink or drugs that s/he does not know the nature of the act being perpetrated and therefore does not display any lack of consent[1]; or where the complainant has been asleep during the sexual intercourse[2]. In each of these cases the appeals have been dismissed with the Court reiterating that the essential ingredient of rape is a lack of consent. How that lack of consent comes about or whether it is made apparent to the defendant is entirely irrelevant – though this is trespassing somewhat onto the issue of mens rea. In *R v Malone*[3] it was held that:

> ... there was no requirement that the absence of consent had to be demonstrated or that it had to be communicated to the defendant for the actus reus of rape to exist and it was thus not the law that the prosecution, in order to prove an offence of rape, had to show that the complainant was either incapable of saying no or putting up some physical resistance or did say no or put up some physical resistance ... in order to obtain a conviction there had to be some evidence of lack of consent to go before the jury, but what that evidence was would depend on the particular circumstances of the case the jury was trying and might consist of the complainant's simple assertion that she did not consent.

1 See, for example, *Camplin* (1845) 1 Den 89.

2 See *Larter and Castleton* [1995] Crim LR 75.

3 [1998] 2 Cr App Rep 447, [1998] Crim LR 834.

1.30 A further complicating feature of the concept of consent and how it might differ with other possible synonyms arose in the case of *DT*[1] where the Court of Appeal criticised a judge for using the word 'wanted' as a synonym for 'consented'. It was decided that the word 'want' should not be used in summing-up to a jury and trial judges should adhere only to the word 'consent', leaving the jury to use their common sense and knowledge of the world to decide if the requisite consent was present. The case involved a couple in a sexual relationship and during the appeal against the conviction for rape it was opined that there may be occasions when a complainant in such a situation may not 'want' to have sexual intercourse, but nonetheless consents to it with his/her partner on that particular occasion.

1 [2000] 7 Archbold News 3, CA.

1.31 It will be seen from the above analysis that, in attempting to explain the concept of consent, both trial judges and the Court of Appeal have sometimes created more problems than have been solved. What can only be said definitively is that in order to prove the actus reus of rape, the prosecution must satisfy the jury that the complainant did not consent to the sexual intercourse. To that extent, consent must be a conscious and intelligent decision by the complainant. He or she must be consenting to sexual intercourse at that time with that particular partner for the act not to be rape. Any less than that standard and the actus reus is made out.

1.32 In saying that the consent must be conscious and intelligent will inevitably create difficulties where the prosecution case is based on the contention that the complainant is mentally incapable of giving consent to sexual intercourse. Although the statutory offence of having sexual intercourse with a defective (sic) woman exists[1] it is sometimes preferable to charge a man who has sexual intercourse with a mentally defective female with rape - not least because the maximum sentence is greater. In such a circumstance it is necessary for the prosecution to prove that she was not capable of forming the necessary consent due to her mental deficiency. Although this is an issue that was considered in Victorian cases – not always with, what would be considered today, proper propriety – it was held in the Australian case of *Morgan*[2] that the prosecution must prove that the woman did not have sufficient knowledge or understanding to comprehend that the man proposed having sexual intercourse (ie penetration of her body with his penis) with her, or that the penetration of her body was a sexual matter as opposed to any other act of a different nature. It is submitted that this approach is far more preferable to that which flows from the earlier English decisions pertaining to this issue.

1 See SOA 1956, s 7 and Chapter 4 of this work.

2 [1970] VR 337.

1.33 In order, therefore, to avoid an allegation of rape against a man, it might be said that it is incumbent upon him to ensure in some way that the man or woman is consenting to sexual intercourse. This, of course, may not be easy to do, and in some circumstances might appear unnecessary, but, unless the situation is absolutely clear, the risk of such an allegation is always present.

Children and Consent

1.34 The issue of consent is no less important or significant when the complainant is a child as when s/he is an adult. In such cases it is still for the prosecution to prove the lack of consent on the part of the complainant. When the child is of such a tender age that he or she is unaware of any sexual matters, little difficulty should arise. However, unlike the offence of indecent assault for example, with rape there is no age restriction to the offence. It remains the role of the jury to decide, in such circumstances, whether or not the complainant consented to sexual intercourse. As was said by Humphreys J in the case of *Harling*[1]:

> In every case of rape it is necessary that the prosecution should prove that the girl or woman [or boy or man] did not consent and that the crime was committed against her will. It may well be that in many cases the prosecution would not need to prove much more than the age of the [complainant] ...

1 (1938) 26 Cr App Rep 127 at 128, CCA.

1.35 If the prosecution is able to satisfy the jury that the complainant could not, and therefore did not, consent to the act of sexual intercourse through ignorance of what that act constitutes, the actus reus of the offence is made out.

Mens Rea

Knowledge or Recklessness as to Lack of Consent

1.36 Assuming that the defendant has the intention of having sexual intercourse with the complainant, the prosecution must prove, as far as his mental state is concerned, either knowledge on his part that the complainant is not consenting, or recklessness as to whether they are consenting. As a result of the Court of Appeal ruling in *Satnam and Kewal*[1] it is possible to say that the necessary form required is so-called *Cunningham* recklessness[2]. In addressing the issue it was said that:

> [A]ny direction as to the definition of rape should be based on [the SO(A)A 1976,] s 1 and upon *Morgan*, without regard to *R v Caldwell* ... or *R v Lawrence* ... which were concerned with recklessness in a different context and under a different statute where different concepts are involved.

1 (1983) 78 Cr App Rep 149, [1985] Crim LR 236.

2 [1957] 2 QB 396, [1957] 2 All ER 412.

1.37 In the case of *Taylor*[1] the topic of recklessness when a man is charged with rape was considered by Lord Lane CJ. The defendant admitted to having been drinking prior to the sexual intercourse but maintained that he genuinely believed the complainant to have been consenting. She gave evidence that she had not been a consenting party. Lord Lane set out the state of the law with regard to recklessness in this way:

> ... in rape the defendant is reckless if he does not believe that the woman is consenting and could not care less whether she is consenting or not but presses on regardless.

1 (1984) 80 Cr App Rep 327, CA.

Genuine Belief in Consent

1.38 During January and February of 1975 four appeals were heard together concerning the issue of whether a defendant's belief that the complainant in a rape allegation was consenting to sexual intercourse must be based on reasonable grounds. The cases were reported as *DPP v Morgan*[1] and the ruling by the House of Lords led to a change in the law and the introduction of the declaratory provision set out in the SO(A)A 1976, s 1(2)[2].

1 [1976] AC 182, 61 Cr App Rep 136.

2 See paragraph 1.3 above.

1.39 In *Morgan* the House of Lords held that where a defendant had a belief the complainant did consent to sexual intercourse, even where there were no reasonable grounds for holding that belief, he could not be guilty of rape. As a result of this decision (which had altered the law as to genuine belief that had stood since 1889[1]) the Government asked the Advisory group on the Law of Rape under Mrs Justice Heilbron to consider the matter. That committee concluded that the law as set out in *Morgan* must be right in principle but felt it important that the SO(A)A 1976, s 1(2) should be introduced into English law, if only for the benefit of juries.

1 See *Tolson* (1889) 23 QBD 168, CCR.

1.40 In *Morgan* both Lord Hailsham and Lord Fraser of Tullybelton summarised the situation with regard to what the prosecution must establish to obtain a guilty verdict. Lord Fraser put it this way:

> If the effect of the evidence as a whole is that the defendant believed, or may have believed, that the woman was consenting, then the crown has not discharged the onus of proving the commission of the offence as fully defined and, as it seems to me, no question can arise as to whether the belief was reasonable or not. Of course, the reasonableness or otherwise of the belief will be important as evidence tending to show whether it was truly held by the defendant, but that is all[1].

1 [1976] AC 182 at 237.

1.41 In saying that the prosecution must prove *Cunningham* type recklessness it should be remembered that the jury have to concern themselves with the state of the complainant's mind rather than with the consequences of the defendant's act. It is for the prosecution to convince the jury that the defendant either knew that the complainant was not consenting or acted as if he didn't care whether they were consenting or not. In the case of *Haughian and Pearson*[1] the trial judge directed the jury, as to recklessness, in the following terms:

> ... a man is reckless if either he was indifferent and gave no thought to the possibility that the woman might not be consenting in circumstances where if any thought had been given to the matter it would be obvious there was a risk she was not, or he would be aware of the possibility she might not be consenting but nevertheless persisted regardless of whether she consented or not and could not care less.

This direction was exactly as set out by the Court of Appeal in the earlier cases of *Pigg*[2] and *Thomas*[3]. The Court of Appeal dismissed the appeal and criticised the direction only slightly in that it did not make it clear to the jury that when they considered the point they must look at the risk as being 'obvious' to the defendant rather than as being obvious to a reasonable man[4].

1 (1984) 80 Cr App Rep 334.

2 (1982) 74 Cr App Rep 352.

3 (1982) 77 Cr App Rep 63.

4 (1982) 74 Cr App Rep 352 at 343.

1.42 In the case of *Adkins*[1] the defendant was convicted of rape and appealed his conviction by contending that in every case of rape where the defendant relies on consent there is an implicit defence that the defendant honestly believed that there was consent. If that were so it was further contended that it is incumbent upon the trial judge to always direct the jury in the terms of the SO(A)A 1976, s 1(2)[2]. It was also said on the appellant's behalf that whenever the question of reckless rape is in issue, the direction should be given. In order to understand why these contentions were rejected, it would be illustrative to set out briefly, the facts of the case.

1 [2000] 2 All ER 185, CA.

2 See paragraph 1.3 above.

1.43 The complainant was a barmaid at a club of which Mr Adkins attended. He was married and she was separated from her husband but had a boyfriend. Adkins attempted on numerous occasions to instigate a relationship with her. His advances were always rebuffed by the complainant, not least of all because he was married. Her evidence was that on the day of the offence – at about 10 am – she was getting ready for work when she heard a knock on her door. She opened the door, dressed in only knickers and a dressing gown, to see the defendant there. She refused him entry but he pushed his way in and, eventually, pushed her onto her bed, pulled her knickers off and forcibly had sex with her. She stated that she struggled throughout and, when it was over he said to her 'I'd better not get a knock on the door' which she took to be a reference to her informing the police of what had happened.

1.44 Mr Adkins' evidence was that she had been a willing party throughout the event, that she responded willingly, even to the extent of helping him to gain an erection and that she had clearly enjoyed the sex. Significantly so far as the issue of recklessness was concerned, though not referred to in the judgment of the Court, in cross-examination he did say that he would not take no for an answer and that he had told the complainant that he wanted sex with her.

1.45 Roch LJ, giving the decision of the Court, reviewed the earlier case law, in particular the dictum of Lord Lane in *Taylor*, and went onto say:

> In our judgment, these cases demonstrate that [counsel for Mr Adkins] is wrong in his primary submission that whenever the issue of consent arises there must be a direction as to honest belief. Such a direction need only be given when the evidence in the case is such that there is room for the possibility of a genuine mistaken belief that the victim was consenting. In our view this accords with the basic principle that the jury should not be subjected to unnecessary and irrelevant directions.

He continued with the following:

> The question of honest belief does not necessarily arise where reckless rape is in issue. The defendant may have failed to address his mind to the question whether or not there was consent, or be indifferent as to whether there was consent or not, in circumstances where, had he addressed his mind to the question, he could not genuinely have believed that there was consent[1].

1 Both quotations are in [2000] 2 All ER 185 at 191, CA.

1.46 It will be seen then that the question of whether a defendant can claim that he held a genuine belief that the complainant was consenting must be borne out by all the circumstances of the evidence. In cases where there is a direct dispute between the two parties as to whether the complainant was consenting, the jury will have to decide which of the two parties they believe before considering the issue of genuine or honest belief in consent. The Court of Appeal in *Adkins* suggested that, if they accept the evidence of the complainant, then there is no room for considering whether or not the defendant held an honest belief in consent. If however, they are not sure as to the truth of the complainant then the issue arises. Saying this, however, is to suggest that the decision was not entirely correct. The ruling in that case was made on the basis that, in accepting the evidence of the complainant, the jury could not have possibly concluded that the defendant held an honest belief that she was consenting, which is deciding an issue on an ex post facto basis. That is, that the verdict of guilty shows they did not believe the defendant's version of events. One must ask what the situation would be if the jury did not fully accept the evidence of the complainant and had not been directed in terms of SO(A)A 1976, s 1(2) – as in *Adkins* – and conclude that his counsel may well have been right after all.

Sentence

1.47 The maximum sentence for rape is life imprisonment. In the renowned case of *Billam*[1] Lord Lane set out the guidelines for sentencing in rape cases which still apply today. Before however going into details of the appropriate sentences for the various features of rape cases he emphasised that it would be rare for any man convicted of rape not to be imprisoned immediately, saying that 'rape is always a serious crime which calls for an immediate custodial sentence other than in wholly exceptional circumstances'[2].

1 [1986] 1 All ER 985, [1986] 1 WLR 349, CA.

2 [1986] 1 All ER 985 at 987.

1.48 Lord Lane then set out, on a rising scale, the appropriate ranges of sentences which would take into account the variable factors involved. These ranges are as follows:

- five years as being the starting point for a contested case;
- eight years for a rape committed by two or more men acting together, for a man who has broken into or otherwise gained access to the complainant's home, for a man taking advantage of a position of trust or responsibility towards the complainant, or by a man who has abducted his victim;
- 15 years or more for a man who has carried out a campaign of rape against a number of different victims;
- a life sentence would not be inappropriate for a man who has carried out a rape during which he has manifested perverted or psychopathic tendencies or gross personality disorder and would therefore be likely to be a danger to women (or men now) for an indefinite time.

1.49 In addition to the above guidelines, it was said that the following features should be regarded as being aggravating features of a rape:

- violence is used over and above the force necessary to commit the rape;
- a weapon is used to frighten or wound the complainant;
- the rape is repeated;
- the rape has been carefully planned;
- the defendant has previous convictions for rape or other serious offences of a violent or sexual nature;

- the victim is subjected to further sexual indignities or perversions;
- the victim is either very old or very young;
- any effect on the victim, whether physical or mental.

It was said by Lord Lane that where any one or more of those features are present the sentence should be substantially higher than the figure suggested as the starting point.

1.50 So far as mitigating features are concerned, his Lordship referred only to the fact that a plea of guilty should be accorded more weight than in other cases because, often, the distress caused to complainants in having to relive the events in the witness box is avoided.

1.51 It was also said in *Billam* that sentences where the defendant is under 21 years of age should follow the same criteria as for adult offenders and that '... the appropriate sentence would be one of youth custody', following the term suggested as terms of imprisonment for adults, but making some reduction to reflect the youth of the offender.

1.52 It was further said that in the case of defendants who were youths, the sentencing court will, in most cases, exercise the power under the Children and Young Persons Act 1933, s 53(2) and that, due to the procedural limitations within that Act, magistrates dealing with a youth should invariably commit the case to the Crown Court for trial.

1.53 So far as the offence of attempted rape is concerned, Lord Lane stated that 'the starting point should normally be less than for the completed offence ...'.

1.54 It might be said that the case of *Billam* was the high watermark of the sentencing regime so far as rape is concerned. Since that case there have been significant legal and social shifts towards certain aspects of the law of rape. For instance, since the case of *R*[1] it is now possible for a man to be convicted of raping his wife, but sentencers have often taken a comparatively lenient approach to such an offender. For example, in that case R pleaded guilty to an attempted rape having forcing his way into his ex-wife's parents' home and assaulting her, and was sentenced to three years' imprisonment. Yet, using the guideline as set out in *Billam* the starting point, for an offence of attempted rape, the sentence should have been somewhere in the region of six years (less perhaps two or so for his guilty plea). In a further apparent departure from the guidelines, Lord Taylor CJ in the case of *Stephen W*[2] opined that '... it should not be thought that a different and lower scale of sentencing attaches automatically to rape by a husband as against that set out in *Billam*'. The Court then went onto approve the sentence of five years even though the man raped his wife the day she had told him she wanted to leave him, using a knife to threaten her[3]!

1 [1992] 1 AC 599, [1991] 4 All ER 481, HL.

2 (1992) 14 Cr App Rep (S) 256, CA.

3 In the case of *Henshall* (28 July 1994, unreported), the defendant received a mere three years in prison following guilty pleas to two counts of rape against his girlfriend of 12 years. He had entered her home, threatened to 'shove' a pair of scissors into her vagina, and then raped her, repeating the events two weeks later.

1.55 Similarly, the courts appear to regard rapes where the defendant is known to the complainant as not so serious as other cases. In cases where the appalling term 'date-rape' raises its head, lesser sentences than accord with the *Billam* guidelines are often imposed. In such circumstances it is understandable why there is the occasional outcry with regard to such sentences, from women's groups in particular.

1.56 As something of a counter-balance to the issues raised above, in the case of *R v G (W)*[1] the defendant was sentenced to 10 years' imprisonment, which was upheld by the Court of Appeal, for three counts of rape on his wife. It is submitted, however, that the sound reasoning that led to the guidelines set out in *Billam* remains just as sound today and sentencing courts should pay more heed to the good sense which appears in Lord Lane's dicta.

1 [2000] 1 Cr App Rep (S) 70, CA.

1.57 Difficulties have sometimes arisen when cases of rape come to light many years after the actual events, for example when adult men and women report rapes which occurred against them when they were children. As with indecent assaults, care should be taken when dealing with an alleged rape that happened in such circumstances. For example, until 1993 there was a presumption that a boy under the age of 14 was incapable of sexual intercourse and therefore any allegation against such a boy having sexual intercourse with a complainant prior to 20 September 1993 would run into difficulties. Similarly, having unlawful sexual intercourse with a boy without his consent did not constitute rape until the introduction of the CJPOA 1994.

1.58 A perfect example of such a situation arose in the case of *Fowler*[1] which concerned a 44-year-old man who pleaded guilty to eight counts of rape, eight counts of indecent assault and eight counts of gross indecency (together with other, non-sexual offences). The offences were committed between 1972 and 1975 and the victim was a boy between the ages of 8 and 11. He was sentenced to six years in prison for each of the rapes, with lesser sentences for the other offences. The sentence was reduced to two years on appeal. However, nobody, apparently throughout the entire proceedings up to the Court of Appeal (and it should be said, Professor Thomas in his commentary to the case) seems to have noticed that at the time of the offences, anal intercourse did not constitute the offence of rape. As James Richardson has put it, '[that] "nobody" includes a circuit judge, two puisne judges and a lord justice of appeal ... [W]hatever other offences this appellant was guilty of, he was not guilty of rape'[2]. It should also include both prosecuting and defending counsel.

1 [2002] EWCA Crim 620, [2002] Crim LR 521.

2 See (2002) Criminal Law Week, 26 December.

1.59 Part I (ss 1 to 6) of the Sex Offenders Act 1997 applies to offences of rape[1]. This part of the SOA 1997 relates to the requirement for, and effect of, people sentenced for the offence to register with their local police force. It is beyond the scope of this book to look at the provisions in great detail, but it is an issue that should be borne in mind by all students and practitioners.

1 See SOA 1997, Sch 1.

1.60 It should also be noted that both rape and attempted rape constitutes a 'serious offence' so far as the Powers of Criminal Courts (Sentencing) Act 2000, s 109 is concerned. The effect of this section is that if a man is convicted of such an offence after 30 September 1997 *and* at the time when that offence was committed, he was 18 or over and had been convicted in any part of the United Kingdom of another serious offence[1], then the court has the power to impose a life sentence for the later offence. Notice should be taken of the fact that it is possible for the earlier offence to have been committed anywhere within the United Kingdom for the provision to come into play.

1 PCC(S)A 2000, s 109(1)(a) and (b). See also sub-ss (5), (6) and (7) for a full list of qualifying offences.

1.61 For an offence of rape a sentencing judge is entitled to invoke PCC(S)A 2000, ss 85 and 86 which allow for the extension of sentences imposed for sexual (or violent) offences. In addition, if the offence is committed against a child complainant, s/he may be ordered to be disqualified from working with children, under Criminal Justice and Court Services Act 2000, ss 26 to 31.

Chapter two

'Unnatural offences'

2.1 The SOA 1956, ss 12 and 13 deal with what are termed, somewhat unfortunately, 'Unnatural Offences'. This is a term that was clearly acceptable during the 1950s but which has taken on insulting and offensive connotations in the 21st century. It is to be deplored that, with the numerous amendments that have been made to various provisions in the original Act, no government has seen fit to dispense with the heading entirely. It is only for convenience and consistency with the Act that the term is used in this chapter.

2.2 The two so-called 'unnatural offences' covered by SOA 1956, ss 12 and 13 are buggery and indecency between men (usually reduced to the phrase 'gross indecency'). Each of these will be considered in turn.

A Buggery

2.3 As will be seen when the SOA 1956, s 12 is considered, the act of buggery can be undertaken between two males, between a man and a woman or between either sex and an animal. The latter form of buggery is usually referred to as bestiality and this will be considered separately below.

2.4 Since the SOA 1956, s 1 was amended to include in the definition of rape both vaginal and anal penetration without consent, the offence of buggery has lost a considerable amount of its original power. Allegations of non-consensual anal intercourse should now be charged as rape, indeed Judge LJ said in the case of *Davies*[1] that:

> [W]hen non-consensual sexual intercourse, whether vaginal or anal, is alleged it must be charged as rape, with (if appropriate) an alternative count of buggery.

Having said that, it will become clear that the only time buggery should be charged alone is when both parties are consenting to the anal intercourse, but, either that one or both participants is/are below the age of consent, more than two persons were present during the act, or the consensual act did not take place in private.

1 [1998] 1 Cr App Rep (S) 380, CA.

2.5 The original SOA 1956, s 12(1) merely set out that it was 'a felony for a person to commit buggery with another person or with an animal' taking its lead from the common law interpretation of what constituted buggery, ie 'sodomy'. Since the inception of the SOA 1956, however, there have been many amendments to this particular section, especially in relation to the age of consent between homosexual partners and the current state of SOA 1956, s 12 is as follows:

> 12(1) It is an offence for a person to commit buggery with another person otherwise than in the circumstances first described in subsection (1A) or (1AA) below or with an animal.
>
> (1A) The circumstances referred to in section (1) are that the act of buggery takes place in private and both parties have attained the age of 16.
>
> (1AA) The other circumstances so referred to are that the person is under the age of 16 and the other person has attained that age.
>
> (1B) An act of buggery by one man with another shall not be treated as taking place in private if it takes place –
> (a) when more than two persons take part or are present; or
> (b) in a lavatory to which the public have or are permitted to have access, whether on payment or otherwise.

(1C) In any proceedings against a person for buggery with another person it shall be for the prosecutor to prove that the act of buggery took place otherwise than in private or that one of the parties to it had not attained the age of 16.

2.6 All very well as far as it goes. However, the offence of buggery actually now comprises three separate offences which are differentiated by each one's factual circumstances. This is said because the sentencing regime is different for each one of those three different offences. When combining the sentences as set out in the SOA 1956, Sch 2 (as amended), together with the SOA 1967, s 3 (as amended), the current maximum sentences for each offence are as follows:

A.	If committed with a person under the age of 16 or with a woman or an animal	Life
B.	If the accused is 21 or over and the other person is under the age of 18	five years
C.	In any other circumstances	two years

These sentencing provisions are of special significance when it comes to charging and, on conviction, dealing with the defendant and for ease of reference in this chapter, the offences being discussed will be referred to as 'A', 'B' or 'C' offences as appropriate.

2.7 This issue was addressed in the case of *Courtie*[1] in which Lord Diplock set out the (then) situation pertaining to the various offences within the term 'buggery'. He said:

> ... the effect of [amendments to the SOA 1967] is that the SOA 1967 creates a number of specific offences for which the maximum punishment prescribed varies upon a descending scale from imprisonment for life, ('the life-offence') ... imprisonment for five years ('the five-year offence') down to imprisonment for two years ('the two-year offence'), according to the existence or absence of particular factual ingredients[2].

The rationale behind Lord Diplock's dictum still stands but the case was decided before at least two further amendments to the age restrictions contained in the present Act and should now be seen in the light of those amendments.

1 [1984] AC 463, [1984] 1 All ER 740, HL.

2 [1984] AC 463 at 471, HL.

2.8 It will be noted that the offence initially encompasses both participants in an act of buggery by the use of the word 'person' and therefore both parties can be charged as principals to the offence. The parlance used in some of the Victorian cases involving buggery is to refer to the 'victim' of the buggery as the 'patient' and the other party as the 'agent'.

2.9 In addition to the SOA 1956, s 12, attention should be paid to a number of different statutes when considering the offence of buggery (and indeed, for gross indecency). The SOA 1967, s 7 reads as follows:

> 7(1) No proceedings for an offence to which this section applies shall be commenced after the expiration of 12 months from the date on which that offence was committed.
>
> (2) This section applies to –
> (a) any offence under section 13 of the Act of 1956 (gross indecency between men);
> (b) *repealed*;
> (c) any offence of buggery by a man with another man not amounting to an assault on that other man and not being an offence by a man with a boy under the age of 16.

The effect of sub-s (2)(c) is that the charge has to be laid within a 12-month period from the date of the commission of the offence *only* when the act was committed otherwise than in private and when both parties were men.

2.10 The SOA 1967, s 8 reads as follows:

> No proceedings shall be instituted except by or with the consent of the Director of Public Prosecutions against any man for the offence of buggery with, or gross indecency with, another man, ... or for aiding, abetting, counselling, procuring or commanding its commission where either of those men was at the time of its commission under the age of 16.

Failure to obtain such consent will lead to the quashing of a conviction for any of the offences listed[1].

1 See, for example, *Angel* [1968] 2 All ER 607n, 52 Cr App Rep 280, CA and *Secretary of State for Defence v Warn* [1970] AC 394, [1968] 2 All ER 300, HL in which it was held that SOA 1967, s 8 applied to a court-martial.

2.11 In addition to the above two provisions, the offence is also governed, to a certain extent, by the SOA 1967, s 1 (as amended by both the Mental Health (Amendment) Act 1982 and the Sexual Offences (Amendment) Act 2000). This provision overlaps somewhat with the SOA 1956, s 12 and reads as follows:

> 1(1) Notwithstanding any statutory or common law provision ...
> (a) a homosexual act in private shall not be an offence provided that the parties consent thereto and have attained the age of 16 years; and
> (b) a homosexual act by any person shall not be an offence if he is under the age of 16 and the other party has attained that age.
>
> (2) An act which would otherwise be treated for the purposes of this Act as being done in private shall not be so treated if done –
> (a) when more than two persons take part or are present; or
> (b) in a lavatory to which the public have or are permitted to have access, whether on payment or otherwise.
>
> (3) A man who is suffering from severe mental handicap cannot in law give any consent which, by virtue of subsection 1 of this section, would prevent a homosexual act from being an offence, but a person shall not be convicted, on account of the incapacity of such a man to consent, of an offence consisting of such an act if he proves that he did not know and had no reason to suspect that man to be suffering from severe mental handicap[1].
>
> (3A) In subsection (3) of this section 'severe mental handicap' means a state of arrested or incomplete development of mind which includes severe impairment of intelligence and social functioning.
>
> (4) Section 128 of the Mental Health Act 1959 (prohibition on men on the staff of a hospital, or otherwise having responsibility for mental patients, having sexual intercourse with women patients) shall have effect as if any reference

therein to having unlawful sexual intercourse with a woman included a reference to committing buggery or an act of gross indecency with another man.

(5) *Repealed.*

(6) It is hereby declared that where in any proceedings it is charged that a homosexual act is an offence the prosecutor shall have the burden of proving that the act was done otherwise than in private or otherwise than with the consent of the parties or that any of the parties had not attained the age of 16 years.

(7) For the purposes of this section a man shall be treated as doing a homosexual act if, and only if, he commits buggery with another man or commits an act of gross indecency with another man or is a party to the commission by a man of such an act.

1 Offences concerning sexual intercourse with 'mental defectives' are dealt with in Chapter 4 below.

2.12 When attempting to pull together all of the dizzying array of statutory provisions that pertain to the offence of buggery, it must be said that some issues are not reconcilable. However, a full analysis produces the following points:

- In order for an act to constitute the offence of buggery the following features are important:
  - at least one party must be under 16 years of age if heterosexual buggery is performed in private,
  - if both parties are 16 or over it must be performed in public.
- Consent is never an issue – lack of it would constitute rape.
- Homosexual buggery is not an offence where the 'agent' is under 16 and the 'patient' is 16 or over (SOA 1967, s 1(1)(b)).
- A 'patient' who is suffering from severe mental handicap cannot give consent so as to prevent the act being an offence (but again such buggery should be charged as rape).
- It is for the prosecution to prove that the act took place otherwise than in private or that one of the parties was under 16 – though it is for the defendant to raise the issue.
- No proceedings for buggery can be instituted more than 12 months after the commission of the offence (for offences 'B' and 'C' only).

- The consent of the DPP is required for any proceedings against any person for the offence where either participant was under 16 years of age.
- Buggery comprises three separate offences depending on the factual circumstances and maximum sentences differ accordingly.

General Issues

Mode of Trial

2.13 Buggery is an offence that can only be tried on indictment[1]. It is a Class 3 offence and as such can be tried by a High Court judge, a circuit judge or a recorder who has been properly authorised by a presiding judge[2]. The same factors apply when the charge is of attempted buggery.

1 See the SOA 1956, s 37(2) and Sch 2, para 3.

2 Practice Direction (Crown Court: allocation of business) (No 3) [2000] 1 All ER 380, [2000] 1 WLR 203.

2.14 It should be noted that in certain circumstances the United Kingdom courts do not have jurisdiction to try 'a member of a visiting force or a civilian component of such a force'. Under the VFA 1952, s 3(1) an offence under SOA 1956, s 12 may come under this provision.

Parties to the Offence

2.15 As has already been noted, both participants in an act of buggery can be charged as principals to the offence. The law sees each participant as equally culpable in the offence and makes no distinction between them. The 'patient' should not be regarded merely as an accessory to the 'agent'[1]. It is also the case that a man can be charged with buggery when his wife is the 'patient'[2]. However, this decision would have to now be looked at in the light of the age considerations, and the issue of consent as they affect the current offence. For example, if the man's wife was not consenting then he should be charged with rape; if she does consent then the offence would only be committed if the wife was under the age of 18 and the husband was over 21 (the 'B' offence) and the offence was committed otherwise than in private.

1 See, for example, *R v DPP, ex p C* [1995] 1 Cr App Rep 136.

2 *Jellyman* (1838) 8 C & P 604.

2.16 Until September 1993 there was a common law presumption that a boy under the age of 14 could not indulge in sexual intercourse, either vaginal or anal. This presumption was abolished by the Sexual Offences Act 1993, s 1. The effect of that provision is to allow the conviction of any male aged 10[1] or over for any sexual offence involving the penetration of the vagina or anus of the complainant by him. Thus there is no reason why a boy between the ages of 10 and 16 cannot be prosecuted for the offence of buggery so long as all of the other criteria are satisfied. Notice should be made of the SOA 1967, s 1(1)(b)[2].

1 The age at which any criminal liability arises: see the CYPA 1933, s 50.

2 See paragraph 2.11 above.

2.17 An interesting topic relating to the fact that both participants can be charged as principals to the offence of buggery arose in the case of *Bourne*[1] which concerned an act of bestiality. In the Court of Appeal, Lord Goddard seemed to suggest that it is not voluntary, but involuntary participation which may provide a defence to buggery. Thus, where a participant performs his or her part under some form of duress, this may afford a defence to the charge of buggery where the victim of the duress is the 'agent' rather than the 'patient'. Having said that, depending on the circumstances, if the duress amounts to a threat of some kind that may amount to the offence of rape.

1 (1952) 36 Cr App Rep 125, CCA.

Complainant's Anonymity

2.18 The 'patient' in an allegation of buggery is entitled to comprehensive anonymity[1]. The question of anonymity would only ever arise when the 'patient' was not being tried as a principal to the offence. The anonymity of the 'patient' stretches to cover the publication of any matter relating to him/her 'if it is likely to lead members of the public to identify that person as the person against whom the offence is alleged to have been committed'[2]. The anonymity in these provisions remains in place throughout the complainant's lifetime. The anonymity provisions can however be over-ridden by an application by the accused to the trial judge to direct that the SO(A)A 1992, s 1 should not apply in relation to the complainant. Under the SO(A)A 1992, s 3(1) in order for such a direction to be made the judge must be satisfied of two things, namely that:

(a) the direction is required for the purpose of inducing persons who are likely to be needed as witnesses at the trial to come forward; and
(b) the conduct of the applicant's defence at the trial is likely to be substantially prejudiced if the direction is not given.

1 SO(A)A 1992, ss 1-4. These provisions apply to a large number of sexual offences.

2 See SO(A)A 1992, s 1(1).

2.19 The trial judge can also direct that the SO(A)A 1992, s 1 should not apply if he is satisfied that such anonymity 'imposes a substantial and unreasonable restriction upon the reporting of proceedings at the trial' and 'that it is in the public interest to remove or relax the restriction'[1].

1 See SO(A)A 1992, s 3(2).

2.20 As both participants in buggery can be charged as principals, Parliament enacted the SO(A)A 1992, s 4(4) which excludes – in rather clumsy language – the anonymity provisions from applying where both parties to the act are charged with the offence.

Alternative Verdicts

2.21 The legal concept of buggery is made up of three distinct offences, differentiated by their factual circumstances and the various ages of the participants. If a person were charged with the 'B' offence and the jury were not satisfied by the evidence that either that person was over 21, or the other person was under 18, then they could find the person not guilty of the 'B' offence but guilty of the 'C' offence[1].

1 Criminal Law Act 1967, s 6(3); *R v Courtie* [1984] AC 463 at 473, HL.

2.22 As will be seen below, the offence of buggery is committed when penetration of the 'patient's' anus is complete. Thus, if the jury are not satisfied that actual penetration occurred, though that was the intention of the 'agent' and acts occurred which were more than merely preparatory to the commission of buggery, then it is open to them to find the defendant guilty of an attempt[1].

1 CLA 1967, s 6(4).

Actus Reus

2.23 The first issue as to the offence of buggery is comparatively straightforward. For the act of buggery to occur, penetration of the anus must take place. As in the offence of rape, the act is complete once penetration is proved and the emission of seed is not required[1].

1 *R v Reekspear* (1832) 1 Mood CC 342.

2.24 The second issue in the offence is rather more complicated and relates to the ages of the participants. As has been shown above, there are, in effect, three distinct offences of buggery (so far as humans are concerned) and each depends upon the ages of the parties.

2.25 The best way of approaching this issue is first to consider that the offence is only committed by consensual partners. Secondly, if the act is performed otherwise than in private, then it is an offence no matter what the age of the participants. Thirdly, if both partners are at least 16 years of age, then no offence has been committed, unless it was performed in public. Fourthly, notice must be paid to the SOA 1967, s 1(1)(b)[1].

1 See paragraph 2.11 above.

2.26 Having said all of that, care should be taken in addressing the evidence of the relative ages of the participants when considering which of the three extant offences has been committed and therefore should be charged. It is for the prosecution to prove the pertinent ages of the participants and also to prove, if necessary, that the act took place otherwise than in private.

Mens Rea

2.27 The mental element in the offence of buggery has the potential to become extremely complicated. It must always be remembered that there are three distinct offences of buggery and the ages of each participant must always be borne in mind. Paragraph 2.6 above sets out the different maximum sentences for the various offences and it will be seen from that table that convictions for the various offences can lead to widely different sentences of imprisonment.

2.28 In addition to the topic of the participants' ages, it will not be unusual for the defendant to raise the issue that he or she thought their partner was older than he or she actually was. For example, a 25-year-old man may have anal sex with a 15-year-old (of either sex) – the 'A' offence leading to a possible life sentence – thinking that his partner was 16. Until the House of Lords decision in *B (a minor) v DPP*[1] such a man would not be entitled to an acquittal simply because of his mistaken belief in the age of his partner. Since that case, however, the courts will have to allow him to put such a defence before the jury for them to decide how honest and reasonable that belief was.

1 [2000] 2 AC 428, [2000] 1 All ER 833, [2000] 2 Cr App Rep 65, HL and see *R v K* [2001] UKHL 41, [2002] 1 AC 462, [2001] 3 All ER 897.

Sentence

2.29 As has been mentioned above, the three distinct offences of buggery attract different maximum sentences and the particular facts of each case must be considered in detail when considering the appropriate sentence.

2.30 A great many of the cases relating to the sentencing exercise pertaining to the offence of buggery have also been responsible for deciding on the various parameters of the offences themselves. Indeed, the leading case of *Courtie*[1] went to the House of Lords following a guilty plea in the Crown Court. The defendant pleaded guilty to what would now constitute the 'B' offence, which then carried a maximum sentence of five years in prison (at that time the age of consent was 21 and the 'patient' was 19). Following his plea it became clear from the Crown's version of the facts that the allegation was of a much more serious offence of buggery carrying a maximum penalty (then) of 10 years in prison. The sentencing judge made it clear that he was sentencing him on the basis of the more serious offence. The Court of Appeal dismissed his appeal, but the House of Lords allowed it and reduced his sentence holding that to sentence someone for an offence graver than that to which they had pleaded guilty was contrary to a basic principle of English criminal law. The case should be the starting point for any sentencing exercise concerning the offence of buggery. It is essential that, in the first place, a defendant knows which of the offences he faces and, if convicted, the sentencing judge is aware of which of the sentencing regimes is open to him or her.

1 [1984] AC 463, [1984] 1 All ER 740, HL.

2.31 It should also be noted that, due to the large number of amendments to the various statutes relating to the offence of buggery over the years, the case law has to be approached with some caution. For example, a number of cases refer to how a person should be sentenced when non-consensual buggery has taken place. Such an act should now be charged as rape and therefore any dicta relating to such matters should be discounted[1]. Further, a number of the earlier cases were decided at a time when homosexual acts were seen in a much less permissive light than they are today.

1 See for example, the comparatively recent case of *Davies* [1998] 1 Cr App Rep (S) 380, CA where, upon conviction for buggery of a 15-year-old girl, the defendant was sentenced for forcibly buggering her.

2.32 Having said that the main principle in sentencing is that the defendant should be sentenced for what he has done wrong in law, an attempt will now be made to extract some other principles from the case law.

2.33 The 'A' offence is without doubt the most serious of buggery offences and, of course, carries a maximum penalty of life in prison. It is committed only where the 'agent' is over 16 years of age and the 'patient' is under that age. It is often referred to as the 'full offence'. The other two offences rarely come to court and any sentences imposed appear not to be appealed against. There is a dearth of such cases that have come before the Court of Appeal.

2.34 In *Willis*[1], a case in which a 24-year-old man pleaded guilty to an offence of buggery on an eight-year-old boy, Lawton LJ said that:

> ... judges should always regard buggery with boys [and, no doubt, girls] under the age of 16 as a serious offence – and the younger the boy the more serious the offence[2].

He went on to say that such an offence in which there were neither aggravating nor mitigating factors (though this would be rare) would attract a sentence of between three and five years in prison.

1 [1975] 1 All ER 620, 60 Cr App Rep 143, CA.

2 (1974) 60 Cr App Rep 143 at146, CA.

2.35 Further, he listed the following factors as being of significance as aggravating factors:

(i) *physical injury to the boy* – and the more serious the violence the higher the sentence,

(ii) *emotional and psychological damage* – but judges should not assume that either of these forms of damage is a probable result or that such an attack will lead to the victim becoming a homosexual in later life,

(iii) *moral corruption* – especially in terms of gifts of money or other incentives,

(iv) *abuse of authority or trust*[1],

and the following as being significant in terms of mitigating features:

(i) *mental imbalance* – special caution should be taken where the imbalance is sufficiently serious as to warrant an alternative to an immediate committal to prison,

(ii) *personality disorders* – such men may require management rather than treatment,

(iii) *emotional stress*.

1 The case was decided before the introduction of this as a particular offence. See Chapter 3 for an analysis of this offence.

2.36 Other attempts have been made to set out guidelines for sentencing in such cases but rarely has the topic been addressed with such good sense, sound logic and sensitivity. Care ought to be taken by sentencing judges not to pander to public opprobrium shown to the kind of people who commit such offences. This issue was addressed by Lord Lawton in *Willis* and the sound reasoning in his decision still stands the test of time. In considering the topic he stated the following:

> One of the difficulties judges have in sentencing offenders of this type is their own reactions of revulsion to what the accused has been proved to have done. Right-thinking members of the public have the same reactions and expect the judges in their sentences to reflect public abhorrence of the graver kinds of criminal homosexual acts. There is a widely held opinion that homosexual offences involving boys lead to the corruption of the boys and cause them severe emotional damage. Judges of experience are often of this opinion because when considering homosexual offences they are frequently told in pleas of mitigation that the accused was made an homosexual as a result of being involved when a boy in homosexual acts by a man.

He then went onto warn judges against simply stopping there and urged them to consider, for example, the Wolfenden Report[1] which considered such matters in great detail and did not conclude that such events necessarily led to a young man becoming homosexual in later life.

1 Report of the Departmental Committee on Homosexual Offences and Prostitution, 1957.

2.37 Part I (ss 1 to 6) and Sch 1 of the Sex Offenders Act 1997 applies to offences of buggery[1]. This part of the Act relates to the requirement for, and effect of, people sentenced for the offence to register with their local police force. It should be remembered that the Act also applies when the offence is committed with an animal. In addition, if the offence is committed against a child complainant, he can be ordered to be disqualified from working with children under CJCSA 2000, ss 26 to 31.

1 See SOA 1997, Sch 1.

Bestiality

2.38 Bestiality is not a distinct offence from buggery and is also governed by the SOA 1956, s 12(1) and the procedural issues relating to mode of trial are identical. The maximum sentence for bestiality is life imprisonment.

2.39 Perhaps understandably there have been very few cases of bestiality to come before the lower courts let alone the Court of Appeal and so it is difficult to extract any significant principles pertaining to the offence. Suffice to say that both men and women can be charged as principles in the offence and both male and female animals can be victims. There is no differentiation between vaginal or anal sex when buggery is performed on the animal and it would seem that any creature within the animal kingdom could be a victim of the offence[1].

1 See for example *Brown* (1889) 24 QBD 357, CCR.

2.40 In essence, the few cases relating to the offence that have come before the higher courts concern two distinct ways of committing the offence. In *Higson*[1] for example, when a man was convicted of attempted buggery on a dog, a prison sentence was replaced with a probation order because, as the court said, it was the man who needed help, not the dog and the sentencing exercise should be aimed at preventing a recurrence of the offence rather than punishing the perpetrator.

1 (1984) 6 Cr App Rep (S) 20, CA.

2.41 Alternatively, in the case of *Tierney*[1], where a man coerced his ex-wife into committing buggery with an Alsatian dog, a prison sentence was upheld due to the particularly distressing effect the offence would no doubt have had upon the man's ex-wife.

1 (1990) 12 Cr App Rep (S) 216, CA.

2.42 The case of *Bourne*[1] involved similar facts to that of *Tierney*, with a man forcing his wife to allow him to insert a dog's penis into her vagina. She was not charged at all and he was charged with aiding and abetting his wife to commit buggery. Upon conviction he appealed on the basis that he should not have been convicted as a principal if his wife could not be convicted. The argument was rejected by Lord Goddard CJ who set out a general principle pertaining to such offences. In essence his argument was that the man was properly convicted because, even had the wife been charged, she would have been acquitted as her defence would have been that she was acting under duress. As he put it, 'the offence does not depend upon consent but on the act'. Thus both man and wife committed the actus reus and both had the requisite mens rea. However, in such circumstances, the woman was to be excused because she had a proper defence available to her. It ought to be the case in future that similar cases will be charged in the same way. However, in the case of *Pamela Jean P*[2] the unfortunate defendant was charged (together with her then boyfriend) with attempted buggery with a cross-breed Alsatian dog. Following a guilty plea she was sentenced to three months in prison with the sentencing judge dismissing her claim that she committed the act unwillingly and only in an attempt to keep the man she loved. The Court of Appeal saw no justification in the judge dismissing her contention and, while not spelling out that a prison sentence was not justified, suggested that the shame that would be suffered as a result of such a conviction might mean that a prison sentence was not necessarily appropriate.

1 (1952) 36 Cr App Rep 125, CCA.

2 (1991) 13 Cr App R (S) 369, CA.

B Gross Indecency

2.43 The SOA 1956, s 13 is another provision that has been amended a number of times through the years (the latest being the reduction to 16 of the age of consent for homosexual acts by the Sexual Offences (Amendment) Act 2000) and now reads as follows:

> 13 It is an offence for a man to commit an act of gross indecency with another man otherwise than in the circumstances described below, whether in public or private, or to be a party to the commission by an act of gross indecency with another man, or to procure the commission by a man of an act of gross indecency with another man.

The circumstances referred to above are that the man is under the age of 16 and the other man has attained that age.

2.44 It will be seen from the statute that SOA 1956, s 13 actually comprises two distinct offences, ie committing 'an act of gross indecency' and procuring the 'commission by a man of an act of gross indecency ...'. The latter aspect of the provision will be considered in Chapter 7 when offences involving the procurement of a number of offences are dealt with. In saying that the provision comprises two distinct offences, as a result of the case of *Courtie*[1] gross indecency, like buggery, is made up of offences differentiated by the ages of the participants and distinguished by the different maximum sentences for each.

1 [1984] AC 463, [1984] 1 All ER 740, HL.

2.45 The SOA 1956, ss 7 and 8 apply to this offence[1]. As the offence can only be committed by men, notice should also be paid to the SOA 1967, s 1[2]. The effect of s 1 is that no offence is committed when the act in question is committed in private and between men who are both aged 16 or over. If the defendants to a charge of gross indecency contend that the act took place in private, it is for them to raise the issue at trial and then it is for the prosecution to prove that the act was committed in a public place[3].

1 See paragraphs 2.9 and 2.10 above.

2 See paragraph 2.11 above.

3 See SOA 1967, s 1(2) and (6). See also the case of *Reakes* [1974] Crim LR 615 where the Court of Appeal said that the test for what is a private place was not subjective.

General Issues

Mode of Trial

2.46 Gross indecency is an offence which is triable either way[1]. It is a Class 4 offence and as such, when committed to the Crown Court, can be tried by a High Court judge, a circuit judge or a recorder[2].

1 See the SOA 1956, s 37(2) and Sch 2, para 16.

2 Practice Direction (Crown Court: allocation of business) (No 3) [2000] 1 All ER 380, [2000] 1 WLR 203.

2.47 In certain circumstances the United Kingdom courts do not have jurisdiction to try 'a member of a visiting force or a civilian component of such a force'. Under the VFA 1952, s 3(1) an offence under the SOA 1956, s 13 may come under this provision.

Actus Reus

2.48 While a comprehensive definition of 'gross indecency' has never been attempted by either Parliament or the courts, Smith and Hogan, in the eighth edition of their *Criminal Law*, quote the definition of the term as set out by the Wolfenden Committee[1]. It would be difficult to better the definition given there which reads:

> ... the offence usually takes one of three forms; either there is mutual masturbation; or there is some form of intercrural contact; or oral genital contact (with or without emission) takes place. Occasionally the offence may take a more recondite form; techniques in heterosexual relations may vary considerably, and the same is true of homosexual relations.

1 [1984] AC 463 at 496.

2.49 One of the difficulties in dealing with the offence is in deciding what exactly does constitute 'gross indecency' as opposed to mere 'indecency'. The ultimate decision must be for the jury or magistrates and so it can be said that what was regarded as grossly indecent many years ago might not be so regarded today. For this reason, case law involving such questions should be considered very carefully, especially the older cases.

2.50 The essence of the offence is that two men willingly participate in an act of gross indecency in public. If one man is not a consenting participant then the offence is not made out – though another offence may be. The point was amply illustrated in the case of *Preece and Howells*[1] where the two defendants were convicted of the offence. The men were in adjacent public toilet cubicles. There was a hole between the cubicles and the evidence was that they were both masturbating while watching each other through the holes. There was no evidence that the two men knew each other or had gone to the toilet in order to meet each other. They appealed, arguing that the word 'with another man' in SOA 1956, s 13 meant 'in concert with him' or 'with his consent'. Lord Scarman, having considered all of the pertinent case law, concluded that:

> We think the complete offence requires the participation, the co-operation, of two men. The offence, now that the

> words 'in private' have been deleted, is one of an indecent exhibition by two men in a public place ... [T]o construe the section so that the complete offence could be committed even though the other man did not consent could lead to the embarrassment of, and injustice to, innocent men.

He went on to give the example of a man who gleans sexual pleasure from masturbating in public. A man who happened to see the other man masturbating would not be a willing participant in an act of gross indecency and would, of course, be innocent of any offence. The first man would also not be guilty of an act of gross indecency, but would be committing another offence – outraging public decency for example.

1 [1977] QB 370, 63 Cr App Rep 28, CA.

2.51 It will also be seen from the case of *Preece and Howells*, that, as was decided in the earlier case of *Hunt*[1], it is not necessary for direct physical contact between the participants to occur for the offence to be committed.

1 (1950) 34 Cr App Rep 135, CCA.

2.52 As it is an essential aspect of the offence that two men must be acting in concert and willingly participating in the grossly indecent act, if the evidence against the two men is identical then it must be the case that they are either both convicted or both acquitted. However, it is possible for one man to be convicted and the other acquitted where the evidence does not support the contention that both men were willing participants. An obvious example would be when one of the men pleads guilty to the offence but the other denies that he was acting in concert with the other. It will of course depend upon the particular circumstances of each offence. Lord Parker CJ in the case of *Pearce*[1] did however say that:

> [T]here is nothing to support the proposition that where two persons are jointly indicted for such an offence, one cannot be convicted and the other acquitted.

1 [1951] 1 All ER 493 at 494, CCA.

Mens Rea

2.53 There is really only one issue to be considered so far as the mens rea of the offence is concerned. That is, were each of the defendants aware that what each man was doing was being done in concert with the other. This issue will be rather more difficult to prove in circumstances such as the facts of *Preece and Howells*, where there was no direct physical contact between the two men, than when such direct contact can be proved. However, it will still be for the prosecution to prove that both men were consenting participants.

Sentence

2.54 As has been mentioned above, the offence has been altered a number of times over the years as the age of consent for homosexuals has been changed, from 21 to 18 and then from 18 to 16. As a result of those changes, the sentences for the offence have been altered by various amending statutes. Both the CJPOA 1994, s 144 and the SO(A)A 2000, s 1 were enacted in order to amend the relevant sentence. The case of *Courtie*[1] made it clear that there are two offences contained within SOA 1956, s 13, each one depending on the ages of the participants, and each one attracting a different maximum sentence. The more serious offence is that perpetrated by a man over the age of 21 with a man under 16, where the maximum sentence is five years in prison; in any other circumstance the maximum sentence is two years in prison. Those sentences apply only when the man or men are tried on indictment. The equivalent sentence for a case tried summarily is six months in prison[2].

1 [1984] AC 463, [1984] 1 All ER 740, HL.

2 See the MCA 1980, s 32.

2.55 There are no significant guideline cases for sentencing gross indecency. However it has been suggested in the Court of Appeal that, certainly for first-time offenders, custodial sentences are not appropriate as, very often, the shame of such a conviction is sufficient to prevent further offending[1].

1 See, for example, *Morgan and Dockerty* [1979] Crim LR 60 and *Clayton* [1981] Crim LR 425.

2.56 Part I (ss 1 to 6) and Sch 1 of the SOA 1997 applies to offences of gross indecency[1]. This part of the Act relates to the requirement for, and effect of, people sentenced for the offence to register with their local police force. In addition, if the offence is committed against a child complainant, he can be ordered to be disqualified from working with children under CJCSA 2000, ss 26 to 31.

1 See the SOA 1997, Sch 1.

C Procuring Others to Commit Homosexual Acts

2.57 The SOA 1967, s 4 reads as follows:

> 4(1) A man who procures another man to commit with a third man an act of buggery which by reason of section 1 of this Act is not an offence shall be liable on conviction on indictment to imprisonment for a term not exceeding two years.
>
> (2) *Repealed.*
>
> (3) It shall not be an offence under section 13 of the Act of 1956 for a man to procure the commission by another man of an act of gross indecency with the first-mentioned man which by reason of section 1 of this Act is not an offence under the said section 13.

2.58 The SOA 1967, s 1 amended the law so as to prevent a homosexual act committed in private between consenting parties who are both (now) 16 being a criminal offence. In those circumstances, an offence under SOA 1967, s 4(1) can only be committed when one of the parties to the buggery is under 16 years old or the buggery takes place otherwise than in private, or there were more than two people present.

2.59 The use of the word 'man' in the section applies just as much to boys. By virtue of SOA 1956, s 46 and the SOA 1967, s 11(3), the two words are interchangeable.

General Issues

Mode of Trial

2.60 This is an offence which is triable either way[1]. It is a Class 4 offence and as such, when committed to the Crown Court, can be tried by a High Court judge, a circuit judge or a recorder[2].

1 MCA 1980, s 17(1) and Sch 1.

2 *Practice Direction (Crown Court: allocation of business) (No 3)* [2000] 1 All ER 380, [2000] 1 WLR 203.

Actus Reus

Procure

2.61 For issues pertaining to the definition of 'procure' see paragraph 4.31 below.

An Act of Buggery

2.62 The offence of buggery is now so constrained that it is an offence that is likely to come before the criminal courts only rarely[1]. For an allegation that a SOA 1967, s 4(1) offence has been committed to succeed, it would have to be proved that the procurement of the second man by the defendant was to commit buggery as currently defined with the third man. If the act intended did not constitute an offence, as the law of buggery currently stands, then it is submitted that no offence under s 4(1) has been committed. Any lesser standard would lead to a situation in which one man could procure another to have anal intercourse with a third man; males 2 and 3 have committed no offence (assuming adulthood, consent and privacy) but male 1 has committed an offence under s 4(1). Although the section only uses the phrase 'an act of buggery', it is submitted that this must mean more than merely an act of anal intercourse.

1 See paragraphs 2.3 to 2.12 above.

Mens Rea

2.63 The prosecution would have to prove that the defendant was aware that he was procuring the complainant so as to have him commit an act of buggery with a third man. If he were to have procured the second man for any other purpose then he would not be guilty of an offence under this section.

Sentence

2.64 For an offence tried on indictment the maximum prison sentence is one of two years. When the offence is tried summarily the maximum penalty is a fine not exceeding the prescribed sum or six months in prison or both[1]. In addition, if the offence is committed against a child complainant, he can be ordered to be disqualified from working with children under CJCSA 2000, ss 26 to 31.

1 See MCA 1980, s 17 and Sch 1.

Chapter three

Offences involving children

A Sexual Intercourse with a Girl under 13

3.1 The SOA 1956, s 5 as amended by the CLA 1967, s 12(5)(a), reads as follows:

> It is an offence for a man to have unlawful sexual intercourse with a girl under the age of 13.

3.2 The use of the word 'man' in this provision should be read as referring to both men and boys[1]. By virtue of the SOA 1956, s 46 the two terms are interchangeable.

1 See paragraph 3.7 below.

3.3 It might be said that the only real difference between this offence and that of rape is that for the latter offence to be proved, there must be no consent to sexual intercourse on the part of the victim. Consent on the girl's part will afford the defendant no defence to an allegation under SOA 1956, s 5, whereas it will to an allegation of rape. If the prosecution are satisfied that it can be proved that the girl did not consent to sexual intercourse, then a charge of rape should be laid.

General Issues

Mode of Trial

3.4 The offence, together with an attempt to commit the offence, is triable on indictment only[1]. Both offences are Class 2 offences and, as such, can be tried only by a High Court judge unless the case is released by or on the authority of a presiding judge for trial by a circuit judge[2].

1 See the SOA 1956, s 37(2) and Sch 2, para 2.

2 Practice Direction (Crown Court: allocation of business) (No 3) [2000] 1 All ER 380, [2000] 1 WLR 203.

3.5 It should be noted that in certain circumstances the United Kingdom courts do not have jurisdiction to try 'a member of a visiting force or a civilian component of such a force'. Under the VFA 1952, s 3(1), an offence under the SOA 1956, s 5 may come under this provision.

Parties to the Offence

3.6 Only a male can commit the offence as a principal and only a girl under the age of 13 years can be a victim. The fact that the alleged victim is under the age of 13 forms part of the actus reus of the offence and is dealt with in paragraphs 3.15 to 3.18 below.

3.7 The presumption that a boy under the age of 14 could not indulge in sexual intercourse was abolished in 1993 by SOA 1993, s 1. The effect of the provision is to allow the conviction of any male aged 10[1] or over for any offence involving sexual intercourse.

1 The age at which any criminal liability arises: see the CYPA 1933, s 50.

3.8 It might be thought that in circumstances in which a girl is a consensual partner to what is a criminal act on the part of the man, that she could be charged as an aider and abettor. Such an idea was laid to rest by the case of *Tyrrell*[1] where one of the reasons given for not charging girls with such an offence was that the legislation (which was a precursor to the present SOA 1956, s 5) cannot have been intended to make criminals of just the people it was put in place to protect.

1 [1894] 1 QB 710, CCR.

3.9 In the case of *Gillick v West Norfolk and Wisbech Area Health Authority*[1] one of the issues considered by the House of Lords was whether or not a doctor could be charged with aiding and abetting the offence (and also the offence under SOA 1956, s 6(1)) by prescribing contraceptives to a girl under 16. The issue was shortly dealt with, in particular by Lord Scarman when he opined that so long as the doctor was making a proper clinical judgment, no criminality can be alleged, saying:

> ... it must be a medical judgment based upon what [the doctor] honestly believes to be necessary for the physical, mental, and emotional health of his patient. The bona fide exercise by a doctor of his clinical judgment must be a complete negation of the guilty mind which is an essential ingredient of the criminal offence of aiding and abetting the commission of unlawful sexual intercourse[2].

1 [1986] AC 112, [1985] 3 All ER 402.

2 [1986] AC 112 at 190.

Complainant's Anonymity

3.10 Complainants in an allegation of an offence under SOA 1956, s 5 are entitled to comprehensive anonymity[1]. The anonymity of the complainant stretches to cover the publication of any matter relating to her 'if it is likely to lead members of the public to identify that person as the person against whom the offence is alleged to have been committed'[2]. The anonymity in these provisions remains in place throughout the complainant's lifetime. The anonymity provisions can however be overridden by an application by the accused to the trial judge to direct that the SO(A)A 1992, s 1 should not apply in relation to the complainant. Under the SO(A)A 1992, s 3(1), in order for such a direction to be made the judge must be satisfied of two things, namely that:

(i) the direction is required for the purpose of inducing persons who are likely to be needed as witnesses at the trial to come forward; and

(ii) the conduct of the applicant's defence at the trial is likely to be substantially prejudiced if the direction is not given.

1 SO(A)A 1992, ss 1 to 4. These provisions apply to a large number of sexual offences.

2 See SO(A)A 1992, s 1(1).

3.11 The trial judge can also direct that the SO(A)A 1992, s 1 should not apply if he is satisfied that such anonymity 'imposes a substantial and unreasonable restriction upon the reporting of proceedings at the trial' and 'that it is in the public interest to remove or relax the restriction'[1].

1 See SO(A)A 1992, s 3(2).

Alternative Verdicts

3.12 An important element of the offence is that sexual intercourse must take place[1] and, therefore, if a jury is not satisfied on the evidence they hear that sexual intercourse actually occurred then it is open to them to convict the defendant of attempting to commit the offence so long as they are satisfied that all the other elements of an attempt to commit the offence are present.

1 See paragraphs 1.19 to 1.21 above.

3.13 It was held in *R v McCormack*[1] that the offence under the SOA 1956, s 6(1) (sexual intercourse with a girl under 16) necessarily included an allegation of indecent assault under the SOA 1956, s 14(1). The reasoning in that case suggests that, depending on the circumstances of the case, it is open to the jury to find the defendant guilty of indecent assault on the girl if they are not satisfied that the evidence proves either unlawful sexual intercourse or an attempt at the full offence. Having said that it is difficult to see how, on an allegation of unlawful sexual intercourse (under either provision) where the evidence does not prove such intercourse, or even an attempt, that the offence of indecent assault could realistically be made out. The offence calls for 'unlawful sexual intercourse' which necessarily involves the insertion of the man's penis into the girl's vagina. If a jury is not satisfied on the evidence that the offence (or an attempt) is made out, then it is submitted that no offence is committed at all. If there is evidence of an indecent assault distinct from the alleged sexual intercourse (or attempt) then a separate count should be included on (or possibly added to) the indictment.

1 [1969] 2 QB 442, [1969] 3 All ER 371, CA.

3.14 It might be argued that if a man is charged with an offence under the SOA 1956, s 5 and the evidence is not enough to satisfy the jury that the girl is under 13 years of age, then he must be acquitted of the offence. However, the question arises as to whether or not he stands to be convicted of an offence under SOA 1956, s 6 (sexual intercourse with a girl under 16). The Criminal Law Act 1967, s 6(3) allows for a defendant to be convicted as an alternative to the offence charged if the evidence amounts to or includes (expressly or by implication) an allegation of another offence. If sexual intercourse is proved but the evidence is not clear that the girl is under 13 then the evidence must amount to an offence under CLA 1967, s 6(1). Thus, in such circumstances, an alternative verdict of guilty to an offence under CLA 1967, s 6 ought to be returned.

Actus Reus

Unlawful Sexual Intercourse

3.15 The first element of the offence is that 'unlawful sexual intercourse' must be proved. The word 'unlawful' in the context of sexual offences has been considered on a number of occasions by the higher courts, most notably in the case of *R*[1] in which the House of Lords, in deciding that a man could be convicted of raping his wife, decreed that the word was mere surplusage in the context of that offence. Indeed, the word 'unlawful' is now no longer used in the statutory definition of rape. However, it does remain in both the provisions relating to sexual intercourse with young girls.

1 [1992] 1 AC 599, [1991] 4 All ER 481.

3.16 The word can only realistically be considered to have any purpose in the context of the offence by regarding it as meaning 'outside the bonds of a legal marriage'. And further, this situation can only arise when the marriage in question is one validly performed in a foreign jurisdiction. Such a situation is highly unlikely to arise in England and Wales because a marriage between a man and a girl under the age of 16 is not legitimate[1]. However, the situation did arise in the case of *Alhaji Mohamed v Knott*[2] in which a Nigerian man was living with his 13-year-old wife. They had married in Nigeria under the law of that country. The Divisional Court decided that the marriage was valid and, though the Court was not asked to consider whether or not criminal offences were being committed by the man each time he had sex with the girl, the reasoning of Lord Parker CJ in giving the decision of the court, would suggest that he was not.

1 See the Marriage Act 1949, s 2.

2 [1969] 1 QB 1, [1968] 2 All ER 563.

3.17 Sexual intercourse has to be proved by the prosecution in order to establish that the offence has been made out. What constitutes sexual intercourse is governed by the SOA 1956, s 44 and is covered in detail in paragraphs 1.18 to 1.20 above.

Under the Age of 13

3.18 The final element that must be proved is that the girl was under the age of 13 at the time of the unlawful sexual intercourse. So long as the prosecution are able to establish that the girl was under that age, the allegation is proved and there is no need to aver her actual age on the indictment. The prosecution are only allowed to prove the girl's age in a proper way. For example, if it is proposed to prove the girl's age by introducing a certified copy of her birth certificate, then there must also be evidence of her proper identity. The prosecution cannot rely on the presumption of age of a child under the CYPA 1933, s 99. In the past evidence has been given as to the age of the victim by her mother[1] and by the girl's teacher[2].

1 *R v Nicholls* (1867) 10 Cox CC 476, CCR.

2 [1989] 1 QB 179.

Mens Rea

Consent

3.19 The only distinction between this offence and rape is that the girl's consent to sexual intercourse is a defence to an allegation of rape. Having said that, it is not a defence to an allegation under the SOA 1956, s 5 for a man to say that the girl consented to the sexual intercourse. To that extent, her consent is entirely immaterial. Thus, her consent prevents the act being rape but does not provide a defence to an allegation under s 5.

Belief that the Girl was not under 13

3.20 An essential ingredient of the offence for the prosecution to prove is that the girl was under the age of 13 at the time of the sexual intercourse. A significant passage from the opinion of Lord Nicholls of Birkenhead in *B (a minor) v DPP*[1] should be borne in mind. The case related to an allegation of indecency with a girl under the age of 14, but the passage is of importance for its statement of a general principle and should therefore be read as applying to all 'age-related' offences. The passage reads as follows:

> In principle, an age-related ingredient of a statutory offence stands on no different footing from any other ingredient. If a man genuinely believes that the girl with whom he is committing a grossly indecent act is over 14, he is not intending to commit such an act with a girl under 14[2].

Thus, in the context of this particular offence, a man must be proved, by the prosecution, not to have a genuine belief that the girl in question was under the age of 13, if they cannot do so, he should be acquitted of the offence. In such circumstances, he may of course be guilty of an offence of having unlawful sexual intercourse with a girl under the age of 16.

1 [2000] 2 AC 428, [2000] 2 Cr App Rep 65, HL.

2 [2000] 2 Cr App Rep 65 at 71, HL.

Sentence

3.21 The maximum penalty for an offence under SOA 1956, s 5 is life imprisonment, and for an attempt, imprisonment for seven years[1].

1 SOA 1956, s 37(3) and Sch 2, para 2(a).

3.22 An offence under SOA 1956, s 5 should invariably attract a custodial sentence other than where the offender is of limited intelligence or is psychologically abnormal. In *A-G's Reference (No 20 of 1994)*[1] it was said by Lord Taylor CJ that:

> ... it is clear that an offence of unlawful sexual intercourse with a girl under 13 would normally attract a prison sentence, even more so when there are aggravating features ...

His Lordship, in ruling that a probation order was too lenient for a man of 40 who had admitted having sex with a 12-year-old girl on eight or nine occasions, went onto say that:

> No doubt the order ... made here was one which would benefit the offender ... [I]t seems to us that [the sentencing judge] laid more emphasis on the need to assist the offender than on other aspects which require to be considered and taken into account in passing sentence, that is to say, deterrence, not only of the offender, but deterrence of others who are in a position of trust in regard to girls of tender age.

1 (1995) 16 Cr App Rep (S) 578, CA.

3.23 Similarly, in *A-G's Reference (No 13 of 1993)*[1] a probation order was replaced with a prison sentence for an offence of attempting to have unlawful sexual intercourse with a nine-year-old girl.

1 (1994) 15 Cr App Rep (S) 292, CA.

3.24 Part I (ss 1 to 6) of the SOA 1997 applies to both the full offence and to an attempt[1]. This part of the Act relates to the requirement for, and effect of, people sentenced for such offences to register with their local police force.

1 See SOA 1997, Schedule 1.

3.25 The full offence constitutes a 'serious offence' so far as the PCC(S)A 2000, s 109 is concerned. The effect of this section is that if a man is convicted of such an offence after 30 September 1997 *and* at the time when that offence was committed, he was 18 or over and had been convicted in any part of the United Kingdom of another serious offence[1], then the court has the power to impose a life sentence for the later offence. Notice should be taken of the fact that it is possible for the earlier offence to have been committed anywhere within the United Kingdom for the provision to come into play.

1 PCC(S)A 2000, s 109(1)(a) and (b). See also sub-ss (5), (6) and (7) for a full list of qualifying offences.

3.26 An offence under the SOA 1956, s 5 constitutes an 'offence against a child' as defined by the CJCSA 2000, ss 26 to 31. The effect of this is that a convicted man must be disqualified from working with children[1]. Such disqualification need not be ordered if the court is satisfied that it is unlikely that the offender will commit any further offence against a child[2].

1 See PCC(S)A 2000, ss 28(4) and 29(4).

2 See PCC(S)A 2000, s 28(5).

B Sexual Intercourse with a Girl under 16

3.27 The SOA 1956, s 6 reads as follows:

> 6(1) It is an offence, subject to the exception mentioned in this section, for a man to have unlawful sexual intercourse with a girl under the age of 16.
>
> (2) Where a marriage is invalid under section two of the Marriage Act 1949, or section one of the Marriage Act 1929 (the wife being a girl under the age of 16), the invalidity does not make the husband guilty of an offence under this section because he has sexual intercourse with her, if he believes her to be his wife, and has reasonable cause for the belief.
>
> (3) A man is not guilty of an offence under this section because he has unlawful sexual intercourse with a girl under

the age of 16, if he is under the age of twenty-four and has not previously been charged with a like offence, and he believes her to be of the age of 16 or over and has reasonable cause for the belief.

In this subsection 'a like offence' means an offence under this section or an attempt to commit one, or an offence under paragraph (1) of section 5 of the Criminal Law Amendment Act 1885 (the provision replaced for England and Wales by this section).

3.28 While the basic issues pertaining to the offence of having unlawful sexual intercourse with a girl under 16 are identical to those of the more serious offence dealt with above (ie 'unlawful sexual intercourse' and proof of the girl's age) there are some significant differences. Perhaps the most important, in practice, of these differences is that the statutory provision which creates the former offence also allows for what is often called 'the young man's defence'. This is a statutory defence to the allegation of having unlawful sexual intercourse with a girl under 16 that does not apply to the offence under SOA 1956, s 5.

General Issues

Mode of Trial

3.29 Unlawful sexual intercourse with a girl under 16, together with an attempt to commit the offence, is an offence that is triable either way[1]. It is a Class 4 offence and as such, when committed to the Crown Court may be tried by a High Court judge, a circuit judge or a recorder[2].

1 See the SOA 1956, s 37(2) and Sch 2, para 10.

2 Practice Direction (Crown Court: allocation of business) (No 3) [2000] 1 All ER 380, [2000] 1 WLR 203.

3.30 In certain circumstances the United Kingdom courts do not have jurisdiction to try 'a member of a visiting force or a civilian component of such a force'. Under the VFA 1952, s 3(1) an offence under the SOA 1956, s 6(1) may come under this provision.

3.31 An offence under the SOA 1956, s 6(1) (or an attempt), unlike one under the SOA 1956, s 5, must be brought within 12 months of the date of the commission of the offence. This is by virtue of the SOA 1956, s 37(2) and Sch 2, para 10(a) and (b). In the case of *Richards*[1] it was said that on the construction of the SOA 1956, s 37(2) it was necessary to consider the words 'the commencement of the prosecution in respect of the offence charged'. In that case the defendant had been charged with a single allegation under the SOA 1956, s 6(1), and that charge had come within the 12-month period. However, when it came to his trial the prosecution successfully applied to amend the indictment so as to include allegations of offences occurring outside that period. The Court of Appeal overturned his conviction because the jury may have convicted him on evidence relating to the earlier allegations which were statute-barred.

1 [1995] Crim LR 894.

3.32 The significant dates in relation to this provision are, first, when the complaint is made, or the information laid; and secondly, when he first comes before the court if he is arrested and charged without an information being laid[1]. If an indictment is to be amended, as in *Richards*, care should be taken that the new allegations do not relate to offences committed more than 12 months earlier, especially if the amendment relates to different offences to that originally charged.

1 See *Wakeley* [1920] 1 KB 688, CCA and *Hughes* (1879) 43 JP 556, CCR.

3.33 A related topic to that considered in the paragraph above is whether or not evidence of earlier allegations of offences not charged (because they are too old) are admissible at trial. In *Shellaker*[1] it was held that such evidence is admissible as corroboration of the girl's testimony. However, in ruling in that way, Isaacs CJ did go onto say that:

> ... the judge may be of opinion that it is of so little real value and yet indirectly so prejudicial to the prisoner, or that it is so remote, that it ought not to be given[2].

1 [1914] 1 KB 414, CCR.

2 [1914] 1 KB 414 at 418, CCR.

Parties to the Offence

3.34 As with an offence under SOA 1956, s 5, only a male can be an offender and the offence can only be committed against girls under the age of 16. Reference should be made to paragraphs 3.6 to 3.9 above on this topic.

Complainant's Anonymity

3.35 Complainants in an allegation of an offence under SOA 1956, s 6 are entitled to comprehensive anonymity[1]. The anonymity of the complainant stretches to cover the publication of any matter relating to her 'if it is likely to lead members of the public to identify that person as the person against whom the offence is alleged to have been committed'[2]. The anonymity in these provisions remains in place throughout the complainant's lifetime. The anonymity provisions can however be over-ridden by an application by the accused to the trial judge to direct that SO(A)A 1992, s 1 should not apply in relation to the complainant. Under the SO(A)A 1992, s 3(1), in order for such a direction to be made the judge must be satisfied of two things, namely that:

(i) the direction is required for the purpose of inducing persons who are likely to be needed as witnesses at the trial to come forward; and
(ii) the conduct of the applicant's defence at the trial is likely to be substantially prejudiced if the direction is not given.

1 SO(A)A 1992, ss 1 to 4. These provisions apply to a large number of sexual offences.

2 See SO(A)A 1992, s 1(1).

3.36 The trial judge can also direct that the SO(A)A 1992, s 1 should not apply if he is satisfied that such anonymity 'imposes a substantial and unreasonable restriction upon the reporting of proceedings at the trial' and 'that it is in the public interest to remove or relax the restriction'[1].

1 See SO(A)A 1992, s 3(2).

Alternative Verdicts

3.37 Reference should be made to paragraphs 3.12 to 3.14 above in relation to alternative verdicts to the full offence under the SOA 1956, s 6(1).

3.38 In the case of *Adragna*[1] it passed without comment by the Court of Appeal that the defendant was charged with an offence of indecent assault against a 13-year-old girl when he had actually had unlawful sexual intercourse with her. It was simply noted by Judge J that he could not be charged with a SOA 1956, s 6(1) offence because the offence was committed beyond the statutory time period for bringing a prosecution. While, on the basis of this case alone, it would appear to be an acceptable course of action for a prosecutor to take in such circumstances, it is a notion that has been rejected in both Australia[2] and New Zealand[3]. The rationale in the latter two cases is that the offence of indecent assault should not be used to circumvent the time-limit on prosecutions for offences when sexual intercourse takes place.

1 (1994) 15 Cr App Rep (S) 693.

2 *Saraswati v R* (1990) 172 CLR 1.

3 *Blight* (1903) 22 NZLR 837.

3.39 It should be noted that in a case where indecent assault has been charged because an offence under SOA 1956, s 6(3) is time-barred, the sentencing judge should regard the maximum sentence being that for the latter offence (ie two years in prison) rather than for the former (ie 10 years in prison). This proposition was made clear by Lord Taylor CJ in the case of *Hinton.*[1]

1 (1995) 16 Cr App Rep (S) 523, CA.

Actus Reus

3.40 Save for the only difference between offences under SOA 1956, s 5 and s 6(1) being the complainant's age, the actus reus for both offences is identical and reference should be made to paragraphs 3.15 and 3.18 above.

Mens Rea

3.41 Again, the issues under this heading are identical to those pertaining to an offence under SOA 1956, s 5 and reference should be made to paragraphs 3.19 and 3.20 above. However, as SOA 1956, s 6(2) and (3) affords statutory defences to some men alleged to have committed this offence, it is thought appropriate to deal with those issues here.

Statutory Defences

3.42 The first of the two statutory defences contained within the section relates to a man believing that the girl he has sexual intercourse with is his wife. It has already been seen that a marriage entered into in this jurisdiction where one of the parties is under 16 years of age is void[1] and, therefore, in such a situation where a man is alleged to have had sexual intercourse with a female he believes to be his wife, that invalidity does not make him guilty of the offence. However, by virtue of SOA 1956, s 47, the burden of proving that the exception applies to him lies on the man in question.

1 MA 1949, s 2.

3.43 Parliament took the opportunity, when enacting the SOA 1956, to clarify an unacceptable situation that had arisen in relation to the issue of a man having reasonable cause to believe that he was married to the girl in question. The present provision makes it clear that the man must also prove that he did in fact believe that he was married to her.

3.44 The second of the statutory defences contained with section 6 relates to what has been called 'the young man's defence' and pertains only to men aged under twenty-four. Again, by virtue of SOA 1956, s 47 the onus of establishing the defence lies on him. It is a defence that is only available to such a man if he has never been charged with a like offence in the past. In effect, the defence can be broken down into four separate elements, all of which must be present in order for him to avail himself of it, namely:

(i) he must be under 24 years of age at the time of the alleged offence;

(ii) he must not have been charged with a like offence at any stage in the past;
(iii) he must believe that the girl was at least 16 years of age at the time of the sexual intercourse;
(iv) he must have reasonable cause for that belief.

3.45 It should be noted that the defence is also available to a man who is charged with attempting to have unlawful sexual intercourse with a girl under 16. This contention was confirmed by the case of *Collier*[1] in which it was said that the words 'an offence under this section' in SOA 1956, s 6(3) refers to an attempt as well as the full offence.

1 [1960] Crim LR 204, but see the commentary thereto which suggests that the decision was incorrect.

3.46 With regard to (i) above, it should be noted that, by virtue of the Family Reform Act 1969, s 9(1) a man attains the age of 24 at the commencement of the 24th anniversary of his birth and so, in order to prove this fact, it would be necessary for him to adduce duly attested proof of the date of his birth.

3.47 The rationale for the issue set out at (ii) above is that when the gravity and serious nature of the allegations made against a man have once been brought to his attention, he will always be aware of the danger of having sexual intercourse with girls who may not have reached the age of consent.

3.48 The leading case on this point is *Rider*[1] which, though it was heard prior to the SOA 1956, dealt with the same point which was then contained in CLA 1922, s 2. Unfortunately, at the time *Rider* was decided, the offence was triable only on indictment and so the decision does not take into account the fact that the offence is now triable either way and, further, the many changes that have occurred in how cases are dealt with in their early stages. In bringing the reasoning in that case up to date, it can be said that the best argument for when a man is 'charged' with a like offence is to consider when he first appears before a court having jurisdiction to determine the case. In *Rider* Streatfield J differentiated between a magistrates' court deciding whether a case should be committed to the Crown Court – ie that a prima facie case existed against the defendant – and the Crown Court which would try the defendant.

Thus, extrapolating from Streatfield's reasoning, and relating it to the current regime, the defence would only be available to a man who had not been tried – or at least had his case determined – by either a magistrates' court or a Crown Court depending on which was to determine his earlier case.

1 [1954] 1 All ER 5, 37 Cr App Rep 209.

3.49 In addition to the above issues, once the man has established that the defence is available to him on what might be called the procedural issues, he must be able to satisfy the jury that he both believed that the girl was at least 16 years of age and that he had reasonable cause to believe that[1]. In such circumstances, a jury may infer from the surrounding circumstances that the defendant had reasonable cause to believe that the girl was at least 16 and, similarly, they may consider her personal appearance and take that into account.

1 See *Forde* [1923] 2 KB 400, 17 Cr App Rep 99, CCA.

3.50 Reference should also be made to paragraph 3.20 above with regard to the man's genuine belief that the girl was over the age of 16.

Sentence

3.51 The maximum sentence for both the full offence and an attempt is two years in prison when the matter is tried on indictment. In cases tried summarily the sentence is governed by the MCA 1980, s 32.

3.52 In 1977 Lawton LJ laid down guidelines for sentencing offences under SOA 1956, s 6(1),[1] and the principles therein still apply. In considering the wide spectrum of circumstances that might constitute the offence in question he stated as follows:

> Nowadays, most judges would take the view ... that when there is a virtuous friendship (when the male is still youthful) which ends in unlawful sexual intercourse, it is inappropriate to pass sentences of a punitive nature. What is required is a warning to the youth to mend his ways. At the other end, a man in a supervisory capacity, who abuses his position of

> trust for his sexual gratification, ought to get a sentence somewhere near the maximum allowed by law, which is two years' imprisonment. In between there come many degrees of guilt.

1 *Taylor* [1977] 3 All ER 527, 64 Cr App Rep 182, CA.

3.53 As has been noted above, the girl's consent to sexual intercourse is entirely immaterial as a defence to the allegation. However, care should be taken that a defendant is not sentenced to a longer term of imprisonment because the sentencing judge takes the view that she did not consent to the act[1]. Where there is any suggestion that the complainant did not consent to the sexual intercourse then the man should be charged with an offence of rape and not an offence under SOA 1956, s 6(1).

1 See *Druce* (1993) 14 Cr App Rep (S) 691, CA for an example of where this happened.

3.54 Part 1 (ss 1 to 6) of the SOA 1997 applies to both the full offence and to an attempt[1]. This part of the Act relates to the requirement for, and effect of, people sentenced for such offences to register with their local police force.

1 See the SOA 1997, Sch 1.

3.55 An offence under SOA 1956, s 6(1) constitutes an 'offence against a child' as defined by the CJCSA 2000, ss 26 to 31. The effect of this is that a convicted man must be disqualified from working with children[1]. Such disqualification need not be ordered if the court is satisfied that it is unlikely that the offender will commit any further offence against a child[2].

1 See the CJCSA 2000, ss 28(4) and 29(4).

2 See the CJCSA 2000, s 28(5).

C Indecent Conduct With or Towards a Child

3.56 The Indecency with Children Act 1960, s 1, as amended by the Crime (Sentences) Act 1997 and the CJCSA 2000, reads as follows:

> 1(1) Any person who commits an act of gross indecency with or towards a child under the age of 16, or who incites a

child under that age to such an act with him or another, shall be liable on conviction on indictment to imprisonment for a term not exceeding 10 years, or on summary conviction to imprisonment for a term not exceeding six months, to a fine not exceeding the prescribed sum, or both.

3.57 The C(S)A 1997 amended the section to increase the maximum sentence from two years in prison to 10. The amendment came into force on 1 October 1997 but does not apply to offences committed before that date.

3.58 It was decided in the case of *Francis*[1] first, that the words 'with or towards' in the section creates just one offence. That is to say that the word 'with' refers to the notion of an action being 'against or directed towards' rather than 'in concert with'. However, it will be clear from a close reading of the provision that it contains two distinct offences; the first being committing an act of gross indecency, and the second being inciting a child to such an act.

1 (1988) 88 Cr App Rep 127, CA.

General Issues

Mode of Trial

3.59 It is clear from the ICA 1960, s 1 that the offence is triable either way. It is a Class 4 offence and as such, when committed to the Crown Court may be tried by a High Court judge, a circuit judge or a recorder[1].

1 Practice Direction (Crown Court: allocation of business) (No 3) [2000] 1 All ER 380, [2000] 1 WLR 203.

3.60 It has been seen that before an offence of gross indecency by a man against a victim who is under 21 can be instituted, the consent of the Director of Public Prosecutions to the proceedings is required. That is not the case for an offence under the ICA 1960, s 1[1].

1 See the CJA 1972, s 48.

3.61 In certain circumstances the United Kingdom courts do not have jurisdiction to try 'a member of a visiting force or a civilian component of such a force'. Under the VFA 1952, s 3(1) an offence under the ICA 1960, s 1(1) may come under this provision.

Parties to the Offence

3.62 Victims of an offence under this provision can be both male or female, but they must be under the age of 16 years. The offence can be committed, as a principal, by both males and females. So far as issues as to proving the age of the complainant at the time of the offence are concerned, reference should be made to paragraph 3.18 above.

Complainant's Anonymity

3.63 Complainants in an allegation of such an offence are entitled to comprehensive anonymity[1]. The anonymity of the complainant stretches to cover the publication of any matter relating to her 'if it is likely to lead members of the public to identify that person as the person against whom the offence is alleged to have been committed'[2]. The anonymity in these provisions remains in place throughout the complainant's lifetime. The anonymity provisions can however be overridden by an application by the accused to the trial judge to direct that the SO(A)A 1992, s 1 should not apply in relation to the complainant. Under the SO(A)A 1992, s 3(1) in order for such a direction to be made the judge must be satisfied of two things, namely that:

(i) the direction is required for the purpose of inducing persons who are likely to be needed as witnesses at the trial to come forward; and
(ii) the conduct of the applicant's defence at the trial is likely to be substantially prejudiced if the direction is not given.

1 SO(A)A 1992, ss 1-4.

2 See SO(A)A 1992, s 1(1).

3.64 The trial judge can also direct that the SO(A)A 1992, s 1 should not apply if he is satisfied that such anonymity 'imposes a substantial and unreasonable restriction upon the reporting of proceedings at the trial' and 'that it is in the public interest to remove or relax the restriction'[1].

1 See SO(A)A 1992, s 3(2).

3.65 The above provision, allowing for a complainant to such anonymity, is in addition to that afforded by the CYA 1933, s 39(1) which allows a court to order that the media do not publish anything which might lead to the identification of any child witness.

Actus Reus

Commits an Act of Gross Indecency

3.66 The actus reus of this offence is, to a large extent, identical to that of gross indecency when the participants are both adults and reference should be made to paragraphs 2.48 to 2.52 above on that issue. Having said that, it should be remembered that in the offence involving two adults, the participants have to be willing parties to the acts in question. That is clearly not the case when an adult is charged under the ICA 1960.

3.67 In *Speck*[1] it was held that a man was rightly convicted of the offence when an eight-year-old girl placed her hand on his penis outside his trousers for about five minutes. He did not invite the touching nor did he do anything to make the girl remove her hand. The pressure of her hand made the man have an erection. In dismissing the appeal, the Court of Appeal merely said that the judge should have directed the jury that in such circumstances the appellant's conduct *might* constitute the offence rather than *would*. Thus this case is some authority for suggesting that, so far as this offence is concerned at least, inactivity on the part of the offender is enough to constitute the offence. Somewhat bizarrely, however, the ruling did go on to say that 'the element of invitation is important' when clearly there was no such element in that case.

1 [1977] 2 All ER 859, 65 Cr App Rep 161, CA.

3.68 In the case of *Francis*[1] a conviction was quashed because the trial judge directed the jury that it was sufficient for the offence to be made out if a man masturbated merely in the presence of children. The Court ruled that, on a true construction of the section, the grossly indecent behaviour had to be directed towards the children, with the man deriving satisfaction from knowing that the children were watching him. What was significant about the events in *Francis* was that two boys claimed that a man was masturbating in a swimming pool cubicle while watching them. He did not speak to them and had no physical contact with them of any kind. The man denied masturbating at all. In the Court's decision, the Lord Chief Justice said that:

> ... it seems to this Court that the act of a man masturbating in the presence of youngsters under the age of [16] may or may not, according to the circumstances, be an act in contravention of [ICA 1960, s 1(1)]. If a man does masturbate in the presence of children, it may be in circumstances where he believes they are not observing what he is doing. In that case there can be, in the view of this Court, no question of his acting towards the children. He does not involve the children in his action[2].

1 (1988) 88 Cr App Rep 127, CA.

2 (1988) 88 Cr App Rep 127 at 129, CA.

Incites a Child

3.69 The second offence contained within the ICA 1960, s 1(1) is that of inciting a child under 16 years of age to perform an act of gross indecency. In order to constitute this aspect of the offence an offender would have to use some form of encouragement or persuasion to get the child to commit an act of gross indecency. Realistically this would involve pressure of any kind, whether physical or psychological.

Mens Rea

3.70 As a result of the case of *B (a minor) v DPP*[1] a defendant is allowed to put before the jury a defence that he genuinely believed that the complainant was over the requisite age. In considering that defence the jury are entitled to take into account all the circumstances of the case, including the physical appearance of the complainant. It is for the prosecution to satisfy the jury that the defendant did not have a genuine belief that the complainant was at least 16 years old. Further reference should be made to paragraph 3.20 above with regard to the man's genuine belief that the girl was over the age of 16.

1 [2000] 2 AC 428, [2000] 1 All ER 833, HL.

Sentence

3.71 The maximum sentence for the offence when it is tried on indictment is 10 years in prison. When a case is tried summarily the maximum sentence is six months in prison, together with a fine. For the current 'prescribed sum' mentioned in ICA 1960, s 1(1) see the MCA 1980, s 32.

3.72 It should be noted that Parliament increased the maximum sentence on indictment for the offence from two years in prison to 10 years in 1997. Thus references made to any similar cases prior to that date are highly unreliable in the present climate.

D Allowing Premises to be Used for Intercourse

Girls Under the Age of 13

3.73 The SOA 1956, s 25 reads as follows:

> 25. It is an offence for a person who is the owner or occupier of any premises or who has, or acts or assists in, the management or control of any premises, to induce or knowingly suffer a girl under the age of 13 to resort to or be on those premises for the purpose of having unlawful sexual intercourse with men or with a particular man.

3.73A An offence under SOA 1956, s 6(1) constitutes an 'offence against a child' as defined by the CJCSA 2000, ss 26 to 31. The effect of this is that a convicted man must be disqualified from working with children[1]. Such disqualification need not be ordered if the court is satisfied that it is unlikely that the offender will commit any further offence against a child[2].

1 See the CJCSA 2000, ss 28(4) and 29(4).

2 See the CJCSA 2000, s 28(5).

General Issues

Mode of Trial

3.74 An offence under this section is triable on indictment only[1]. It is a Class 3 offence and, as such, can be tried only by a High Court judge, a circuit judge or a recorder who has been properly authorised by a presiding judge[2].

1 See the SOA 1956, s 37(2) and Sch 2, para 6.

2 Practice Direction (Crown Court: allocation of business) (No 3) [2000] 1 All ER 380, [2000] 1 WLR 203.

3.75 It should be noted that in certain circumstances the United Kingdom courts do not have jurisdiction to try 'a member of a visiting force or a civilian component of such a force'. Under the VFA 1952, s 3(1) an offence under SOA 1956, s 25 may come under this provision.

Parties to the Offence

3.76 As the provision refers to a 'person', it is clear that both males and females can commit the offence as principals. In addition, as the offence can be committed by 'the owner ... of any premises' it is possible for the offence to be committed by a corporation so long as all of the other conditions of the offence are satisfied.

Alternative Verdict

3.77 One necessary aspect of the offence is that the girl in question 'be on those premises for the purpose of having unlawful sexual intercourse with men ...'. If the prosecution are unable to satisfy the jury that she was on the premises for that particular reason, then the defendant can be convicted of an offence under the CYPA 1933, s 3. This offence consists of allowing a child between the ages of four and 16 of whom they have custody, charge or care to reside or frequent a brothel. Such an offence would come within the ambit of the CLA 1967, s 6(3).

Actus Reus

Occupier

3.78 There are no decided cases in the context of what constitutes an 'occupier' but in the case of *Tao*[1], which concerned a case under the Misuse of Drugs Act 1971, it was decided that anyone who occupies a premises with the power to exclude any person from those premises qualifies as an 'occupier'. If the question were ever to arise in relation to an offence under this section, the decision in *Tao* would at least be helpful.

1 [1977] QB 141, [1976] 3 All ER 65, CA.

3.79 It is important to remember that the 'occupier' must have real and significant control of the premises in question. It is not necessary for the defendant to have legal possession of the premises but they must have more control than merely the ability to invite people into, or prevent people from entering, the premises[1].

1 See for example *Mogford* [1970] 1 WLR 988, 63 Cr App Rep 168n.

Under the Age of 13

3.80 For a definition of this phrase, refer to paragraph 3.18 above.

Unlawful Sexual Intercourse

3.81 For a discussion of this phrase, see paragraphs 3.15 to 3.17 above.

Mens Rea

3.82 It is necessary for the defendant to 'knowingly suffer a girl under the age of 13 ...' which means that the prosecution must prove that s/he knew that the girl in question was under that age. Until the cases of *B (a minor) v DPP*[1] and *R v K*,[2] such a matter was regarded as one of strict liability, in that no defence existed of reasonable belief that the girl was over the requisite age. Those cases altered that situation and such a defence is now available to a defendant charged with any 'age-related' offence. The cases are discussed in detail at paragraphs 6.43 to 6.46. The decisions in both cases would apply just as much to an offence under this section.

1 [2000] 2 AC 428, [2000] 1 All ER 833, [2000] 2 Cr App Rep 65, HL.

2 [2001] UKHL 41, [2002] 1 AC 462, [2001] 3 All ER 897.

Sentence

3.83 By the SOA 1956, s 37 and Sch 2, para 6, the maximum penalty for this offence is life imprisonment. An offence under SOA 1956, s 25 constitutes an 'offence against a child' as defined by the CJCSA 2000, ss 26 to 31. The effect of this is that a convicted man must be disqualified from working with children[2]. Such disqualification need not be ordered if the court is satisfied that it is unlikely that the offender will commit any further offence against a child[3].

1 See the CJCSA 2000, ss 28(4) and 29(4).

2 See the CJCSA 2000, s 28(5).

Girls Under the Age of 16

3.84 The SOA 1956, s 26 reads as follows:

> 26 It is an offence for a person who is the owner or occupier of any premises or who has, or acts or assists in, the management or control of any premises, to induce or knowingly suffer a girl under the age of 16 to resort to or be on those premises for the purpose of having unlawful sexual intercourse with men or with a particular man.

General Issues

MODE OF TRIAL

3.85 An offence under this section is triable either way[1]. It is a Class 4 offence and, as such, when committed to the Crown Court, may be tried by a High Court judge, a circuit judge or a recorder[2].

1 MCA 1980, s 17(1) and Sch 1.

2 Practice Direction (Crown Court: allocation of business) (No 3) [2000] 1 All ER 380, [2000] 1 WLR 203.

3.86 In certain circumstances the United Kingdom courts do not have jurisdiction to try 'a member of a visiting force or a civilian component of such a force'. Under the VFA 1952, s 3(1) an offence under SOA 1956, s 26 may come under this provision.

PARTIES TO THE OFFENCE

3.87 As with the offence under SOA 1956, s 25, the provision refers to a 'person' so that both males and females can commit the offence as principals. In addition, as the offence can be committed by 'the owner ... of any premises' it is possible for the offence to be committed by a corporation so long as all of the other conditions of the offence are satisfied.

Actus Reus

OCCUPIER

3.88 For a discussion of this term, refer to paragraphs 3.78 and 3.79 above.

UNDER THE AGE OF 16

3.89 For a definition of this phrase, refer to paragraph 3.18 above. It should be noted that the rules pertaining to proving the age of a girl under 16 are the same for those when proving the girl is under 13.

UNLAWFUL SEXUAL INTERCOURSE

3.90 For a discussion of this phrase, see paragraphs 3.15 to 3.17 above.

Mens Rea

3.91 As with the offence under SOA 1956, s 25, for an offence under this section to be proved, it must be shown that the defendant knew the girl to be under 16. Refer to paragraph 3.82 above for a discussion of this aspect of the offence.

Sentence

3.92 By the SOA 1956, s 37 and Sch 2, para 26, the maximum penalty for this offence, when tried on indictment, is two years in prison. When the offence is tried summarily the maximum penalty is six months in prison or a fine[1]. An offence under SOA 1956, s 26 constitutes an 'offence against a child' as defined by the CJCSA 2000, ss 26 to 31. The effect of this is that a convicted man must be disqualified from working with children[2]. Such disqualification need not be ordered if the court is satisfied that it is unlikely that the offender will commit any further offence against a child[3].

1 See the MCA 1980, s 32 and Sch 2.

2 See the CJCSA 2000, ss 28(4) and 29(4).

3 See the CJCSA 2000, s 28(5).

E Abuse of a Position of Trust

3.93 The SO(A)A 2000, s 3[1] reads as follows:

> 3(1) Subject to subsections (2) and (3) below, it shall be an offence for a person of 18 or over –
> (a) to have sexual intercourse (whether vaginal or anal) with a person under that age; or
> (b) to engage in any other sexual activity with or directed towards such a person, if (in either case) he is in a position of trust in relation to that person.

(2) Where a person ('A') is charged with an offence under this section of having sexual intercourse with, or engaging in any other sexual activity with or directed towards another person ('B'), it shall be a defence for A to prove that, at the time of the intercourse or activity –

(a) he did not know, and could not reasonably have been expected to know, that B was a person in relation to whom he was in a position of trust; or
(b) he was lawfully married to B.

(3) It shall not be an offence under this section for a person ('A') to have sexual intercourse with, or engage in any other sexual activity with or directed towards, another person ('B') if immediately before the commencement of this Act –

(a) A was in a position of trust in relation to B; and
(b) a sexual relationship existed between them.

(4) A person guilty of an offence under this section shall be liable —

(a) on summary conviction, to imprisonment for a term not exceeding six months, or to a fine not exceeding the statutory maximum, or to both;
(b) on conviction on indictment, to imprisonment for a term not exceeding five years, or to a fine, or to both.

(5) In this section 'sexual activity' –

(a) does not include any activity which a reasonable person would regard as sexual only with knowledge of the intentions, motives or feelings of the parties; but
(b) subject to that, means any activity which such a person would regard as sexual in all the circumstances.

1 The SO(A)A 2000 was brought into force on 8 January 2001 by the Sexual Offences (Amendment) Act 2000 (Commencement No 1) Order 2000, SI 2000/3303.

3.94 SO(A)A 2000, s 4 sets out the definitions of the term 'position of trust'. In effect the section creates four conditions that must be met in order to establish that a person over the age of 18 ('A') was indeed in a 'position of trust' over a person under that age ('B'). These are as follows:

(i) 'A' must look after persons under 18, and be looking after 'B', who is detained in an institution by virtue of an order of the court or under an enactment (SO(A)A 2000, s 4(2));
(ii) 'A' must look after persons under 18 who are resident in a home or other place in which:
   (a) accommodation and maintenance are provided by an authority under the Children Act 1989, s 23(2), or
   (b) accommodation is provided by a voluntary organisation under the Children Act 1989, s 59(1),
   (c) ... (SO(A)A 2000, s 4(3));
(iii) 'A' must look after persons under 18 who are accommodated and cared for in an institution which is:
   (a) a hospital,
   (b) a residential care home, nursing home, mental nursing home or private hospital,
   (c) a community home, voluntary home, children's home or residential establishment, or
   (d) a home provided under the Children Act 1989, s 82(5)

   and 'B' is accommodated and cared for in that institution. (SO(A)A 2000, s 4(4));
(iv) 'A' looks after persons under 18 who are receiving full-time education at an educational institution, and 'B' is receiving such education at that institution (SO(A)A 2000, s 4(5)).

3.95 SO(A)A 2000, s 4(7) defines a person 'A' as being 'regularly involved in caring for, training, supervising or being in sole charge of such persons'. Reference should be made to SO(A)A 2000, s 4(8) and (9) for further definitions of terms.

3.96 This is an extremely peculiar piece of legislation that was enacted as a sop to misguided public opinion that such offences were common. If it is ever used in order to prosecute a man alleged to have transgressed its labyrinthine strictures, it is submitted that the higher courts will have a Herculean task in unravelling it all. That is to say nothing of the potential constitutional arguments as to how an Act can criminalise consensual sexual acts between two partners over the legal age of consent.

General Issues

Mode of Trial

3.97 The offence is triable either way. It is a Class 4 offence and as such, when committed to the Crown Court may be tried by a High Court judge, a circuit judge or a recorder[1].

1 *Practice Direction (Crown Court: allocation of business) (No 3)* [2000] 1 All ER 380, [2000] 1 WLR 203.

Sentence

3.98 The maximum sentences for the offence are set out in SO(A)A 2000, s 3(4).

3.99 Part 1 (ss 1 to 6) of the SOA 1997 applies to this offence[1]. That part of the Act relates to the requirement for, and effect of, people sentenced for such offences to register with their local police force. An offence under SO(A)A 2000, s 3 constitutes an 'offence against a child' as defined by the CJCSA 2000, ss 26 to 31. The effect of this is that a convicted man must be disqualified from working with children[2]. Such disqualification need not be ordered if the court is satisfied that it is unlikely that the offender will commit any further offence against a child[3].

1 See SOA 1997, Sch 1.

2 See the CJCSA 2000, ss 28(4) and 29(4).

3 See the CJCSA 2000, s 28(5).

3.100 SO(A)A 2000, s 6 added this offence to the list of offences termed 'sexual offences' listed in the PCC(S)A 2000, s 161.

F Conspiracy or Incitement to Commit Sexual Acts Abroad Against Children

3.101 On 1 October 1996, the Sexual Offences (Conspiracy and Incitement) Act 1996 came into force[1]. The preamble to the Act describes it as an Act 'to make provision about conspiracy, or incitement, to commit certain sexual acts outside the United Kingdom'[1]. It was enacted in the belief that so-called 'sex tourism', especially in the Far East was getting out of hand and, without it, the courts in this country could do nothing to stop the growth in such activity.

1 See the Sexual Offences (Conspiracy and Incitement) Act 1996 (Commencement) Order 1996, SI 1996/2262.

3.102 SO(CI)A 1996, s 1 reads as follows:

> 1(1) Where each of the following conditions is satisfied in the case of any agreement, Part 1 of the Criminal Law Act 1977 (conspiracy) has effect in relation to the agreement as it has effect in relation to an agreement falling within section 1(1) of that Act.
>
> (2) The first condition is that the pursuit of the agreed course of conduct would at some stage involve –
> (a) an act by one or more of the parties, or
> (b) the happening of some event,
> intended to take place in a country or territory outside the United Kingdom.
>
> (3) The second condition is that that act or other event constitutes an offence under the law in force in that country or territory.
>
> (4) The third condition is that the agreement would fall within section 1(1) of that Act as an agreement relating to the commission of a listed sexual offence but for the fact that the offence would not be an offence triable in England and Wales if committed in accordance with the parties intentions.
>
> (5) The fourth condition is that –
> (a) a party to the agreement, or a party's agent, did anything in England and Wales in relation to the agreement before its formation, or
> (b) a party to the agreement became a party in England and Wales (by joining it either in person or through an agent), or
> (c) a party to the agreement, or a party's agent, did or omitted anything in England and Wales in pursuance of the agreement.

(6) In the application of Part 1 of that Act to such an agreement, any reference to an offence is to be read as a reference to what would be the listed sexual offence in question but for the fact that it is not an offence triable in England and Wales.

3.103 SO(CI)A 1996, s 2 sets out the offence of incitement to commit certain sexual acts in similar terms to the offence of conspiracy. It is clear from SO(CI)A 1996, s 1 that, before an offence of conspiracy to commit a particular sexual act can be proved, four conditions must be met by the prosecution. If the four conditions are made out then the act comes into the ambit of CLA 1977, s 1(1) and the people in question can be tried for conspiracy to commit the relevant criminal act(s), even though they were committed outside the United Kingdom.

3.104 In reading the sections to the SO(CI)A 1996 carefully one might wonder why it is printed here in a chapter concerning offences committed against children. It is only when one refers to the list of relevant sexual offences that one discovers that the Act does not apply to offences which can be committed against adults when the victim of the offence 'has attained the age of 16 years'[1].

1 See SO(CI)A 1996, s 1(2) and the Schedule.

3.105 It is to be taken as satisfied that the act in question was contrary to the law of the country in which it was perpetrated unless the defence can prove otherwise and SO(CI)A 1996, s 3 provides for the procedural steps involved.

3.106 The list of offences contained within the Schedule to the SO(CI)A 1996 is as follows:
(i) rape
(ii) sexual intercourse with a girl under 13
(iii) sexual intercourse with a girl under 16
(iv) buggery
(v) indecent assault on a girl
(vi) indecent assault on a boy
(vii) the ICA 1960, s 1 (indecent conduct towards a young child).

3.107 It should be noted that there is no requirement for the accused person to be a British citizen at the time of the commission of the offence[1].

1 See SO(CI)A 1996, s 3(6).

3.108 In addition to the above Act, the SOA 1997 extended the jurisdiction of the courts of England and Wales to deal with such offences involving citizens of the United Kingdom.

Chapter four

Offences involving 'defectives' and patients

4.1 The term 'defective' is a word used in the SOA 1956 when dealing with offences committed against women (but not men) suffering from 'severe impairment of intelligence and social functioning'. It is yet another word that was no doubt deemed acceptable in 1956, but has come to be thought of as insulting and demeaning to such people in the 21st century. Again it is unfortunate that no government has thought it fit to use one of the myriad of Acts that have amended the SOA 1956 over the years to dispense with the term and replace it with a more acceptable one. It is a word that will be used in this chapter merely for the sake of convenience and consistency with the relevant legislation pertaining to the different offences perpetrated against so-called 'defectives'.

4.2 It should be noted also that, while the laudable aim of the legislation has been to protect such vulnerable people, the particular provisions of the Act dealing with 'defectives' has been criticised as being over-protective in the sense that, in the first place, such people may well have perfectly legitimate sexual urges and desires which may be prevented or controlled by the legislation and, secondly, that the overall canon of existing sexual offences is sufficient to protect such people. It is beyond the scope of this work to consider the philosophical principles behind such criticism but it is worth noting that both the Sexual Law Reform Society and the National Council for Civil Liberties have, in the past, made submissions on the topic to the Criminal Law Revision Committee.

4.3 On a related topic to that above, it should also be noted that, in practice, men who suffer a severe mental incapacity who indulge in sexual relationships, albeit with the encouragement of the staff of institutions in which they may live, with women under similar disabilities are not likely to be prosecuted for any offence considered in this chapter.

4.4 This chapter deals with offences where the statutory regime has been aimed specifically at protecting vulnerable people – in particular women – who suffer from some kind of mental disorder. Indecent assaults against 'defective' men and women are dealt with in Chapter 6 and so are not considered here.

A Unlawful Sexual Intercourse with a 'Defective'

4.5 The SOA 1956, s 7, as amended by the MHA 1959, s127(1)(a), reads as follows:

> 7(1) It is an offence, subject to the exception mentioned in this section, for a man to have unlawful sexual intercourse with a woman who is a defective.
>
> (2) A man is not guilty of an offence under this section because he has unlawful sexual intercourse with a woman if he does not know and has no reason to suspect her to be a defective.

4.6 The use of the word 'man' in the section should be read as referring to both men and boys. By virtue of the SOA 1956, s 46 the two words are interchangeable.

General Issues

Mode of Trial

4.7 Unlawful sexual intercourse with a female defective, or an attempt to commit it, is an offence that can only be tried on indictment[1]. They are both Class 3 offences and as such can be tried by a High Court judge, a circuit judge or a recorder who has been properly authorised by a presiding judge[2].

1 See the SOA 1956, s 37(2) and Sch 2, para 11.

2 Practice Direction (Crown Court: allocation of business) (No 3) [2000] 1 All ER 380, [2000] 1 WLR 203.

4.8 In certain circumstances the United Kingdom courts do not have jurisdiction to try a 'member of a visiting force or a civilian component of such a force'. Under the VFA 1952, s 3(1), an offence under SOA 1956, s 7 may come under this provision.

Parties to the Offence

4.9 As can be seen from the wording of the section, only a male can be a defendant to such an allegation and only females can be victims. It is not possible for a woman to be charged under this provision with having unlawful sexual intercourse with a male defective; however, depending on the circumstances, she may be guilty of an offence of indecent assault[1].

1 See SOA 1956, ss 14 and 15 and Chapter 6 below.

Complainant's Anonymity

4.10 The complainant in an allegation of an offence under SOA 1956, s 7 is entitled to comprehensive anonymity[1]. The anonymity of the complainant stretches to cover the publication of any matter relating to him/her 'if it is likely to lead members of the public to identify that person as the person against whom the offence is alleged to have been committed'[2]. The anonymity in these provisions remains in place throughout the complainant's lifetime. The anonymity provisions can however be over-ridden by an application by the accused to the trial judge to direct that SO(A)A 1992, s 1 should not apply in relation to the complainant. Under SO(A)A 1992, s 3(1), in order for such a direction to be made the judge must be satisfied of two things, namely that:

(a) the direction is required for the purpose of inducing persons who are likely to be needed as witnesses at the trial to come forward; and

(b) the conduct of the applicant's defence at the trial is likely to be substantially prejudiced if the direction is not given.

1 SO(A)A 1992, ss 1-4. These provisions apply to a large number of sexual offences.

2 See SO(A)A 1992, s 1(1).

4.11 The trial judge can also direct that SO(A)A 1992, s 1 should not apply if he is satisfied that such anonymity 'imposes a substantial and unreasonable restriction upon the reporting of proceedings at the trial' and 'that it is in the public interest to remove or relax the restriction'[1].

1 See SO(A)A 1992, s 3(2).

Actus Reus

4.12 As in offences under the SOA 1956, ss 5 and 6, s 7 uses the phrase 'unlawful sexual intercourse'. Reference should be made to paragraphs 3.15 to 3.17 above for a discussion on the definition of 'unlawful' in this context and to paragraphs 1.18 to 1.20 for the legal definition of 'sexual intercourse'.

4.13 In order for the prosecution to prove their case, they must satisfy the jury that the woman in question was, at the time of the offence, a 'defective'. The definition of 'defective' in this context is given in the SOA 1956, s 45[1] and reads as follows:

> 45 In this Act 'defective' means a person suffering from a state of arrested or incomplete development of mind which includes severe impairment of intelligence and social functioning.

1 The section was provided by the MHA 1959, s 127(1)(b), which itself has been amended by the MH(A)A 1982, Sch 3.

4.14 The SOA 1956 does no more than that to define the term, but it may be of some use to refer to the MHA 1983, s 1(2) which sets out definitions of terms such as 'severe mental impairment' and 'mental disorder'. It is interesting to note that nowhere in the MHA 1983 is the word 'defective' used in relation to people suffering such mental disorders and the position so far as the criminal law is concerned remains as set out in the SOA 1956, s 45.

4.15 The case of *Hall*[1] dealt with the issue in that it was said by the appellant that the victim of the indecent assaults had been convicted of was of moderate impairment, although by comparison with normally developed persons she was severely impaired, and did not therefore come within the ambit of the SOA 1956, s 45. Parker LJ, in dismissing the appeal, said the following:

> As to the first matter, we regard the submission as untenable. The words of the phrase 'severe impairment of intelligence and social functioning' are ordinary English words. They are not terms of art. The ... section ... is ... designed to protect women ... defectives from exploitation. We can see no reason to suppose that Parliament intended to protect only those who were severely impaired compared with other mentally defective persons, but not those who were severely impaired as compared with normally developed persons. (O)n a natural reading of the words, it is ... clear that severe impairment is to be measured against the standards of normal persons[2].

1 (1987) 86 Cr App Rep 159, CA.

2 (1987) 86 Cr App Rep 159 at 162, CA.

4.16 The appellant in *Hall* further argued that the degree of a complainant's impairment can only be proved by expert evidence, and this was not done at the trial. Lord Parker dealt with this point with the following words:

> It is clear that [expert] evidence is admissible to establish the extent of the victim's intelligence, but we are unable to accept that a medical expert's opinion that a woman of, say, 30, with the intelligence of a girl of five is not severely impaired is of any real weight, if indeed admissible at all. If, having heard such evidence, the jury observe the victim happily playing with toys suitable for a child of five, unable to cope with toys for slightly older girls, and only able to converse like a child of five, the doctor's opinion cannot be regarded as being preferable to the observation of the jury[1].

1 (1987) 86 Cr App Rep 159 at 162 and 163, CA.

4.17 The effect of this dictum is that, while the prosecution may feel it desirable to call expert evidence as to the complainant's level of mental development, such evidence is not required, and the ultimate decision as to whether or not the woman comes within the ambit of the section is that of the jury's, even to the extent of rejecting any opinion given by an expert witness. Without any expert evidence it is likely that the prosecution will need or want to call the complainant herself to give evidence so that the jury have an opportunity to assess her capabilities. Notice should be made of the rules pertaining to the evidence of vulnerable witnesses which is considered in Chapter 12.

Mens Rea

4.18 The only issue to be considered under this heading is as to the man's knowledge or otherwise that the woman in question was a 'defective'. SOA 1956, s 7(2) allows for a statutory defence if the man can satisfy the jury[1] that he did not know, and had no reason to know, that the woman was indeed a 'defective'.

1 SOA 1956, s 47 puts the onus of proving the exception on him.

4.19 The case of *Hudson*[1] makes it clear that the approach as to whether or not the man knew of the woman's mental capacity is a subjective one. Ashworth J, in allowing the appeal, stated:

> ... the view of this court is that the proper approach to [SOA 1956,] s 7(2) is the subjective approach, that is to say that, if an accused man succeeds in establishing to the extent known as the balance of probabilities test that he himself did not know and that he himself had no reason to suspect the woman to be a defective, then he succeeds in his defence[2].

1 [1966]1 QB 448, [1965] 1 All ER 721, CCA.

2 [1965] 1 All ER 721 at 724B, CCA.

4.20 It should however be noted that Ashworth J did go on to say that a man who shuts his eyes to the obvious cannot avail himself of the statutory defence. While this is an important issue to bear in mind, it might be said that the latter point was no more than stating the obvious in that the provision does contain the words 'and has no reason to suspect her to be a defective'. It is submitted that if a man shuts his eyes to the obvious, then he ought not to be able to rely on the fact that he had no reason to suspect the woman to suffer from a mental impairment.

Sentence

4.21 By SOA 1956, s 37 and Sch 2, paras 11(a), (b), the maximum penalty for an offence under s 7 is imprisonment for two years. In spite of the many increases of maximum sentences for other offences, the maximum for this offence has remained the same. It is sometimes the case that men accused of having sexual intercourse with mentally impaired woman are charged with rape on the grounds that (a) the prosecution allege that the woman was not mentally able to consent to sexual intercourse, and (b) any sentence imposed for an offence under s 7 is unlikely to reflect the criminality involved in the act.

4.21A In addition, if the offence is committed against a child complainant, the offender can be ordered to be disqualified from working with children under CJCSA 2000, ss 26 to 31.

B Unlawful Sexual Intercourse with Patients

4.22 The current MHA 1959, s 128 reads as follows:

> 128(1) Without prejudice to section seven of the Sexual Offences Act 1956, it shall be an offence, subject to the exception mentioned in this section –
> (a) for a man who is an officer on the staff or is otherwise employed in, or is one of the managers of, a hospital, independent hospital or care home, to have unlawful sexual intercourse with a woman who is for the time being receiving treatment for mental disorder in that hospital or home, or to have such intercourse on the premises of which the hospital or home forms part with a woman who is for the time being receiving such treatment there as an outpatient;
> (b) for a man to have unlawful sexual intercourse with a woman who is a mentally disordered patient and who is

subject to his guardianship under the Mental Health Act 1983 or is otherwise in his custody or care under the Mental Health Act 1983 or in pursuance of arrangements under ... Part III of the National Assistance Act 1948 ... or the National Health Service Act 1977, or as a resident in a care home.

(2) It shall not be an offence under this section for a man to have sexual intercourse with a woman if he does not know and has no reason to suspect her to be a mentally disordered patient.

(3) Any person guilty of an offence under this section shall be liable on conviction on indictment to imprisonment for a term not exceeding two years.

(4) No proceedings shall be instituted for an offence under this section except by or with the consent of the Director of Public Prosecutions.

(5) This section shall be construed as one with the Sexual Offences Act 1956; and section 47 of that Act (which relates to proof of exceptions) shall apply to the exception mentioned in this section.

(6) In this section 'independent hospital' and 'care home' have the same meaning as in the Care Standards Act 2000.

4.23 The SOA 1967, s 1(4) states that the above section is to have effect as if the reference to 'unlawful sexual intercourse with a woman' includes committing buggery or an act of gross indecency with another man.

4.24 To a large extent the statutory provision speaks for itself and contains all that is required to be known about the offence. A complainant to such an offence is entitled to the same anonymity as for an offence under the SOA 1956, s 7[1] and the provision makes it clear that it is an offence that can only be tried on indictment. For all other issues pertaining to the offence, reference should be made to the corresponding paragraphs set out above in relation to an offence under s 7.

1 See paragraphs 4.10 and 4.11 above.

C Procurement of a Female 'Defective' to have Unlawful Sexual Intercourse

4.25 The SOA 1956, s 9 reads as follows:

> 9(1) It is an offence, subject to the exception mentioned in this section, for a person to procure a woman who is a defective to have unlawful sexual intercourse in any part of the world.
>
> (2) A person is not guilty of an offence under this section because he procures a defective to have unlawful sexual intercourse, if he does not know and has no reason to suspect her to be a defective.

General Issues

Mode of Trial

4.26 An offence under this provision, or an attempt to commit it, is an offence that can only be tried on indictment[1]. They are both Class 3 offences and as such can be tried by a High Court judge, a circuit judge or a recorder who has been properly authorised by a presiding judge[2].

1 See the SOA 1956, s 37(2) and Sch 2, para 13.

2 Practice Direction (Crown Court: allocation of business) (No 3) [2000] 1 All ER 380, [2000] 1 WLR 203.

4.27 In certain circumstances, the United Kingdom courts do not have jurisdiction to try a 'member of a visiting force or a civilian component of such a force'. Under the VFA 1952, s 3(1) an offence under SOA 1956, s 9 may come under this provision.

Parties to the Offence

4.28 The essence of the offence is that of 'procurement' and therefore both males and females can be defendants to such an allegation. The victim must, however, be female.

Complainant's Anonymity

4.29 The complainant in an allegation of an offence under SOA 1956, s 9 is entitled to comprehensive anonymity[1]. The anonymity of the complainant stretches to cover the publication of any matter relating to him/her 'if it is likely to lead members of the public to identify that person as the person against whom the offence is alleged to have been committed'[2]. The anonymity in these provisions remains in place throughout the complainant's lifetime. The anonymity provisions can however be over-ridden by an application by the accused to the trial judge to direct that SO(A)A 1992, s 1 should not apply in relation to the complainant. Under SO(A)A 1992, s 3(1), in order for such a direction to be made the judge must be satisfied of two things, namely that:

(a) the direction is required for the purpose of inducing persons who are likely to be needed as witnesses at the trial to come forward; and
(b) the conduct of the applicant's defence at the trial is likely to be substantially prejudiced if the direction is not given.

1 SO(A)A 1992, ss 1-4. These provisions apply to a large number of sexual offences.

2 See SO(A)A 1992, s 1(1).

4.30 The trial judge can also direct that the SO(A)A 1992, s 1 should not apply if he is satisfied that such anonymity 'imposes a substantial and unreasonable restriction upon the reporting of proceedings at the trial' and 'that it is in the public interest to remove or relax the restriction'[1].

1 See SO(A)A 1992, s 3(2).

Actus Reus

4.31 On an allegation of an offence under this section the prosecution need to prove, first, that an act of 'procurement' took place, secondly, that the woman so procured was a 'defective' and, thirdly, that the procurement led to 'unlawful sexual intercourse'. So far as the first point is concerned, 'procurement' involves a positive act on the part of the accused. If there is any doubt as to whether or not the victim initiated the action then the defendant should be acquitted.

4.32 For issues pertaining to the definition of 'defective', see paragraphs 4.14 to 4.18 above.

4.33 For issues pertaining to the term 'unlawful sexual intercourse', see paragraphs 3.15 to 3.17 and paragraphs 1.18 to 1.20 above.

4.34 In the case of *Johnson*[1] the appellant was convicted of an offence of procuring a girl under the age of 21 to have sexual intercourse. He appealed on the ground that in order to satisfy the section actual sexual intercourse must take place, and it did not do so between himself and the woman in question. His appeal was successful with Lord Parker CJ stating the following:

> This court has come to the clear conclusion that it is necessary before a man can be found guilty of [the] offence to prove that unlawful sexual intercourse did take place ... It is further to be observed that this same expression [ie 'for the purposes of ...'] occurs in three other sections [of the SOA 1956]: section 2; ... section 3; ... and section 9, dealing with mental defectives. I only mention that because in those cases, particularly the last one, the real vice occurs through the sexual intercourse taking place.

1 [1964] 2 QB 404, [1963] 3 All ER 577, CA.

4.35 It should be noted, however, that it was decided in *Johnson* that in circumstances where no sexual intercourse takes place, but all the other factors are proved, the man should be convicted of an attempt to commit the full offence.

Mens Rea

4.36 The same statutory defence is available to an accused under this provision as to an offence under SOA 1956, s 7 and reference should be made to paragraphs 4.18 to 4.20 above.

Sentence

4.37 By the SOA 1956, s 37 and Sch 2, para 13(a) and (b), the maximum sentence for an offence under this section is two years in prison. In addition, if the offence is committed against a child complainant, the offender can be ordered to be disqualified from working with children under CJCSA 2000, ss 26 to 31.

D Abduction of a Female 'Defective' from her Parent or Guardian

4.38 The SOA 1956, s 21 reads as follows:

> 21(1) It is an offence subject to the exception mentioned in this section, for a person to take a woman who is a defective out of the possession of her parent or guardian against his will, if she is so taken with the intention that she shall have unlawful sexual intercourse with men or with a particular man.
>
> (2) A person is not guilty of an offence under this section because he takes such a woman out of the possession of her parent or guardian as mentioned above, if he does not know and has no reason to suspect her to be a defective.
>
> (3) In this section 'guardian' means any person having the lawful care or charge of the woman.

General Issues

Mode of Trial

4.39 An offence under this provision, or an attempt to commit it, is an offence that can only be tried on indictment[1]. They are both Class 3 offences and as such can be tried by a High Court judge, a circuit judge or a recorder who has been properly authorised by a presiding judge[2].

1 See the SOA 1956, s 37(2) and Sch 2, para 22.

2 Practice Direction (Crown Court: allocation of business) (No 3) [2000] 1 All ER 380, [2000] 1 WLR 203.

4.40 In certain circumstances the United Kingdom courts do not have jurisdiction to try a 'member of a visiting force or a civilian component of such a force'. Under the VFA 1952, s 3(1), an offence under the SOA 1956, s 21 may come under this provision.

Parties to the Offence

4.41 The provision makes it clear that either a male or female can be a defendant to such an offence but the victim must be female.

Actus Reus

4.42 For a definition of the word 'defective' see paragraphs 4.13 to 4.17 above.

4.43 For a definition of the words 'unlawful sexual intercourse' see paragraphs 3.15 to 3.17 and 1.18 to 1.20 above.

4.44 With regard to the notion of 'take ... out of the possession of' the leading case was decided in 1866 and the subject has not been significantly altered in any way since then. In the case of *Olifier*[1] it was said that in order to satisfy the jury that the defendant did indeed 'take' the girl in question, they have to be satisfied that there was some form of positive inducement by way of persuasion or blandishment on his part. There did not need to be any force used upon the girl and even if the girl were to go willingly with the man (for example as an elopement) then any assistance afforded to her would constitute 'taking'. On the other hand, there is no 'taking' if the woman goes to the man under her own free will and the man does nothing to dissuade her from joining him.

1 (1866) 10 Cox CC 402.

4.45 So far as the issue of the woman being in the possession of her parent or guardian is concerned, this is a question of fact for the jury to decide[1]. It would of course be necessary for the prosecution to prove that she was indeed in such possession of her parent or guardian in line with the section.

1 See, for example, *Mace* (1886) 50 JP 776.

4.46 With regard to the phrase 'against his will' in the section, this can realistically only mean without the consent of the parent or guardian. Again, the prosecution would have to prove that the taking of the woman was without the consent of the parent or guardian in order to establish that the offence was committed.

Mens Rea

4.47 Again, the same statutory defence is available to an accused under this provision as to an offence under SOA 1956, s 7 and reference should be made to paragraphs 4.19 to 4.21 above.

Sentence

4.48 By SOA 1956, s 37 and Sch 2, para 22, the maximum sentence for an offence under this section is two years in prison. In addition, if the offence is committed against a child complainant, the offender can be ordered to be disqualified from working with children under CJCSA 2000, ss 26 to 31.

E Permitting a 'Defective' to Use Premises for Intercourse

4.49 SOA 1956, s 27 reads as follows:

> 27(1) It is an offence, subject to the exception mentioned in this section, for a person who is the owner or occupier of any premises, or who has, or acts or assists in, the management or control of any premises, to induce or knowingly suffer a woman who is a defective to resort to or be on those premises for the purpose of having unlawful sexual intercourse with men or with a particular man.
>
> (2) A person is not guilty of an offence under this section because he induces or knowingly suffers a defective to resort to or be on any premises for the purpose mentioned, if he does not know and has no reason to suspect her to be a defective.

General Issues

Mode of Trial

4.50 An offence under this provision, or an attempt to commit it, is an offence that can only be tried on indictment[1]. They are both Class 3 offences and as such can be tried by a High Court judge, a circuit judge or a recorder who has been properly authorised by a presiding judge[2].

1 See the SOA 1956, s 37(2) and Sch 2, para 27.

2 Practice Direction (Crown Court: allocation of business) (No 3) [2000] 1 All ER 380, [2000] 1 WLR 203.

4.51 In certain circumstances the United Kingdom courts do not have jurisdiction to try a 'member of a visiting force or a civilian component of such a force'. Under the VFA 1952, s 3(1), an offence under SOA 1956, s 27 may come under this provision.

Parties to the Offence

4.52 The provision makes it clear that either a male or female can be a defendant to such an offence but the victim must be female.

Actus Reus

4.53 For a definition of the word 'defective' see paragraphs 4.13 to 4.17 above.

4.54 For a definition of the words 'unlawful sexual intercourse' see paragraphs 3.15 to 3.17 and 1.18 to 1.20 above.

4.55 For a discussion of the word 'occupier', refer to paragraphs 3.78 and 3.79 above.

4.56 With regard to the word 'resort' used in the section, it was said in the case of *Brown*[1] that the word is an ordinary English verb and analogous terms would be 'go to', 'frequent' and 'go in and out of'.

1 [1895] 1 QB 119, CCR.

Mens Rea

4.57 Again, the same statutory defence is available to an accused under this provision as to an offence under SOA 1956, s 7 and reference should be made to paragraphs 4.18 to 4.20 above.

Sentence

4.58 By SOA 1956, s 37 and Sch 2, para 27, the maximum sentence for an offence under this section is two years in prison. In addition, if the offence is committed against a child complainant, the offender can be ordered to be disqualified from working with children under CJCSA 2000, ss 26 to 31.

F Causing or Encouraging Prostitution of a 'Defective'

4.59 SOA 1956, s 29 reads as follows:-

> 29(1) It is an offence, subject to the exception mentioned in this section, for a person to cause or encourage the prostitution in any part of the world of a woman who is a defective.
>
> (2) A person is not guilty of an offence under this section because he causes or encourages the prostitution of such a woman, if he does not know and has no reason to suspect her to be a defective.

4.60 Offences pertaining to prostitution in general are dealt with in Chapter 8. However, it is felt appropriate to consider the offence relating to the prostitution of 'mental defectives' here.

Mode of Trial

4.61 An offence under this provision, or an attempt to commit it, is an offence that can only be tried on indictment[1]. They are both Class 3 offences and as such can be tried by a High Court judge, a circuit judge or a recorder who has been properly authorised by a presiding judge[2].

1 See the SOA 1956, s 37(2) and Sch 2, para 29.

2 Practice Direction (Crown Court: allocation of business) (No 3) [2000] 1 All ER 380, [2000] 1 WLR 203.

4.62 In certain circumstances the United Kingdom courts do not have jurisdiction to try a 'member of a visiting force or a civilian component of such a force'. Under the VFA 1952, s 3(1), an offence under SOA 1956, s 29 may come under this provision.

Parties to the Offence

4.63 The provision makes it clear that either a male or female can be a defendant to such an offence but the victim must be female.

Actus Reus

4.64 For a definition of the word 'defective' see paragraphs 4.13 to 4.17 above.

4.65 For a definition of the words 'unlawful sexual intercourse' see paragraphs 3.15 to 3.17 and 1.18 to 1.20 above.

4.66 There is no statute that defines the word 'prostitution' and therefore regard must be had to decided cases on the issue. What is clear is that it is not necessary, for prostitution to be proved, for sexual intercourse to have taken place[1]. Further reference should be made to paragraphs 8.10 to 8.14 below for guidance on issues pertaining to 'prostitution'.

1 See, for example, *de Munck* [1918] 1 KB 635, CCA.

Mens Rea

4.67 Again, the same statutory defence is available to an accused under this provision as to offences under earlier sections and reference should be made to paragraphs 4.18 to 4.20 above.

Sentence

4.68 By SOA 1956, s 37 and Sch 2, para 29, the maximum sentence for an offence under this section is two years in prison. In addition, if the offence is committed against a child complainant, the offender can be ordered to be disqualified from working with children under CJCSA 2000, ss 26 to 31.

Chapter five

Incest

5.1 There is a small body of offences that prohibit sexual intercourse between blood relations. It should be noted that the list of relationships prevented from such intercourse is somewhat different than a list of those who are barred from marrying. So that, for example, a man may legally have sexual intercourse with his adopted daughter – so long as she is above the age of 16 and is a consensual partner – but he is disallowed from marrying her. As is made clear below, it is the fact that there is a direct blood relationship between the partners that is the crux of this offence.

5.2 A great many of the offences that come before the courts – but by no means all – concern sexual intercourse between fathers and their daughters and, more often than not, the sexual intercourse takes place in an abusive situation. In some circumstances such a situation inevitably leads to the same act constituting a number of criminal offences. Care should be taken to ensure that the overall criminality of the particular situation is reflected in the offence charged. Further care should be taken in that there are also inevitably, a number of offences that can be alternatives to any offence of incest.

5.3 Incest is another criminal offence that has been criticised in the past as being over-protective and unnecessary. It has been argued in thc past that the offence reflects the horror and disgust that society feels towards such behaviour, but the better view, especially when one considers that it is only blood relations that are affected by the offence, is that the basis of the law is eugenic.

A Incest by a Man

5.4 SOA 1956, s 10 reads as follows:

> 10(1) It is an offence for a man to have sexual intercourse with a woman whom he knows to be his grand-daughter, daughter, sister or mother.
>
> (2) In the foregoing subsection 'sister' includes half-sister and for the purposes of that subsection any expression importing a relationship between two people shall be taken to apply notwithstanding that the relationship is not traced through lawful wedlock.

5.5 The use of the word 'man' in this provision should be read as referring to both men and boys[1]. By virtue of SOA 1956, s 46 the two words are interchangeable.

1 See paragraph 5.11 below.

5.6 SOA 1956, s 37(2) and Sch 2, para 14(a) and (b) makes it clear that no prosecution for this offence, or an attempt to commit the offence, may be commenced except by or with the permission of the Director of Public Prosecutions.

General Issues

Mode of Trial

5.7 An offence under SOA 1956, s 10(1), together with an attempt, is triable only on indictment[1]. Both are Class 3 offences, unless the victim is under 13 years old, in which case they are Class 2 offences. As a Class 3 offence the matter can be tried by a High Court judge, a circuit judge or a recorder who has been properly authorised by a presiding judge. As Class 2 offences they can be tried only by a High Court judge unless the case is released by or on the authority of a presiding judge for trial by a circuit judge[2].

1 See the SOA 1956, s 37(2) and Sch 2, para 14.

2 Practice Direction (Crown Court: allocation of business) (No 3) [2000] 1 All ER 380, [2000] 1 WLR 203.

5.8 In certain circumstances the United Kingdom courts do not have jurisdiction to try 'a member of a visiting force or a civilian component of such a force'. Under VFA 1952, s 3(1) an offence under SOA 1956, s 10(1) may come under this provision.

Parties to the Offence

5.9 It is clear that only a male can be accused of an offence under this section. It is equally clear that only females within the requisite blood relationship to the man can be victims. The absolute essence of this offence is consanguinity. Without there being a blood relationship between the man and the complainant, incest should not be charged. Thus, daughters of men who have been adopted or who are step-daughters cannot be victims of incest.

5.10 It is further made clear (in SOA 1956, s 10(2)) that 'half-sisters' are included in the offence together with children born out of wedlock. Much of the case law pertaining to the offence of incest stems from the early part of the 20th century where the unfortunate term 'illegitimate' is often used to refer to such children.

5.11 Until September 1993 there was a common law presumption that a boy under the age of 14 could not indulge in sexual intercourse, either vaginal or anal. This presumption was abolished by the SOA 1993, s 1. The effect of that provision is to allow the conviction of any male aged 10[1] or over for any sexual offence involving the penetration of the vagina or anus of the complainant by him.

1 The age at which any criminal liability arises: see CYPA 1933, s 50.

Complainant's Anonymity

5.12 Complainants in an allegation of an offence under SOA 1956, s 10(1) are entitled to comprehensive anonymity[1]. The anonymity of the complainant stretches to cover the publication of any matter relating to her 'if it is likely to lead members of the public to identify that person as the person against whom the offence is alleged to have been committed'[2]. The anonymity in these provisions remains in place throughout the complainant's lifetime. The anonymity provisions can however be overridden by an application by the accused to the trial judge to direct that the SO(A)A 1992, s 1 should not apply in relation to the complainant. Under the SO(A)A 1992, s 3(1) in order for such a direction to be made the judge must be satisfied of two things, namely that:

(i) the direction is required for the purpose of inducing persons who are likely to be needed as witnesses at the trial to come forward; and
(ii) the conduct of the applicant's defence at the trial is likely to be substantially prejudiced if the direction is not given.

1 SO(A)A 1992, ss 1 to 4. These provisions apply to a large number of sexual offences.

2 See SO(A)A 1992, s 1(1).

5.13 The trial judge can also direct that SO(A)A 1992, s 1 should not apply if he is satisfied that such anonymity 'imposes a substantial and unreasonable restriction upon the reporting of proceedings at the trial' and 'that it is in the public interest to remove or relax the restriction'[1].

1 See SO(A)A1992, s 3(2).

Alternative Verdicts

5.14 On a charge of the full offence under SOA 1956, s 10, it is open to the jury to find the man guilty of offences of unlawful sexual intercourse with a girl under 13[1] or of having unlawful sexual intercourse with a girl under 16[2]. This is allowed under the SOA 1956, s 37(5) and later made plain in Sch 2, para 14(a).

1 SOA 1956, s 5. See Chapter 3 above.

2 SOA 1956, s 6. See Chapter 3 above.

5.15 It should be noted that, in the case of *McCormack*[1] it was decided that an offence under SOA 1956, s 6 implicitly included an allegation of indecent assault and so, in the right circumstances, it would be open for a jury to return verdicts of not guilty to incest and having unlawful sexual intercourse with a girl under 16 but guilty of indecent assault. This issue was addressed in the case of *Josef Rogina*[2] even though the appeal was only against sentence. Scarman LJ concluded that, though SOA 1956, s 37 used rather tortuous language to make the point that indecent assault could be an alternative verdict, it did indeed get there in the end.

1 [1969] 2 QB 442, [1969] 3 All ER 371, CA; and see paragraph 3.13 above.

2 (1975) 64 Cr App Rep 79.

5.16 It should also be remembered that an offence under SOA 1956, s 6 must be brought within 12 months of the date of the commission of the alleged offence. Depending on the circumstances, this may create difficulties, especially in terms of the trial judge's summing-up and his directions on this point.

Actus Reus

5.17 The first element of the offence for the prosecution to prove is that sexual intercourse has taken place. This is a topic that has been fully considered in Chapter 1 and reference should be made to paragraphs 1.18 to 1.20 for a definition of 'sexual intercourse'.

5.18 The next element that the prosecution must prove is that there was indeed a blood relationship between the parties. The prosecution may seek to prove this relationship in a number of ways but, whichever method is chosen, the proof must be conclusive. In the case of *Evan Jones*[1], for example, the only evidence that the victim – who was 22 at the time of the offence – was the man's daughter was by the defendant's admission. This was held, on appeal, to be permissible to go before the jury as evidence of the relationship. This is a case that is still, today, cited as support for the contention that such an admission is sufficient evidence to prove consanguinity. It is submitted, however, that in these days of artificial insemination and IVF treatment for infertile couples, as well as a more permissive age than that enjoyed by Mr Jones, such authority should be treated cautiously.

1 (1933) 24 Cr App Rep 55, CCA.

5.19 Other forms of evidence may be acceptable, for example oral evidence from the victim's mother or from an entry in a copy of the Register of Births for the particular individual. However, again it is submitted that, from the point of view of the defendant, a DNA test should be required to prove consanguinity between the man and the complainant, if there is any doubt of the matter[1].

1 See *Hemmings* [1939] 1 All ER 417, CCA and *Carmichael* [1940] 1 KB 630, 27 Cr App Rep 183, CCA for examples of cases where the defendants relied on things told them by the complainant's mother as part of their defence.

Mens Rea

5.20 Consent is not a defence to an allegation of incest. If there is any doubt as to whether the complainant consented to the sexual intercourse then a charge of rape should be included on the indictment.

5.21 The man must know that the person he is having sexual intercourse with is a blood relation; ie one of the relations specified in the provision. In *Bailie-Smith*[1] the defendant was accused of having sexual intercourse with his 13-year-old daughter. Following his arrest he gave a statement to the police saying that he thought that he was having sex with his wife. At his trial the girl was not called to give evidence and the judge directed the jury that he had admitted knowing that the girl was his daughter, neglecting to direct them that they should consider his full defence; that is, that he did not realise he was having sex with his daughter. His conviction was quashed on appeal with Shaw LJ saying:

> The jury were left to consider only those matters which were not in dispute. They were not invited to apply their minds to the fundamental question of whether or not the appellant was aware at the time he had intercourse which he admitted, that the woman with whom he was having intercourse was his 13-year-old daughter and not, as he asserted he supposed at the time, was his wife[2].

1 (1976) 64 Cr App Rep 76, CA.

2 (1976) 64 Cr App Rep 76 at 78, CA.

5.22 Thus, if the man is unaware that the female he has sexual intercourse with is a blood relation, or makes a genuine mistake as to her identity, then he is not guilty of the offence. Such a situation is further illustrated by the case of *Carmichael*[1] in which the defendant was disallowed from adducing evidence that he had been told by his wife that her daughter was not his. When he later had sexual intercourse with her, it transpired that she was indeed his daughter and he was thus charged with incest. His conviction was later quashed by the Court of Appeal, that evidence being held relevant as to the issue of whether or not the defendant knew that the girl was his daughter.

1 [1940] 1 KB 630, 27 Cr App Rep 183, CCA.

Evidence

5.23 In certain circumstances, evidence of previous incestuous behaviour is admissible to substantiate the offence charged. This is something of a break from the norm in relation to issues touching on so-called 'similar fact' evidence. In the normal course of events the prosecution would not normally be allowed to adduce evidence that a defendant has undertaken similar acts in the past that may or may not have constituted criminal acts in order to bolster the case in question. A common example given in this context is the case of *Ball and Ball*[1]. That case involved a brother and sister who shared a double bed and lived as if husband and wife. The prosecution was allowed to adduce evidence that together they had conceived a child before 1910 (when incest first became a criminal offence) to support the contention that they were guilty of incest in July 1910. This ruling should be considered with some circumspection as, clearly, the exact same situation could not arise today. Though the logic in the ruling still stands, it is submitted that the conception of a child between blood relations would be extremely powerful proof of incest having taken place, for which the parties could be charged.

1 [1911] AC 47, CCA

5.24 In two cases that came before the Court of Appeal shortly after the offence was first introduced, evidence was deemed permissible of sexual intercourse between the parties prior to the act charged[1] and subsequent to the act[2].

1 *Arthur Allen* (1910) 4 Cr App Rep 181.

2 *Alfred Stone* (1910) 6 Cr App Rep 89.

5.25 Similarly, in the case of *DPP v P*[1] it was held by the House of Lords to be permissible for the prosecution to adduce evidence of more than one complainant against the defendant on charges of incest. The defendant was charged with rape and incest against his two daughters and, having ruled that there should not be separate trials, the trial judge allowed the evidence of each girl to be given, the Crown relying on all the evidence to substantiate all of the charges. The Court of Appeal quashed the convictions, but this ruling was overturned by the House of Lords. In dealing with the issue of evidence that is said to be 'strikingly similar' Lord Mackay of Clashfern LC said:

> ... the essential feature of the evidence which is to be admitted is that its probative force in support of the allegation that an accused person committed a crime is sufficiently great to make it just to admit the evidence, notwithstanding that it is prejudicial to the accused in tending to show that he was guilty of another crime[2].

Having set out the various aspects off the evidence in question in relation to the two girls who were the victims of the man's sexual acts, Lord Mackay went onto say:

> In my view these circumstances taken together gave strong probative force to the evidence of each of the girls in relation to the incidents involving the other, and was certainly sufficient to make it just to admit the evidence, notwithstanding its prejudicial effect[3].

1 [1991] 2 AC 447, [1991] 3 All ER 337.

2 [1991] 2 AC 447 at 460.

3 [1991] 2 AC 447 at 461.

5.26 In cases where the allegations against the man are that he had incestuous relations with more than one of his daughters, it is the case of *DPP v P* that will govern the admissibility of each of the girl's evidence.

Sentence

5.27 If the victim of the charge is a girl under the age of 13 then the full offence, together with an attempt, carries a maximum penalty of life imprisonment. If the victim is over 13 years then the maximum penalty for both offences is seven years[1]. It is for this reason that the age of the victim should be averred in the indictment.

1 SOA 1956, s 37(3) and Sch 2, para 14(a) and (b).

5.28 The factual circumstances in offences of incest can, of course, vary enormously from comparatively stable and long-term sexual relationships between partners down to extremely abusive and exploitative sexual activity on the part of a father or grandfather. Equally, the deleterious effects on the 'victim' of incest can range from non-existent up to severe psychological trauma. The sentencing regime for the offence recognises these issues and has been developed accordingly.

5.29 The leading case in relation to sentencing incest is *A-G's Reference (No 1 of 1989)*[1] in which Lord Lane, in recognising that the development of sentencing guidelines for an offence that can be committed under a vast array of circumstances was extremely difficult, attempted a broad formula to be considered when sentencing for the offence. It should be noted that the reference by the Attorney-General followed a guilty plea by the defendant and the guidelines formulated by Lord Lane concerned only offences committed by a father against his daughter. They should not therefore be regarded as the standard for considering the appropriate sentence in all instances of incest but remain extremely helpful.

1 [1989] 3 All ER 571, [1989] WLR 1117, 90 Cr App R 141, CA.

5.30 Before considering both aggravating and mitigating factors Lord Lane emphasised that 'the younger the girl when the sexual approach is started, the more likely it will be that the girl's will was overborne and accordingly the more serious the crime'. Having said that he went onto list the possible aggravating features first. These were:

- if there is evidence of physical or psychological injury
- if the incest has continued at frequent intervals over a long period of time
- if the girl was threatened or treated violently by or was terrified of the father
- if the incest was accompanied by perversions abhorrent to the girl (eg fellatio or buggery)
- if the girl has become pregnant by reason of the father failing to take contraceptive precautions
- if the defendant has committed similar offences against more than one girl.

So far as mitigating features are concerned, he listed the following:

- a plea of guilty
- if it seems there was genuine affection for the girl on the part of the defendant rather than an intention to merely use the girl as an outlet for his sexual gratification
- where the girl has had previous sexual experience
- where the girl has made deliberate attempts at seduction
- where a shorter term of imprisonment for the father may be of real benefit to the victim and the family as a whole.

5.31 So far as the actual sentencing guidelines aspect of the case is concerned, Lord Lane set out the following suggestions, depending on the particular circumstances, as being of general assistance:

(i)	where the girl is over 16	three years in prison down to a nominal sentence
(ii)	where the girl is aged between 13 and 16	about five years in prison down to about three years
(iii)	where the girl is under 13	a prison term of about six years.

In relation to (iii) above Lord Lane accepted that this was the most difficult aspect of incest to sentence as it is likely to be the most serious in terms of the effect it will have had on the family unit and of psychological damage caused to the victim. For that reason it is likely to attract the widest range of sentences.

5.32 Although strictly speaking not part of a sentence that should be imposed following a conviction of this offence, notice should be made of the SOA 1956, s 38 which reads as follows:

> 38(1) On a person's conviction of an offence under section 10 of this Act against a girl under the age of eighteen, or of an offence under section 11 of this Act against a boy under that age, or of attempting to commit such an offence, the court may by order divest that person of all authority over the girl or boy.
>
> (2) An order divesting a person of authority over a girl or boy under the foregoing subsection may, if that person is the guardian of the girl or boy, remove that person from the guardianship.
>
> (3) An order under this section may appoint a person to be the guardian of the girl or boy during his or her minority or any less period.
>
> (4) An order under this section may be varied from time to time or rescinded by the High Court and, if made on conviction of an offence against a girl or boy who is a defective, may, so far as it has effect for any purposes of the Mental Health Act 1983, be rescinded either before or after the girl or boy has attained the age of 18.

5.33 Part I (ss 1 to 6) of the SOA 1997 applies to offences under this section[1]. This part of the Act relates to the requirement for, and effect of, people sentenced for the offence to register with their local police force. In addition, if the offence is committed against a child complainant, the offender can be ordered to be disqualified from working with children under CJCSA 2000, ss 26 to 31.

1 See SOA 1997, Sch 1.

B Incest by a Woman

5.34 The SOA 1956, s 11 reads as follows:

> 10(1) It is an offence for a woman of the age of 16 or over to permit a man whom she knows to be her grandfather,

father, brother or son to have sexual intercourse with her by her consent.

(5) In the foregoing subsection 'brother' includes half-brother and for the purposes of that subsection any expression importing a relationship between two people shall be taken to apply notwithstanding that the relationship is not traced through lawful wedlock.

5.35 SOA 1956, s 37(2) and Sch 2, para 14(a) and (b) makes it clear that no prosecution for this offence, or an attempt to commit the offence, may be commenced except by or with the permission of the Director of Public Prosecutions.

General Issues

Mode of Trial

5.36 An offence under the SOA 1956, s 11(1) is triable only on indictment[1]. It is a Class 3 offence. As a Class 3 offence the matter can be tried by a High Court judge, a circuit judge or a recorder who has been properly authorised by a presiding judge[2].

1 See the SOA 1956, s 37(2) and Sch 2, para 15.

2 Practice Direction (Crown Court: allocation of business) (No 3) [2000] 1 All ER 380, [2000] 1 WLR 203.

5.37 In certain circumstances the United Kingdom courts do not have jurisdiction to try 'a member of a visiting force or a civilian component of such a force'. Under VFA 1952, s 3(1) an offence under the SOA 1956, s 11(1) may come under this provision.

Parties to the Offence

5.38 It is clear that only a female over the age of 16 can be accused of an offence under this section. It is equally clear that only males within the requisite blood relationship to the woman can be victims. As with an offence under the SOA 1956, s 10(1), the essence of the offence is consanguinity. Without there being a blood relationship between the woman and the complainant, incest should not be charged.

5.39 It is further made clear (in the SOA 1956, s 10(2)) that 'half-brothers' are included in the offence together with sons born out of wedlock. Much of the case law pertaining to the offence of incest stems from the early part of the 20th century where the unfortunate term 'illegitimate' is often used to refer to such children.

5.40 Until September 1993 there was a common law presumption that a boy under the age of 14 could not indulge in sexual intercourse, either vaginal or anal. This presumption was abolished by SOA 1993, s 1. The effect of that provision in the context of this offence is that a woman can be charged with incest if she has sexual intercourse with her natural son who is between the ages of 10 and 14.

Complainant's Anonymity

5.41 Complainants in an allegation of an offence under SOA 1956, s 11(1) are entitled to comprehensive anonymity[1]. The anonymity of the complainant stretches to cover the publication of any matter relating to her 'if it is likely to lead members of the public to identify that person as the person against whom the offence is alleged to have been committed'[2]. The anonymity in these provisions remains in place throughout the complainant's lifetime. The anonymity provisions can however be over-ridden by an application by the accused to the trial judge to direct that SO(A)A 1992, s 1 should not apply in relation to the complainant. Under SO(A)A 1992, s 3(1), in order for such a direction to be made the judge must be satisfied of two things, namely that:

(i) the direction is required for the purpose of inducing persons who are likely to be needed as witnesses at the trial to come forward; and
(ii) the conduct of the applicant's defence at the trial is likely to be substantially prejudiced if the direction is not given.

1 SO(A)A 1992, ss 1-4.

2 See SO(A)A 1992, s 1(1).

5.42 The trial judge can also direct that SO(A)A 1992, s 1 should not apply if he is satisfied that such anonymity 'imposes a substantial and unreasonable restriction upon the reporting of proceedings at the trial' and 'that it is in the public interest to remove or relax the restriction'[1].

1 See SO(A)A 1992, s 3(2).

Alternative Verdicts

5.43 Unlike the offence under SOA 1956, s 10(1), Sch 2 does not allow for any specific alternative verdict for an offence under SOA 1956, s 11(1). However, by reason of CLA 1967, s 6(4), it is possible for a woman charged with incest to be found guilty of indecent assault as an alternative to the full offence.

Actus Reus

5.44 The actus reus for this offence is identical to that of the offence under SOA 1956, s 10(1), mutatis mutandis, and reference should be made to paragraphs 5.17 to 5.19 above.

5.45 It would be for the prosecution to satisfy the jury that the defendant had attained the age of 16 at the time of the commission of the offence. This aspect of the offence can be proved in a number of ways including, of course, an admission by the defendant herself. CYPA 1933, s 99(2) and Sch 1, as amended by SOA 1956, s 48 allows for a court to draw an inference as to the girl's age from her appearance, and this provision may be relied upon by the prosecution. It is submitted that for a young woman to be cast in the role of a criminal, the prosecution ought to be made to prove their case, on this point, with rather stronger evidence than a mere inference.

Mens Rea

5.46 The mens rea for this offence is identical to that of the offence under the SOA 1956, s 10(1) and reference should be made to paragraphs 5.20 to 5.22 above.

5.47 It would of course be for the prosecution to prove, to the satisfaction of the jury, that the sexual intercourse was consensual on the part of the defendant. It is not difficult to think of a situation where a woman charged under this section might claim that she did not consent to the sexual intercourse and would, in effect, be claiming that she was raped by her sexual partner. If the jury were to acquit her of the offence of incest, it is submitted that it is unlikely that the man would later be charged with the offence of rape[1].

1 See *Dimes* (1911) 7 Cr App Rep 43 for an example of how the Court of Appeal found a way around just such a conundrum.

Sentence

5.48 The maximum sentence for this offence is seven years in prison. For an attempt the maximum sentence is two years in prison. There is no distinction in sentence depending on the age of the victim. It is rare for cases under this section to come before the courts, least of all the higher courts and the only case of any real significance was that of *Jacqueline F*[1]. In that case the appellant had committed incest with her 13-year-old son on a number of occasions. Her sentence of 18 months in prison was upheld by the Court of Appeal.

1 (1991) 13 Cr App Rep (S) 358.

5.49 Reference should also be made to paragraphs 5.32 and 5.33 above.

C Incitement of Girls under 16 to Commit Incest

5.50 The CLA 1977, s 54 of reads as follows:

> 54(1) It is an offence for a man to incite to have sexual intercourse with him a girl under the age of 16 whom he knows to be his grand-daughter, daughter or sister.
>
> (2) In the preceding subsection 'man' includes boy, 'sister' includes half-sister, and for the purposes of that subsection

any expression importing a relationship between two people shall be taken to apply notwithstanding that the relationship is not traced through lawful wedlock.

(3) The following provisions of section 1 of the Indecency with Children Act 1960, namely –

subsection (3) (references in Children and Young Persons Act 1933 to the offences mentioned in Schedule 1 to that Act to include offences under that section);

subsection (4) (offences under that section to be deemed offences against the person for the purpose of section 3 of the Visiting Forces Act 1952),

shall apply in relation to offences under this section.

(4) A person guilty of an offence under this section shall be liable –

(a) on summary conviction, to imprisonment for a term not exceeding six months or to a fine not exceeding the prescribed sum or both;

(b) on conviction on indictment to imprisonment for a term not exceeding two years.

5.51 This provision was introduced into the criminal canon following the case of *Whitehouse*[1]. That case discovered a lacuna in the law as it then stood and the CLA 1977, s 54 was enacted to close that lacuna. As it is put in the head-note to the case:

> As pursuant to [the SOA 1956,] s 11(1) a daughter under the age of 16 is incapable of committing the crime of incest with her father, the latter cannot be guilty of the common law offence of inciting her to commit that offence with him. Nor can he be guilty of inciting his daughter to aid and abet him in the commission of the crime of incest.

1 [1977] QB 868, 65 Cr App Rep 33, CA.

5.52 The appellant did not have sexual intercourse with his daughter; he merely importuned her to have sexual intercourse, which advances she rejected. Thus it became clear at the Court of Appeal that he had pleaded guilty to offences that did not then exist and his appeal was allowed. The statute now criminalises any such importuning of a female within the said blood relationships to have sexual intercourse.

General Issues

Mode of Trial

5.53 CLA 1977, s 54(4) makes it clear that this offence can be tried either way and as such is a Class 4 offence. The effect of this classification is that the offence can be tried by a High Court judge, a circuit judge or a recorder[1].

1 *Practice Direction (Crown Court: allocation of business) (No 3)* [2000] 1 All ER 380, [2000] 1 WLR 203.

Parties to the Offence

5.54 As with the offence of incest under SOA 1956, s 10(1), only a male can be charged as a principal of this offence and the complainant must be a female under the age of 16. Such female must also come within one of the designated blood relationships set out in the provision.

Complainant's Anonymity

5.55 Complainants in an allegation of an offence under this section are entitled to comprehensive anonymity[1]. The anonymity of the complainant stretches to cover the publication of any matter relating to her 'if it is likely to lead members of the public to identify that person as the person against whom the offence is alleged to have been committed'[2]. The anonymity in these provisions remains in place throughout the complainant's lifetime. The anonymity provisions can, however, be overridden by an application by the accused to the trial judge to direct that the SO(A)A 1992, s 1 should not apply in relation to the complainant. Under the SO(A)A 1992, s 3(1), in order for such a direction to be made the judge must be satisfied of two things, namely that:

(i) the direction is required for the purpose of inducing persons who are likely to be needed as witnesses at the trial to come forward; and
(ii) the conduct of the applicant's defence at the trial is likely to be substantially prejudiced if the direction is not given.

1 SO(A)A 1992, ss 1-4. These provisions apply to a large number of sexual offences.

2 See SO(A)A 1992, s 1(1).

5.56 The trial judge can also direct that the SO(A)A 1992, s 1 should not apply if he is satisfied that such anonymity 'imposes a substantial and unreasonable restriction upon the reporting of proceedings at the trial' and 'that it is in the public interest to remove or relax the restriction'[1].

1 See SO(A)A 1992, s 3(2).

Actus Reus

5.57 The offence is committed when a man incites a girl under the age of 16 who is a blood relative of his to have sexual intercourse with him. It is not an ingredient of the offence that sexual intercourse actually takes place as, if it did, the offence under SOA 1956, s 10(1) should be charged.

5.58 As in the full offence, the prosecution will need to prove that the girl in question was under the age of 16 at the time of the commission of the offence and that she came within one of the relationships set out in the provision. Reference should be made to paragraphs 5.18 and 5.19 above with regard to these points.

Mens Rea

5.59 The man must be shown to know that the girl in question satisfies the relationship criterion in the provision and reference should be made to paragraphs 5.21 and 5.22 above with regard to this aspect of the offence.

Sentence

5.60 CLA 1977, s 54(4) of the section sets out the particular sentences for the offence. Reference should be made to the MCA 1980, s 32(2) and (9) for the 'prescribed sum'.

5.61 Part I (ss 1 to 6) of the SOA 1997 applies to offences under this section[1]. This part of the Act relates to the requirement for, and effect of, people sentenced for the offence to register with their local police force. In addition, if the offence is committed against a child complainant, the offender can be ordered to be disqualified from working with children under CJCSA 2000, ss 26 to 31.

1 See SOA 1997, s 1.

Chapter six

Sexual assaults

A Indecent Assault

6.1 The SOA 1956, s 14 reads as follows:

> 14(1) It is an offence, subject to the exception mentioned in subsection (3) of this section, for a person to make an indecent assault on a woman.
>
> (2) A girl under the age of sixteen cannot in law give any consent which would prevent an act being an assault for the purposes of this section.
>
> (3) Where a marriage is invalid under section two of the Marriage Act 1949, or section one of the Age of Marriage Act 1929 (the wife being a girl under the age of sixteen), the invalidity does not make the husband guilty of any offence under this section by reason of her incapacity to consent while under that age, if he believes her to be his wife and has reasonable cause for the belief.
>
> (4) A woman who is a defective cannot in law give any consent which would prevent an act being an assault for the purposes of this section, but a person is only to be treated as guilty of an indecent assault on a defective by reason of that incapacity to consent, if that person knew or had reason to suspect her to be a defective.

6.2 The SOA 1956, s 15 reads as follows:

> 15(1) It is an offence for a person to make an indecent assault on a man.
>
> (2) A boy under the age of sixteen cannot in law give any consent which would prevent an act being an assault for the purposes of this section.
>
> (3) A man who is a defective cannot in law give any consent which would prevent an act being an assault for the purposes of this section, but a person is only to be treated as guilty of an indecent assault on a defective by reason of that incapacity to consent, if that person knew or had reason to suspect him to be a defective.

6.3 As can be seen, the offences contained in each section are set out in identical terms. What is also set out in identical terms are the subsections pertaining to an indecent assault on a 'defective' victim, and the statutory defence contained therein. The only significant differences between the two sections are, first, of course, the sex of the complainant; and, secondly, the statutory defence available to a man alleged to have indecently assaulted a girl he reasonably believes to be his wife even though she is under 16 years of age.

6.4 The analysis of the offences below does not distinguish between the two sections of the SOA 1956 because, in general terms, the issues that are addressed in the case law pertaining to one offence applies equally to both offences. Where this is not the case it will be made apparent.

General Issues

Mode of Trial

6.5 Indecent assault, whether committed against a woman or a man, is an offence that is triable either way[1]. It is a Class 4 offence and, as such, when committed to the Crown Court, may be tried by a High Court judge, a circuit judge or a recorder[2].

1 MCA 1980, s 17(1) and Sch 1.

2 Practice Direction (Crown Court: allocation of business) (No 3) [2000] 1 All ER 380, [2000] 1 WLR 203.

6.6 In certain circumstances the United Kingdom courts do not have jurisdiction to try 'a member of a visiting force or a civilian component of such a force'. Under the VFA 1952, s 3(1) offences under SOA 1956, ss 14 and 15 may be affected by this provision.

Parties to the Offence

6.7 Offences under SOA 1956, ss 14 and 15 may be committed by either a man or a woman. In *Hare*[1], it was held that a woman can be convicted of an indecent assault on a boy and Avory J went onto say that '... there is no reason for saying that a woman cannot be guilty of an indecent assault on another female'[2]. The case was concerned with the Offences Against the Person Act 1861, s 62 of which used a form of words which read '[W]hosoever ... shall be guilty ... of any indecent assault upon any male person shall be guilty of a misdemeanour' and was decided on the basis that the word 'whosoever' includes a woman. As the law is now set out in SOA 1956, ss 14 and 15, each of which contains the formula 'It is an offence ... for *a person* to make an indecent assault on a woman/ man', it is logical to conclude that the Court of Appeal, if it were asked to decide, would rule that the words 'a person' also includes a woman.

1 [1934] 1 KB 354, CCA.

2 [1934] 1 KB 354 at 356, CCA.

6.8 A man may be guilty of an indecent assault on his wife. In a time when the law was that a man could not rape his wife, the Court of Appeal held in the case of *Kowalski*[1] that even as a preliminary to an act of sexual intercourse, a man forcing his wife to perform an act of fellatio against her will was capable of constituting an indecent assault, notwithstanding that it was an act that had been performed in the past willingly by the wife. Now that a man can be found guilty of raping his wife, the picture has not changed at all in relation to the question of a man indecently assaulting her.

1 (1988) 86 Cr App Rep 339.

6.9 When the words 'woman' and 'girl' are used in SOA 1956, s 14, it realistically means 'female'. This is because the SOA 1956, s 46 sets out that wherever, in the Act, the word 'woman' or 'girl' are used, this does not prevent the provision applying to either – as if both words were used. The section makes the same provision for the use of the words 'man' and 'boy' in the Act.

6.10 As a result of the case of *Tan*[1], a person who is born a man and remains, biologically speaking, a man, even though he has undergone surgical treatment in order to change his apparent sex and hormone treatment in order to become, psychologically, female, remains a man for all legal purposes. One of the effects of this decision is that, were such a person to become the victim of an indecent assault, the charge would have to be brought under the SOA 1956, s 15 rather than under the SOA 1956, s 14. It is to be presumed that the same principle applies, mutatis mutandis, to a woman who attempts to alter her sex, in which case the charge against her would have to be brought under the SOA 1956, s 14.

1 [1983] QB 1053, 76 Cr App Rep 300, CA.

6.11 While it is right, up to a point, to say that, by the SOA 1956, ss 14(2) and 15(2), consent is no defence to an allegation of indecent assault against a complainant under the age of 16, this aspect of the offence should now be seen in the light of *B (a Minor) v DPP*[1] and *R v K*[2]. The outcome of these two cases is that the House of Lords has now ruled that an honest belief that the complainant was at least 16 is a defence that should go before the jury. The effects of these cases are dealt with in more detail in paragraphs 6.43 to 6.46 below.

1 [2000] 2 AC 428, [2000] 1 All ER 833, [2000] 2 Cr App Rep 65.

2 [2001] UKHL 41, [2002] 1 AC 462, [2001] 3 All ER 897.

6.12 The exception set out in the SOA 1956, s 14(3) is unlikely to be of any great concern to the courts. For it to apply the man would have had to marry a girl who was under the age of 16. Such a marriage would automatically be void as a result of the Marriage Act 1949, s 2. Having said that, however, it is possible to imagine an unconventional community or group that allows for the marriage of girls under the age of 16, even though such practice would be contrary to English law. If such a 'marriage' were to be solemnised between a man and a girl he knew to be under 16, then if he was charged with an offence of indecent assault against her he would no doubt be in a position to claim that he '... believe[d] her to be his wife and had reasonable cause for the belief'. Under the SOA 1956, s 47 the burden of proving that he came under the exception in sub-s (3) falls on the defendant.

6.13 Just as a boy or a girl under the age of 16 cannot give any consent which would prevent an act being an assault under the SOA 1956, ss 14(2) or 15(2), a 'defective' equally cannot give such consent. However, unlike the provisions relating to children, that pertaining to 'defectives' does have a qualifying clause. A person accused of an indecent assault on a 'defective' cannot be guilty if the victim's lack of consent is only because of his or her incapacity and that the accused did not know and had no reason to suspect him or her to be a defective. The wording of this particular provision leads to the conclusion that it is for the prosecution to adduce evidence, first that the victim did not give any consent to the (indecent) act of the accused; secondly that that lack of consent was because of their incapacity to consent; and thirdly, that the accused knew or had reason to suspect the victim to be a defective. Without all three issues being proved by the prosecution, the accused is entitled not to be treated as guilty and the trial judge would be obliged to withdraw the matter from the jury.

6.14 The SOA 1956, s 45, as substituted by the MHA 1959, s 127(1) and as amended by the MH(A)A 1982 sets out that a 'defective' means a person suffering from 'a state of arrested or incomplete development of mind which includes severe impairment of intelligence and social functioning'. The words of the section are to be regarded as ordinary English words and a jury should analyse and consider the evidence in accordance with them. In *Hall (JH)*[1] the trial judge's direction to the jury that it was a matter for them, taking into account all of the evidence they have heard, whether the victim was 'severely impaired' within the ordinary meaning of the words of the statute, was upheld in the Court of Appeal. Reference should be made to paragraphs 4.13 to 4.17 for further analysis of this term.

1 (1987) 86 Cr App Rep 159, CA.

Complainant's Anonymity

6.15 Complainants in allegations of indecent assault are entitled to comprehensive anonymity[1]. The anonymity of the complainant stretches to cover the publication of any matter relating to her 'if it is likely to lead members of the public to identify that person as the person against whom the offence is alleged to have been committed'[2]. The anonymity in these provisions remains in place throughout the complainant's lifetime. The anonymity provisions can however be over-ridden by an application by the accused to the trial judge to direct that the SO(A)A 1992, s 1 should not apply in relation to the complainant. Under the SO(A)A 1992, s 3(1), in order for such a direction to be made the judge must be satisfied of two things, namely that:

(i) the direction is required for the purpose of inducing persons who are likely to be needed as witnesses at the trial to come forward; and
(ii) the conduct of the applicant's defence at the trial is likely to be substantially prejudiced if the direction is not given.

1 SO(A)A 1992, ss 1 to 4.

2 See SO(A)A 1992, s 1(1).

6.16 The trial judge can also direct that the SO(A)A 1992, s 1 should not apply if he is satisfied that such anonymity 'imposes a substantial and unreasonable restriction upon the reporting of proceedings at the trial' and 'that it is in the public interest to remove or relax the restriction'[1].

1 See SO(A)A 1992, s 3(2).

6.17 The consequence of the SO(A)A 1992, s 3(6) is that where a case is being tried summarily, 'judge' means any justice of the peace acting for the petty sessions concerned. Thus, either a District Judge or a bench of lay magistrates have the power to direct that nothing may be published that may possibly identify the victim.

Particulars of Offence

6.18 It is not uncommon for the particulars of a count on an indictment alleging indecent assault to aver the age of the alleged victim. Strictly speaking, this is not necessary as the age of the victim is not an essential ingredient of the offence. The only time that the victim's age can become a relevant issue is when he or she is under the age of 16 and the issue of consent raises its head[1]. As a victim under 16 years of age cannot, by the SOA 1956, s 14(2), give consent, preventing an act being an indecent assault, proving his or her age is an important aspect of the prosecution case. However, save in the circumstances mentioned, the fact that the age of the victim is either averred in the particulars or not cannot open the indictment up to any form of criticism.

1 *R v Hodgson* [1973] 1 QB 565, [1973] 2 All ER 552, CA

6.19 It should be noted that the SOA 1985, s 33(3) increased the maximum penalty for indecent assault to 10 years in prison. The amendment took effect on 16 September 1985. Prior to that date the maximum penalty was imprisonment for a period not exceeding two years except where the victim was under the age of 13 and her age was averred in the indictment, in which case the maximum period of imprisonment was five years. Difficulties have arisen in the past when indictments have been framed to reflect allegations of indecent assault committed against children many years before. As a consequence of the maximum penalties pertaining to offences committed before the SOA 1985, it would be preferable for the particulars of the offence, where the victim was under 13, to specify the age of the victim at the time of the offence, especially[1].

1 *R v R* [1993] Crim LR 541, CA

6.20 Further difficulties may arise where the prosecution relies on specimen charges relating to offences, some of which occurred before 16 September 1985 and some after. Only if it can be shown that the offences were committed after 16 September 1985 will the greater maximum sentence apply[1]. Prosecutors should take care to frame indictments so that separate counts – specimen if necessary – are included, one covering a period up to 15 September 1985 and one commencing the following day. Such a course of action will make the sentencing exercise much clearer and easier for the sentencing judge.

1 *R v S* (1991) 13 Cr App Rep (S) 306, CA

Actus Reus

Assault or Battery

6.21 Although contrary to the statement of the offence, it is better to approach the issue of the actus reus of indecent assault by considering the question of 'assault' first. This aspect of the offence takes its lead from the Criminal Justice Act 1988, s 39, which reads:

> Common assault and battery shall be summary offences and a person guilty of either of them shall be liable to a fine ... to imprisonment ... or to both.

Even a cursory reading of the provision shows that it clearly creates two distinct offences; assault and battery. An assault is any act by which a person intentionally, or recklessly, causes the victim to apprehend immediate and unlawful personal violence[1]. A battery is any act by which a person inflicts unlawful personal violence upon the victim[2]. Thus, the former does not need any physical contact although it does require the victim to be aware of the 'threat of violence'; and the latter requires physical (not necessarily violent) touching, but does not require the victim to be aware of it. Difficulties have arisen in practice from this question of whether an alleged indecent assault is actually an indecent assault or an indecent battery. However, the courts have tended to gloss over the issue and have consistently regarded either an indecent assault or an indecent battery as constituting the offence of 'indecent assault'.

1 See, for example, *Fagan v Metropolitan Police Comr* [1969] 1 QB 439, [1968] 3 All ER 442, where it was said that 'assault', as opposed to 'battery' is a separate offence and should be treated as such.

2 *Rolfe* (1952) 36 Cr App Rep 4, CCA.

6.22 It could be argued, for example, on the basis of the case of *DPP v Taylor; DPP v Little*[1] that an indictment that merely charged 'indecent assault' was duplicitous as the offence in SOA 1956, s 14(1) creates two distinct offences. Such a course has not, thus far, been attempted and the courts continue to allow charges of indecent assault to continue without considering the question, and cases are allowed to progress on the basis that the offence of indecent assault includes both a battery or an assault. It can, however, only be a matter of time before the issue will need to be addressed by the higher courts.

1 [1992] QB 645, [1992] 1 All ER 299.

6.23 It has been stated in the Court of Appeal, and not criticised by the House of Lords, that:

> The offence of indecent assault includes both a battery, or touching, and psychic assault without touching. If there was touching, it was not necessary to prove that the victim was aware of the assault or of the circumstances of indecency. If there was no touching, then to constitute an indecent assault the victim must be shown to be aware of the assault and of the circumstances of indecency[1].

So where there was alleged to be some physical contact between D and V – an example might be where a man is seen to intentionally caress a female's bottom in a crowded room – the victim may not be aware of what has happened but an indecent assault (strictly speaking a battery) has occurred. An example of the latter scenario would be where a man made a gesture towards a (non-consenting) woman as if he was about to touch her breasts. The prosecution would have to prove that the woman was aware of the gesture and that she was also aware that the man was intent on touching her breasts – as opposed to her arm for example. Following this logic it is submitted that it can properly be said that there can be no such offence known to English law as attempted indecent assault. If a man touches a (non-consenting) woman – whether she is aware of it or not – in circumstances of indecency then he is guilty of the offence. Equally, if, in similar circumstances, he tries to touch her but fails – and she is aware of his attempt – he is guilty of indecent assault. If, however, he tries to touch her and fails, and she is not aware of his attempt, then no offence has been committed.

1 *R v Court* [1987] QB 156 at 158, [1987] 1 All ER 120 at 122, CA.

6.24 Although the examples given above may appear to be trivial and minor examples of indecent assaults, it is important to appreciate that the Court of Appeal has recognised that any indecent assault can be serious for the victim and that our law should protect all such victims. In *Ananthanarayanan*[1] Laws J made the laudable statement that:

> In our judgement [to suggest that an indecent assault may be trivial] would [be] a pernicious approach ... to take. It would amount to saying that so far as our law is concerned women have to put up with minor indecent assaults ... in principle there should be no doubt that under the modern law any deliberate and non-consensual touching accompanied by circumstances of indecency constitutes the criminal offence of indecent assault. There is no room in this area of the law for any de minimis exception[2].

1 (1994) 98 Cr App Rep 1.

2 (1994) 98 Cr App Rep 1 at 5.

Indecent

6.25 The question of whether or not a proven assault is indecent is one for the jury, to be considered only once the judge has decided that the act either was inherently indecent or was capable of being indecent. It has already been stated that the victim of the assault need not be aware, either of the assault itself, or of its indecent nature, but it is an objective test that should be applied. When the case of *Court* came before the House of Lords[1], Lord Ackner established the following:

> The judge in assisting the jury in his summing up ... [stated that] ...'indecent' may be defined as 'overtly sexual.' This is a convenient shorthand expression, since most, but not necessarily all, indecent assaults will be clearly of a sexual nature although they ... may have only sexual undertones. A simpler way of putting the matter to the jury is to ask them to decide whether 'right-minded persons would consider the conduct indecent or not.' It is for the jury to decide whether what occurred was so offensive to contemporary standards of modesty and privacy to be indecent[2].

In his dissenting speech, Lord Goff opined that in order to satisfy the jury that an indecent assault has been proven, the prosecution would have to show that the assault was 'objectively indecent'. By this he meant either that it is either inherently indecent or is rendered indecent by the surrounding, physical, circumstances[3].

1 [1989] 1 AC 28, [1988] 2 All ER 221.

2 [1989] 1 AC 28 at 42.

3 The word 'physical' is used here to differentiate the circumstances from questions of motive on the part of the defendant. This issue is addressed later under the heading of mens rea.

6.26 In saying that the question is an objective one for the jury, it should be noted that issues of motive are irrelevant[1]. While this point strays into the area of the requisite mens rea in order to establish an offence, there is some overlap here. So that, for example, where, as in the case of *DPP v H*[2] the defendant claimed that in order to stop a baby from crying he had pushed his thumb into her anus; or, as in the case of *Leather*[3] where the grabbing of a policeman's testicles was held to be indecent even though the defendant claimed that she had only done it because the officer was attempting to arrest her boyfriend, the motive of each defendant was deemed to be irrelevant because their acts were held to be objectively indecent.

1 But see paragraph 6.37 below.

2 [1992] COD 266.

3 (1993) 14 Cr App Rep (S) 736, CA.

6.27 Thus one of the points to be gleaned from *Court* on this topic is that motive is irrelevant where the assault is innately indecent or is rendered indecent by its accompanying circumstances. So that, in the case of a man who touches without consent the ankles of a female in a public house, that act might not be regarded as indecent, whereas the same touching in the female's bedroom is capable of being so. The circumstances of both scenarios would be a relevant issue for the jury to consider. The relationship between the two parties would be important so as to establish, for example, what level of intimacy would be appropriate. Similarly, how and why the defendant was acting in the way alleged would be of significance. In *Leeson*[1] it was held that an assault by kissing a girl against her will could be considered indecent by the fact that the man was also suggesting at the time that she indulge in sexual intercourse with him.

1 (1968) 52 Cr App Rep 185, CA.

6.28 It is far from clear whether merely kissing an unwilling victim is an indecent assault. It might be thought that the jury would consider that a simple kiss on the lips of the victim would not be seen as being inherently indecent, whereas a kiss in which the defendant's tongue was forced into the victim's mouth (as occurred in *Leeson*) is.

6.29 A second point to come from *Court* is that if the assault cannot be considered indecent in any way the prosecution are not entitled to adduce evidence of a secret motive on the part of the defendant. In the case of *George*[1] the defendant attempted on a number of occasions to take a girl's shoe off purely in order to obtain sexual enjoyment. It was held that such a circumstance could not amount to an indecent assault because there was nothing overtly indecent in the man's actions and his reasons for attempting to remove the shoe were thus entirely irrelevant. Such a set of circumstances should be differentiated from those where the physical circumstances of the conduct renders the assault capable of being considered indecent, such as in *Leeson*[2].

1 [1956] Crim LR 52.

2 See paragraph 6.27 above.

6.30 It is important to remember that, as a result of *Court*, the prosecution do not have to prove a sexual motive behind the act in order to establish that an indecent assault took place. As has been set out by Professor Williams:

> [In *Court*] [T]he Crown wished to establish that on a charge of indecent assault it was not necessary to prove a sexual motive, but it was permissible to do so. The Lords accepted both propositions, at any rate as applied to the facts of the particular case.[1]

1 The Meaning of Indecency (1992) Legal Studies 20. A masterly deconstruction of, and trenchant criticism of, their Lordships' reasoning in upholding the appellant's conviction in *Court*.

Consent

6.31 In the normal course of events, consent can negative the question of whether an assault has occurred. However, that has to be considered with a number of caveats so far as indecent assault is concerned. The first is of course that, by the SOA 1956, ss 14(2) and 15(2), a child under the age of 16 years cannot give any consent that would prevent an act being an indecent assault.[1] The second is that, by SOA 1956, ss 14(4) and 15(3), a defective similarly cannot give consent which would prevent an assault being indecent.

1 But see *B v DPP* [2000] 2 AC 428; [2000] 2 WLR 452; [2000] 2 Cr App R 65, *R v K* [2001] 3 WLR 471, HL and paragraphs 6.43 to 6.46 as to the issue of an honest belief by the defendant that the victim was at least 16.

6.32 A third situation which should be considered here is that of where consent is obtained by fraud or force. The case law shows that neither of these is, strictly speaking, really a species of consent. The case of *Case*[1] concerned a medical practitioner who, in 1850, was treating a 14-year-old girl for an undisclosed illness, one of whose symptoms was suppressed menstruation. His earlier treatment had not worked and he then told her that he 'must try further means with [her]'. He lifted her onto a table and had 'carnal connection' with her, she not resisting in any way. At trial she declared that she did not resist because she was submitting to what she thought was medical treatment. Following the doctor's conviction an appeal was lodged at which it was held that:

> what she consented to was something wholly different from that which was done, and therefore, that which was done, was done without her consent[2].

1 (1850) 4 Cox CC 220, CCR.

2 (1850) 4 Cox CC 220 at 223.

6.33 The later case of *Tabassum*[1] concerned a man who persuaded three woman to take part in a breast cancer survey so that he could prepare a computer software package. The survey involved, among other things, examining their own breasts. In order however for them to examine their breasts properly, the women agreed to let Mr Tabassum show them how to perform the examination. This involved removing their clothes and allowing the defendant to feel their breasts. Each of the three complainants stated that they only became involved because they thought the defendant had either medical qualifications or relevant training. He had neither. He was convicted and appealed on the ground that the trial judge was wrong to rule that the prosecution did not have to prove the absence of consent. The appeal was dismissed, Rose LJ stating:

> ... consent was given because they mistakenly believed that the defendant was medically qualified ... and that, in

> consequence, the touching was for a medical purpose. As this was not so, there was no true consent. They were consenting to touching for medical purposes not to indecent behaviour, that is, there was consent to the nature of the act but not its quality. ... Whether the defendant had any sexual motive or intent was irrelevant.[2]

1 [2000] 2 Cr App Rep 328, CA.

2 [2000] 2 Cr App Rep 328 at 336, CA.

6.34 A potentially complicating feature of this area of the law is that, according to the case of *Donovan*,[1] consent cannot be a defence to an assault if a probable outcome of the assault is the likelihood of, or intention to do, bodily harm[2]. The conclusion to be drawn from the case law is that, if the alleged indecent assault was either intended to cause some bodily harm, or the likely outcome was some bodily harm – as opposed to, say, stroking – then consent cannot be a defence. This is very much a public policy decision of the higher courts and can only be sustained if it is right to accept the view of the majority decision in *Brown* that it is a proper public policy that a person cannot validly consent to the infliction on himself of bodily harm[3]. That case revolved around the activities of a group of sado-masochistic men who involved themselves in sessions of consensual acts of torture, bondage, beatings, branding and other unconventional pastimes. All of the men were consenting adults, the acts were conducted in private and arrangements had been made for the sterilisation of all instruments used. Further, specific passwords had been agreed at the outset for 'victims' to use should they want the activity to stop. The majority of the Lords concluded that consensual sado-masochistic acts should not be afforded the privilege of being excepted from the public policy referred to in *Donovan*.

1 [1934] 2 KB 498, CCA.

2 See also *Brown* [1993] 2 All ER 75, [1993] Crim LR 583, HL.

3 But see *Wilson* [1996] 2 Cr App Rep 241, CA where a conviction was quashed of a man who had branded his initials on his (consenting) wife's buttocks.

6.35 It was not the view of Lord Mustill in presenting a dissenting opinion. His view was that when a man has involved himself in consensual violence, which of course also includes a violent sexual scenario, the question of whether an indecent assault has occurred must be addressed in the light of the complete picture and not simply that violence has been inflicted. His view was that in the light of the fact that all participants were consenting adults, the OAPA 1861, ss 47 and 20 (the provisions that the men were charged under) did not need to be interpreted in such ways as to make the men's activities criminal.

6.36 In conclusion, then, it is established law that consent can be a defence to an allegation of indecent assault only in the following circumstances:

(i) if the complainant is at least 16 years of age, or the defendant honestly believed that s/he was;
(ii) if the complainant is not a defective within the meaning of the SOA 1956, s 45; and
(iii) if the assault complained of either was not likely to cause, or was not intended to cause, actual bodily harm.

Mens Rea

Motive

6.37 It has already been said that if an assault cannot possibly be said to be indecent then the defendant's motive cannot be adduced by the prosecution to make such an assault indecent, and that motive is also irrelevant where an assault is inherently indecent. There is however a third category of assault that was considered in the case of *Court*[1]. This is when the assault is capable of being considered indecent, but only depending on, among other things, the reason why the defendant acted as he did. The rationale for this category of offence stems from the facts of the case itself. The defendant worked as a shop-assistant in a shop and struck the complainant a dozen times on the outside of her shorts on her buttocks. Upon arrest he was asked by the police why he did it and his reply was 'I don't know – buttock fetish.' At trial the prosecution successfully argued that this statement was admissible to show why the man did what he did. On appeal it was decided that it was the correct approach. The House of Lords ultimately agreed and the conviction was upheld. The case can be distinguished from the case of *George*[2] because, according to that decision, taking a girl's shoe off cannot possibly be regarded as indecent and taking into account the reason why it was done does not bring it into the 'indecent' ambit, whereas smacking a girl's bottom, while being described by Lord Griffiths as an 'equivocal act', is capable of being considered indecent depending on the circumstances. It is ultimately for the jury (as 'right-minded persons') to decide whether the act actually was indecent having taken into account all of the surrounding factors, including the relationship between the parties and the reasons why the man did what he did.

1 [1989] AC 28, [1988] 2 All ER 221.

2 [1956] Crim LR 52.

6.38 Both Lords Ackner and Griffiths gave a further example of a possible indecent assault not dissimilar to the case of *Tabassum*[1] concerning a medical examination of a young girl. If the medical examination of, say, the vagina, was not necessary then this would be capable of being an indecent assault. Having heard evidence that the examination was unnecessary, the jury would have to decide whether the defendant's intention was indecent. If however, the examination was necessary then the tribunal would be unlikely to conclude that this was an indecent assault even if the defendant obtained some sexual gratification from it.

1 [2000] 2 Cr App Rep 328.

6.39 When the facts of a case point to a conclusion that right-minded persons *might* decide that an assault is indecent, then the defendant's motive is admissible. This is so only where the act by the defendant can properly be said to be equivocal. If any right minded person would determine that an act was inherently indecent, or that the act could not possibly be seen as indecent, then the defendant's motive is entirely irrelevant. His motive only becomes an issue if the jury might conclude that his actions could be indecent, but that would depend on the overall circumstances of the case.

6.40 In practice these principles ought not, but can create very real difficulties. Indeed, *Court* came before the Court of Appeal and then the House of Lords primarily because the trial judge introduced, in his summing-up to the jury, the notion that the prosecution had to prove an indecent motive. In considering the ruling in that case the following points can be made:

(i) Act inherently indecent – motive irrelevant:
The trial judge must direct the jury that it is a matter for them to decide as 'right-thinking people' if the act was indeed indecent and in so doing, they should regard any possible motive behind the act as being of no relevance;

(ii) Act equivocal – motive relevant:
The defendant may admit to assaulting the victim but deny that it was indecent (as in *Court*). Evidence as to the circumstances of the offence is admissible for either side[1] – although it is likely to be of use to only one. If the evidence supports the prosecution version of events, then the judge must direct the jury that if they believe the defendant's account then they must not take into account the evidence that the prosecution say provides the motive for the act in the first place and must acquit. If however they accept the prosecution case then they are entitled to take into account the evidence of motive in deciding whether the act was indecent and was intended to be so. In such circumstances it might reasonably be said that a conviction is a foregone conclusion.

(iii) Act incapable of being indecent – motive irrelevant:
In such circumstances any evidence of a secret motive is inadmissible and, in the circumstances, one imagines that a submission of no case to answer should be allowed and the defendant acquitted.

1 See for example *R v Pratt* [1984] Crim LR 41, approved by the House in *Court*, where a man came across two boys night fishing. He made them both undress so as to reveal their genitals. He did not touch either boy and gave evidence that he made them undress because he thought they had stolen cannabis from him. This was his sole motive and there was no indecent intent. The Court of Appeal held that the evidence was rightly admitted (though for the wrong reasons).

Basic Intent

6.41 In the case of *R v C*[1] the appellant was convicted of indecent assault by inserting his finger into a young girl's vagina. He had been drinking and at trial claimed that he had no memory of the event because of his state of intoxication. He based his appeal on the dicta in *Court* which, it was argued, made indecent assault an offence of specific intent. Such an argument can only have been based on the second principle set out in paragraph 6.40 above. As

Court concerned an act which was described as 'equivocal' in terms of whether it might or might not be indecent, it was decided that, in such cases, the defendant's actual (ie specific) intention was relevant to go before the jury so that they could be in a position to consider all of the surrounding circumstances of the case. In any other set of circumstances (ie principles (i) and (iii) above) the defendant's specific intention was not relevant either way. In *R v C* it was decided that a case involving the insertion of a finger into a young girl's vagina was inherently indecent and therefore the appellant's intention was irrelevant, thus reiterating that 'indecent assault remains an offence of basic intent, so that self-induced voluntary intoxication is not a defence'[2].

1 [1992] Crim LR 642, CA.

2 [1992] Crim LR 642 at 643, CA.

6.42 Lord Griffiths in *Court*[1] addressed, what had become over the years, the confusion as to what it was that constituted the necessary intention for the offence. Referring to the reasoning in the case when it came before the Court of Appeal[2] he said:

> I cannot accept the Court of Appeal's definition of the mental element which they defined as proof 'that the accused intentionally assaulted the victim with knowledge of the indecent circumstances of what he did or was being reckless as to the existence of them.

He went on to say that:

> ...the necessary intent is to commit an assault which the jury as right-thinking people consider to be sexually indecent. The motive for such an act will usually be to obtain sexual gratification but it need not necessarily be so.

1 [1989] 1 AC 28 at 35 and 36.

2 [1987] QB 156, [1987] 1 All E R 120.

Belief as to the Age of the Victim

6.43 We have already seen that according to the statute a complainant under 16 years of age cannot give any consent to an assault that will prevent it being indecent. As a result of two cases that went to the House of Lords in 2001 and 2002 it is now a defence for an accused to set before the jury that he genuinely believed that the complainant was 16 or over and was consenting, or that he genuinely believed that the victim was consenting.[1] In *B (a minor) v DPP*, the first of the cases to be considered by the House, their Lordships produced a ruling that stands as a paragon of clarity and sound logic in an area that has been dogged by confusion for many years. It was unanimously held that whether or not a defendant held a genuine belief as to the age of the victim being over the requisite age, and that belief was based on reasonable grounds, was a matter that could and should properly go before the jury. The decision was based primarily on the common law principle that a defendant is entitled to a verdict of not guilty if the prosecution cannot prove that he was fully aware that he was committing the offence in question.

1 See *B (a minor) v DPP* [2000] 2 AC 428, [2000] 1 All ER 833, [2000] 2 Cr App Rep 65 and *R v K* [2001] UKHL 41, [2002] 1 AC 462, [2001] 3 All ER 897

6.44 *B (a minor) v DPP* was primarily concerned with an offence under the ICA 1960, s 1, though it is made quite apparent in the decisions of their Lordships that their ruling pertained to all 'age-related offences' and so it can be said to have general application to any offence where the age of the victim is a significant feature of the offence. The opinions – particularly of Lords Nicholls of Birkenhead, Steyn and Hutton – were based on the renowned statement of Lord Reid in the case of *Sweet v Parsley*[1] in which he said:

> ... there has for centuries been a presumption that Parliament did not intend to make criminals of persons who were in no way blameworthy in what they did. That means that whenever a section is silent as to mens rea there is a presumption that, in order to give effect to the will of Parliament, we must read in words appropriate to require mens rea ... it is firmly established by a host of authorities that mens rea is an essential ingredient of every offence unless some reason can be found for holding that that is not necessary[2].

1 [1970] AC 132, 53 Cr App Rep 221, HL.

2 Quoted in [2000] 2 Cr App Rep 65 at 68.

6.45 Prior to these cases it was always believed that offences against victims who were, in the case of indecent assault, under the age of 16, were ones of strict liability in the sense that, once the prosecution had proved the victim to be under 16, he or she could not consent and therefore no such defence was available to the defendant. Such a view stemmed from the Victorian case of *Prince*[1] and stood as the law for more than a hundred years[2]. This is no longer the case and it must be left to the jury to decide, first, whether the defendant did indeed believe the victim to be of an age when he or she could consent; and secondly, whether or not that belief was reasonable.

1 (1875) LR 2 CCR 154.

2 The case of *Prince* was given fairly short shrift by Lord Hutton [2000] 2 Cr App Rep 65 at 91.

6.46 *B (a minor) v DPP* is a case of immense importance to all age-related sexual offences and undoubtedly repays close reading. It might be said that the overall impact of the closely reasoned opinions given can be summed up in the following concise statement of Lord Nicholls of Birkenhead:

> In principle, an age-related ingredient of a statutory offence stands on no different footing from any other ingredient. If a man genuinely believes that the girl with whom he is committing a grossly indecent act is over 14, he is not intending to commit such an act with a girl under 14[1].

1 [2000] 2 Cr App Rep 65 at 71, HL.

Hostile Act

6.47 Hostility is not a requisite element to the offences of assault or battery, and nor is it one for the offence of indecent assault. It is obvious that some indecent assaults will have an element of hostility to them and some will not. The problem relating to whether or not a hostile act is required in order to prove an indecent assault, and the view that hostility was an essential ingredient of the offence stems from the case of *Beal v Kelley*[1] which came before the Divisional Court and in which it was held that the defendant was guilty of an indecent assault 'as he had performed a hostile act towards the boy accompanied with circumstances of indecency.'

The defendant had approached a young boy with his erect penis sticking out of his trousers and asked the boy to handle it. The boy refused and started to move away. The defendant then grabbed the boy's arm and pulled him towards himself. The boy pulled away from the defendant and made good his escape. It was contended at trial on behalf of the defendant that the 'assault' – ie the pulling of the boy – was not indecent in itself and, in such circumstances, the state of mind of the person committing the assault was immaterial. The point was not taken by the Peterborough justices as they dismissed the charge on other grounds. However, when the prosecution appealed to the Divisional Court, Lord Goddard CJ gave the argument short shrift. He couched his words though in terms of the pulling of the boy as being 'a hostile act' and therefore an assault, giving the impression that in order for an assault to be proved a hostile act had to take place. This view has been erroneously relied upon in a number of appeals to support an argument that a hostile act is a requisite element of the offence of indecent assault.

1 [1951] 2 All ER 763, 35 Cr App Rep 128.

6.48 The case of *Beal v Kelley* can be properly compared to the second principle set out in *Court* and considered above in paragraph 6.40. The pulling of a boy by the arms could be said to be equivocal when one is considering the issue of an indecent assault. By the reasoning of *Court*, evidence would be admissible as to why the defendant was pulling the boy and the jury would be entitled to hear evidence of the man's erect penis being visible and the request to the boy to handle it.

6.49 The question of whether a hostile act was necessary for an indecent assault was taken up in a number of cases during the early 1950s which concerned invitations by men, to a young girl (*Fairclough v Whipp*[1]) and to a young boy (*Burrows*[2]), to touch them in circumstances of indecency, culminating in the case of *DPP v Rogers*[3]. All three convictions in those cases were quashed on the basis that no hostile act had occurred and therefore no indecent assault. In the last of the cases mentioned, the defendant had invited the girl to touch him indecently and, while doing so, led her upstairs by the shoulders. The case was regarded as being distinguishable from *Beal v Kelley* because there was no threatening gesture made by the man, nor was there any physical force used by the man to get the girl to go upstairs with him. It might be said that the Court of Appeal in *Court* had this case in mind when it used the phrase 'psychic assault' in defining the offence of indecent assault[4].

1 (1951) 35 Cr App Rep 138.

2 (1951) 35 Cr App R 180, CCA.

3 [1953] 2 All ER 644, [1953] 1 WLR 1017.

4 See paragraph 6.23 above.

6.50 The question of a hostile act being required to be proved by the prosecution was addressed in various cases and attempts were undoubtedly made to prevent the requirement of a hostile act undermining the whole purpose of the 1956 legislation. Those attempts reached fruition in the case of *Faulkner v Talbot*[1] in which Lord Lane made the following statement:

> An assault is any intentional touching of another person without the consent of that person and without lawful excuse. It need not necessarily be hostile, rude or aggressive, as some of the cases seem to indicate.

That case involved a woman having sexual intercourse with a 14-year-old boy. She was charged with indecent assault and the particulars of the offence were that she had handled the boy's penis immediately prior to insertion of it into her vagina. Perhaps understandably, she claimed that there was no hostile act and therefore no indecent assault. The Court of Appeal rejected the argument and concluded that as the boy could not in law give any consent to prevent the 'assault' being indecent she was guilty of the offence.

1 [1981] 3 All ER 468, [1981] 1 WLR 1528.

Summary

6.51 In order then to satisfy a jury that an indecent assault has been perpetrated by the defendant, the prosecution must prove the following matters:

- an assault (or battery) has occurred in circumstances of indecency (*Court*)

- the victim of the assault was either, not consenting, or was unable in law to give any consent which would prevent the assault being an indecent assault
- if the victim was a non-defective adult, and the act was one of violence, that the act was intended to, and was likely to, cause bodily harm to the victim – thereby negativing consent (*Brown*)
- if the act is capable of being 'indecent' in the minds of right-thinking people, that the motive behind the act was indecent, ie sexually motivated (*Court*).

Defences available to the defendant – apart from the obvious ones of, for example, alibi or mistaken identity – are the following:

- the victim was consenting – except in the circumstances envisaged by the statute
- if the victim was either a defective or under 16 years of age, the defendant honestly believed him/her to not be a defective or at least 16 years old (*B (a minor) v DPP*)
- the act was a violent act but the victim was his consenting partner (*Wilson*[1])
- the act was not inherently indecent (*Beal v Kelly* and *Court*)
- the act was capable of being deemed indecent but the defendant's motive was not sexually motivated (*Court*).

1 [1996] 2 Cr App Rep 241, CA.

Sentence

6.52 The maximum penalty for indecent assault is ten years' imprisonment. This maximum was increased by way of an amendment to the SOA 1956 by the SOA 1985 (s 3(3)). The amendment came into effect on 16 September 1985, before which date the maximum penalty was two years in prison (for an offence under SOA 1956, s 15) unless the victim was under 13 and her age was averred in the indictment, in which case it was five years. As has been mentioned before[1], when an allegation is that indecent assaults have occurred either a long time ago, or over an extensive period, care should be taken that a count on an indictment does not cover offences either side of 16 September 1985[2].

1 See paragraph 6.20.

2 See for example *R* [1993] Crim LR 531, CA.

6.53 Part I (ss 1 to 6) of the SOA 1997 applies to the offence of indecent assault[1]. This part of the Act relates to the requirement for, and effect of, people sentenced for the offence to register with their local police force. It is beyond the scope of this book to look at the provisions in great detail, but it is an issue that should be borne in mind by all students and practitioners.

1 See SOA 1997, Sch 1.

6.54 Registration with the convicted person's local police force applies to young sex offenders just as it does to adult sex offenders and neither person needs to have been sentenced to periods of custody for the provisions to apply.

6.55 It is possible for the Crown Court or the Court of Appeal to impose a restraining order on a convicted person. The order may prohibit the offender from doing anything described in the order[1].

1 See SOA 1977, s 5A(3).

6.56 By way of the PCC(S)A 2000, s 91, as amended, an offender under the age of 18 can be sentenced to be detained for such period, up to the maximum period for adult offenders, as is felt appropriate. Such a course can only be taken if the court is of the opinion that no other method which is legally available to the sentencing judge is suitable[1].

1 For guidelines governing the use of this power, see *R v AM* [1998] 1 All ER 874, [1998] 1 WLR 363, CA.

6.57 Notice should also be taken of the PCC(S)A 2000, s 79(2)(b) which refers to one of the criteria for imposing a custodial sentence being that a sexual offence is concerned.

6.58 The various acts which can constitute an indecent assault form a very wide spectrum, ranging from frottage on a crowded train or bus, up to an act just short of rape. In addition each such offence can have varying degrees of aggravation attached to them. The Court of Appeal has, on a number of occasions, made it clear that there should not be any attempt to set guidelines for the sentencing of such offences. There has, however, been some desire to adumbrate certain principles that sentencers should concern themselves with. In the case of *L*[1] for example, Henry LJ, said:

> It is not the purpose of this judgment to seek to lay down guidelines for sentencing in cases of indecent assault. It is never easy to sentence in such cases. The circumstances of each case will ... vary greatly. What the judge must do ... is to tailor the sentence to the particular facts of the case before the court. In most cases the personal circumstances of the offender will have to take second place behind the plain duty of the court to protect the victims of sexual attacks and to reflect the clear intention of Parliament that offences of this kind are to be met with greater severity than may have been the case in former years when the position of the victim may not have been so clearly focussed in the public eye[2].

1 [1999] 1 Cr App Rep 117, CA.

2 [1999] 1 Cr App Rep 117 at 124, CA.

6.59 While it cannot be said that mitigation on behalf of the offender is not important, as is clear from the quotation above, sentencers are encouraged to have greater regard to any aggravating features of the case when deciding on how to deal with the defendant. In *A-G's Reference (No 12 of 1994) (Phillip Dyke)*[1] the aggravating features that the Court were urged to consider – and appear to have done so – were: (i) the number of different children involved, (ii) the age(s) of the child(ren), (iii) the period of time over which the offences were committed, (iv) whether a breach of trust was concerned, and (v) the impact of the offences on the victims. Having said that in terms of aggravating features of a case, a defendant who pleads guilty should, logically, be entitled to rather more credit when being sentenced than for other, non-sexual, offences because the victim has not had to re-live the traumatic event(s) by giving evidence.

1 (1994) 16 Cr App Rep (S) 559, CA.

6.60 The impact of the offences upon the victim might properly be said to be the most important of the aggravating features to be considered in sentencing. If the sentencing judge has heard evidence during a trial from the victims as to the effect the offences have had on them, then s/he is entitled to take that into consideration when deciding upon the proper sentence. However, what is most important is that thc proscutor should not, when opening the case following a guilty plea, refer to any such impact without evidence in support. That is what happened in the case of *Hobstaff*[1], in which two young children had been indecently assaulted by their neighbour. The Court of Appeal criticised the practice in no uncertain terms. The Court stated:

> ...what counsel for the prosecution said was wholly improper; there was no evidence before the court touching the matter ... Such [admissible] evidence must be available in proper form whether as an expert's report, witness statement or otherwise[2].

The reasons for having such admissible evidence before the court are, as was set out by the Court, twofold: first, the defence would have it in advance and may wish to address the court on it, and, secondly, it would form part of the judge's papers.

1 [1993] Crim LR 318.

2 [1993] Crim LR 318 at 319.

6.61 Somewhat perversely, if a man has sexual intercourse with, say, a, consenting 15-year-old girl and the fact of the offence does not come to light until more than a year later, because of the time bar for prosecutions in the SOA 1956, s 37(2) and Sch 2, para 10, he cannot be prosecuted for an offence of unlawful sexual intercourse. He can however, be charged with an indecent assault as there is no time limit for bringing such a charge. According to the case of *Roy Hinton*[1] (who pleaded guilty in just such circumstances) he should be sentenced bearing in mind that the maximum punishment for unlawful sexual intercourse is two years, rather than 10 years for indecent assault. In such circumstances it was held fairer to sentence him *as if* he was being dealt with for the former offence.

1 (1995) 16 Cr App Rep (S) 523, CA.

6.62 There is no principle that comparably minor offences, for example of frottage, should not be met with a sentence of imprisonment although the case of *Neem*[1] has often been used to submit that there was. In that case a 42-year-old professional man of good character was convicted of persistently rubbing himself up against a woman on the London Underground. The woman felt his erect penis pushing against her backside. MacPherson J stated, somewhat ambiguously that '[A] sentence of imprisonment was ... wrong in principle. This man should have been fined and should have been ordered to pay a sum in compensation and costs[2].' This comment, almost certainly referring to that particular defendant, became, in the headnote to the case, 'Held: a sentence of imprisonment was wrong in principle;' and thus, the case was relied upon to submit that imprisonment should not be used for such offenders. Although *Neem* was followed in at least one appeal, in *Townsend*[3] Glidewell LJ, said:

> ... we have concluded that the Court in *Neem* was wrong in saying that as a matter of principle an indecent assault of this kind, for the first conviction, should not carry a sentence of custody. We think it is open to a sentencing court in its discretion to impose a custodial sentence for such an offence. We are not saying of course that it must do so; in many cases it is properly dealt with by a non-custodial sentence.

1 (1992) 14 Cr App Rep (S) 18, CA.

2 (1992) 14 Cr App Rep (S) 18 at 20, CA.

3 (1994) 16 Cr App Rep (S) 553, CA.

6.62A In addition, if the offence is committed against a child complainant, the offender can be ordered to be disqualified from working with children under CJCSA 2000, ss 26 to 31.

B Assault With Intent to Commit Buggery

6.63 The SOA 1956, s 16(1) reads as follows:

> It is an offence for a person to assault another person with intent to commit buggery.

6.64 An offence under SOA 1956, s 16 is, it is submitted, unlikely to be encountered with any great frequency. This is said because almost any set of circumstances which would fall within this curiously worded provision would constitute an offence of a different nature, and one which is likely to be much easier to prove and for a jury to understand. The few cases concerning the section that have come before the Court of Appeal have met with not a little confusion, and certainly no clarity.

General Issues

Mode of Trial

6.65 The offence is triable only on indictment[1] and is a Class 3 offence[2].

1 See the SOA 1956, s 37(2) and Sch 2, para 19.

2 See Practice Direction (Crown Court: allocation of business) (No 3) [2000] 1 All ER 380, [2000] 1 WLR 203.

6.66 In certain circumstances the United Kingdom courts do not have jurisdiction to try 'a member of a visiting force or a civilian component of such a force.' Under the VFA 1952, s 3(1) offences under SOA 1956, s 16 may be affected by the provision.

Parties to the Offence

6.67 It is possible for a female to be prosecuted as a principal offender in an offence under this provision, but in practical terms it is unlikely to happen. This is said because there is no reason why a female cannot commit the offence of buggery as a principal and, therefore, assault with intent to commit buggery. However, the typical offender of such an allegation will be a male.

6.68 Buggery does not have a statutory definition but under common law it has been defined as 'anal intercourse by a man with another man or a woman, and anal or vaginal intercourse by a man or a woman with an animal'[1]. Thus it is possible to imagine a case where a man was charged with assaulting a farmer, intent on having intercourse with one of the farm animals.

1 *Wiseman* (1718) Fortes Rep 91; *Bourne* (1952) 36 Cr App Rep 125, CCA

Complainant's Anonymity

6.69 A complainant to such an offence is entitled to anonymity. See paragraphs 6.15 to 6.17 above for the full extent of the pertinent statutory provisions.

Particulars of the Offence

6.70 There are realistically two elements to this offence; first, an assault[1] and, secondly, an intention to commit buggery. There is nothing in the Act to suggest that the intention to commit buggery is an intention to commit buggery with the person assaulted, although this will normally be the case. A possible scenario, for example, might be where a man, intent on buggering a boy, assaults the boy's mother or father, in order to get at the boy. If the man is unsuccessful in his desire then a prosecution for, say, common assault would be wholly inappropriate.

1 See paragraphs 6.21 to 6.24 above for issues relating to the actus reus of 'assault'.

6.71 An act which would constitute the offence under the SOA 1956, s 16(1) is also an assault with intent to commit rape because the provision appears to imply a non-consensual act of buggery. However, the section does not say that explicitly and it may be read so as to criminalise an assault when a man intends to commit buggery with a consenting victim – consenting to buggery that is. As it is put rather elliptically by Smith and Hogan:

> presumably ... the intent required is to 'commit buggery', which it is, not to 'commit the offence of buggery', which it is not[1]

1 Smith & Hogan *Criminal Law* (8th ed) 495.

Consent

6.72 As consent is a defence to an assault[1] and there is not the statutory provision to the contrary as for indecent assault, even where the victim is under 16, if he or she consents, then no offence has been committed under the SOA 1956, s 16(1). Such a circumstance would however be likely to be an indecent assault.

1 Save in the circumstances set out in the case of *Brown* [1993] 2 All ER 75, [1993] Crim LR 583, see paragraphs 6.31 to 6.36 above.

Mens rea

6.73 The intention in the offence is to commit buggery and so, while a female can be a victim to the offence, it must be proved that the defendant was intent on having anal intercourse with her as opposed to vaginal. Such a charge would only be appropriate if an assault occurred, during which the offender was intent on committing buggery. Such an occurrence would suggest that the victim was unwilling and if anal intercourse took place then a charge of rape would be more appropriate – or perhaps attempted rape if the full offence were not made out.

Sentence

6.74 The maximum punishment for this offence is 10 years in prison[1].

1 See the SOA 1956, s 37(3) and Sch 2, para 19.

6.75 Part I (ss 1 to 6) of the SOA 1997 applies to the offence of assault with intent to commit buggery[1]. This part of the Act relates to the requirement for, and effect of, people sentenced for the offence to register with their local police force. In addition, if the offence is committed against a child complainant, the offender can be ordered to be disqualified from working with children under CJCSA 2000, ss 26 to 31.

1 See the SOA 1997, Sch 1.

C Indecent Exposure and Outraging Public Decency

6.76 The offences commonly known as 'indecent exposure' and 'outraging public decency' are not, of course, assaults as such, but as they are undoubtedly affronts to the well-being of the complainant in each case, it is felt appropriate to deal with them here.

Indecent Exposure

6.77 The Vagrancy Act 1824, s 4, as amended, concerns itself with a large number of offences. Set out within the large body of the section are the following words:

> ... every person wilfully, openly, lewdly, and obscenely exposing his person ..., with intent to insult any female; ... shall be deemed a rogue and vagabond, within the true intent and meaning of this Act.

The provision goes on to state that the maximum sentence for a first offence of this kind is three months in prison. By virtue of the MCA 1980, s 34(3), the sentencing court can also now impose a fine up to level 3 on the standard scale. VA 1824, s 5 allows for a man convicted on further occasions for such an offence to be deemed an 'incorrigible rogue' and allows for him to be committed to the Crown Court to be sentenced. In such circumstances, the Crown Court may sentence the man to a term of imprisonment not exceeding one year.

6.78 In addition to the above provision, the Town and Police Clauses Act 1847, s 28 states that '[E]very person who wilfully and indecently exposes his person ... shall be liable to a penalty not exceeding level 3 on the standard scale for each offence, or ... prison ... for a period not exceeding 14 days.'

General Issues

Mode of Trial

6.79 Offences under both provisions can only be tried summarily.

Parties to the Offence

6.80 Both offences can only be committed by males. However, the offence under the VA 1824 can only be committed when the male defendant exposes himself to a female. That is not the case with an offence under the TPCA 1847.

Actus Reus

6.81 The word 'person' in both provisions refers purely and simply to the penis. The offence is not committed if any other part of the man's body is exposed. In *Evans v Ewells*[1] the defendant was convicted of an offence under the VA 1824, s 4 when he exposed, to the complainant, a patch of skin low down on his stomach in a 'V' shape. In allowing his appeal, Ashworth J made it crystal clear that the word 'person' in the Act relates only to the man's penis and to no other part of his body.

1 [1972] 2 All ER 22, 1972] 1 WLR 671.

6.82 Somewhat bizarrely, the case of *Hunt v DPP*[1] is authority for the suggestion that the penis does not have to be seen by a woman in order for the offence to be committed. Mr Hunt was seen by a WPC to be standing up against a window inside his house with his trousers round his ankles and his right hand moving up and down in the vicinity of his penis. He was convicted of the offence and, on appeal, it was held that the magistrates were entitled to infer from the evidence before them that his penis had been exposed and that he knew his actions could be seen by passers-by. Thus circumstantial evidence is permitted in order to prove the offence. However, if the man's penis could not be seen how can it be said that he was exposing himself? As was put, in the commentary to *Hunt v DPP*, 'if the sharp eyes of the trained observer looking for evidence could not see it, how could anyone else?'

1 [1990] Crim LR 812.

6.83 It was held in *Ford v Falcone*[1] that it was not necessary for the commission of an offence under the VA 1824 for the act in question to be done in a public place. Mr Falcone exposed his penis to a woman inside his own flat and the Queen's Bench Division held that his actions came under the provision as there was no stipulation that the criminal deed must take place in public.

1 [1971] 2 All ER 1138, [1971] 1 WLR 809.

6.84 The offence under the Town and Police Clauses Act 1847 however, must take place in public by virtue of the words in the TPCA 1847, s 28, 'who in any street'. TPCA 1847, s 3 defines 'street' so as to include 'any road, square, court, alley and thoroughfare, or public passage.' This definition was extended by the Public Health Acts (Amendment) Act 1907 to include 'any place of public resort or recreation ground belonging to, or under the control of, the local authority and any unfenced ground adjoining or abutting any street'.

6.85 An element of the offence, when one considers the wording of the TPCA 1847, s 28 that must be proved by the prosecution is that the act in question 'annoyed' residents or passengers. It is not a requirement that an actual witness needs to be called to give evidence that s/he was actually annoyed by the exposure but it is permissible for the magistrates to infer from the circumstances of the case that a person was likely to be annoyed by the act[1].

1 See for example *Cheeseman v DPP* [1992] QB 83, [1991] 3 All ER 54 in which the witnesses were police officers, and also *Lunderbeech* [1991] Crim LR 784, CA.

Mens Rea

6.86 Both provisions use the word 'wilfully' and so it is the case that the defendant must be proven to have had a guilty mind in perpetrating the act under review. That is to say that the defendant must be proved to have intended his action to be an indecent exposure or that he was reckless as to whether it was. With the addition of the words 'insult any female' in the VA 1824, s 4, proof of the man's wilfulness can come from a proven desire to insult or it may even be inferred from the surrounding circumstances of the offence.

Outraging Public Decency

6.87 It is a common law offence to say or do or exhibit anything in public which outrages public decency, whether or not it also tends to corrupt and deprave those who see or hear it[1]. The essence of the offence is that something is done in public that is lewd, disgusting or obscene. In the context of sexual offences, the offence is usually committed by an act of indecent exposure. As was said by Lord Simon of Glaisdale in *Knuller v DPP*[2] the aim of the law is to ensure that 'reasonable people should be able to venture into public without their sense of decency being outraged'[3].

1 See Lord Reid's speech in *Shaw v DPP* [1962] AC 220, 45 Cr App Rep 113, HL.

2 [1973] AC 435, 56 Cr App Rep 633, HL.

3 [1973] AC 435 at 493 and 56 Cr App Rep 633 at 696.

General Issues

Mode of Trial

6.88 The offence, being a common law offence, is triable only on indictment. It is a class 3 offence and, as such can be tried by a High Court judge, a circuit judge or a recorder who has been properly authorised by a presiding judge[1].

1 See *Practice Direction (Crown Court: allocation of business) (No 3)* [2000] 1 All ER 380, [2000] 1 WLR 203.

Parties to the Offence

6.89 Both males and females can commit this offence as principals as there is no restriction on the ways in which the lewd, obscene or disgusting behaviour can be undertaken. It should also be noted that if the action in question amounts to an indecent exposure, there is no requirement that the complainant must be a member of the opposite sex[1].

1 See *Evans v Ewells* [1972] 2 All ER 22, [1972] 1 WLR 671.

Actus Reus

Lewd, Obscene or Disgusting

6.90 The act itself must be lewd, obscene or disgusting and the test is objective rather than subjective. Further, the lewd, obscene or disgusting behaviour must be of an extreme nature, so that public decency would be likely to be outraged. Having said that, it is not necessary to prove that people actually were outraged, merely that, in the circumstances of the particular case, members of the public, had they witnessed the act, would have been outraged.

6.91 In *Rowley*[1] it was said that it was the nature and effect of the act itself that was important and not any motive or intention behind the act. In that case the prosecution had asserted that a schoolmaster's diary, some entries of which indicated a desire on his behalf to have sexual activity with certain boys, supported its contention that notes he had written to the boys were lewd or disgusting. Following his conviction, the Court of Appeal decided that such evidence was not admissible because the appellant's motive or intention could not supply lewdness or obscenity to the act if in itself it lacked those qualities.

1 (1991) 94 Cr App Rep 95, CA.

In Public

6.92 The offence must be committed in public. In *Walker*[1] the defendant exposed his penis to young girls while in the sitting-room of his own house. At his appeal Laws J considered the earlier case of *Mayling*[2] which involved a man masturbating in a public lavatory and said:

> In our judgment *Mayling* establishes ... no more than this: that it is a necessary condition for guilt of the offence that at least two people must have been able to witness what happened. ... The requirement is that the offence be committed in a place where there exists a real possibility that members of the general public might witness what happens.

Thus the requirement that the act must take place in public is no more than that the man's 'person' must be visible from a place to which the public have access. It is not necessary for the defendant to be in a public place, so long as the complainants are, even if they have no right to be where they are[3]. In the context of this particular offence, help on this issue is likely to come from the statutory definitions that apply to the offences under the TPCA 1847, s 28. Reference should be made to paragraph 6.84 above.

1 [1996] 1 Cr App Rep 111, CA.

2 [1963] 2 QB 717, 47 Cr App Rep 102, CCA.

3 See *Wellard* (1884) 15 Cox CC 559, CCR on this latter point.

Mens Rea

6.93 There is, in effect, no particular mens rea that is required for the commission of this offence. All that the prosecution must prove is that an act was committed and that that act was undertaken in public and that, had it been seen by members of the public, they would have been outraged by it. So long as it can be shown that the defendant performed a deliberate act that is considered, objectively, to outrage public decency, the defendant is guilty of committing the offence. That is the current state of the law.

6.94 It is submitted that this common law offence is one that, as the law currently stands, does not sit well with the general tenet of English criminal law that those who commit criminal offences must be shown to be blameworthy in what they do. It ought to be the case that a man charged with this offence must be shown to have either intended to outrage public decency or to be reckless as to whether he did. Support for this argument comes from the quotation of Lord Reid in the case of *Sweet and Parsley* that is set out in paragraph 6.44 above.

Sentence

6.95 As the offence is one under common law there is no maximum sentence and the sentence is at large and in the discretion of the trial judge. It is to be hoped that, as the offence is akin to the statutory offences under the VA 1824, s 4 and the TPCA 1847, s 28, sentences would be somewhat similar.

Chapter seven

Procurement and abduction

7.1 This chapter is concerned with a number of offences relating to the procurement and abduction of individuals, for the most part in order for them to have sexual intercourse. The offences of procuring a female 'defective' to have unlawful sexual intercourse and abducting a 'defective' woman from her parents or guardian are dealt with in Chapter 4 above. The offence of procuring others to commit homosexual offences is dealt with in Chapter 2 above.

7.2 A number of the offences considered below grew out of Victorian legislation that was introduced with the perceived dangers of a so-called 'white slave market' in mind. As a consequence of this, and because the actus reus of each of the offences is likely to constitute a different offence, they seem to be charged only rarely, and their appearance before the criminal courts is even more rare. For that reason there is very little case law pertaining to these offences.

A Procurement of a Woman by Threats or Intimidation

7.3 The SOA 1956, s 2(1) reads as follows:

> 2(1) It is an offence for a person to procure a woman, by threats or intimidation, to have sexual intercourse in any part of the world.

7.4 The SOA 1956, s 2(2) was repealed by the CJPOA 1994, s 33(1). CJPOA 1994, s 168(1), (3) and Sch 9, para 2 and Sch 11 amended SOA 1956, s 2(1) to remove the word 'unlawful' before the word 'sexual'.

7.5 The use of the word 'woman' in the section applies just as much to girls. By virtue of the SOA 1956, s 46, the two words are interchangeable.

General Issues

Mode of Trial

7.6 This offence, together with an attempt to commit it, can only be tried on indictment[1]. They are both Class 3 offences and as such can be tried by a High Court judge, a circuit judge or a recorder who has been properly authorised by a presiding judge[2].

1 See the SOA 1956, s 37(2) and Sch 2, para 7.

2 Practice Direction (Crown Court: allocation of business) (No 3) [2000] 1 All ER 380, [2000] 1 WLR 203.

7.7 It should be noted that in certain circumstances the United Kingdom courts do not have jurisdiction to try 'a member of a visiting force or a civilian component of such a force'. Under the VFA 1952, s 3(1) an offence under SOA 1956, s 2(1) may come under this provision.

Parties to the Offence

7.8 By the use of the word 'person' in the provision it is clear that the offence can be committed, as a principal, by both males and females. The complainant must of course be a female.

Complainant's Anonymity

7.9 Complainants in an allegation of an offence under SOA 1956, s 2(1) are entitled to comprehensive anonymity[1]. The anonymity of the complainant stretches to cover the publication of any matter relating to her 'if it is likely to lead members of the public to identify that person as the person against whom the offence is alleged to have been committed'[2]. The anonymity in these provisions remains in place throughout the complainant's lifetime. The anonymity provisions can however be over-ridden by an application by the accused to the trial judge to direct that SO(A)A 1992, s 1 should not apply in relation to the complainant. Under SO(A)A 1992, s 3(1) of the SO(A)A 1992, in order for such a direction to be made the judge must be satisfied of two things, namely that:

(i) the direction is required for the purpose of inducing persons who are likely to be needed as witnesses at the trial to come forward; and
(ii) the conduct of the applicant's defence at the trial is likely to be substantially prejudiced if the direction is not given.

1 SO(A)A 1992, ss 1-4.

2 See SO(A)A 1992, s 1(1).

7.10 The trial judge can also direct that SO(A)A 1992, s 1 should not apply if he is satisfied that such anonymity 'imposes a substantial and unreasonable restriction upon the reporting of proceedings at the trial' and 'that it is in the public interest to remove or relax the restriction'[1].

1 See SO(A)A 1992, s 3(2).

Actus Reus

Procure

7.11 For issues pertaining to the definition of 'procure' see paragraph 4.31 above.

7.12 'Procure' involves a positive act on the part of the defendant. For an offence under this provision the act of procuring of the woman must be motivated by an intention of having sexual intercourse. Without such a motivation the offence is not committed.

Threats or Intimidation

7.13 The term 'threats or intimidation' is not defined in the SOA 1956. As the offence follows immediately on from the offence of rape in the Act, it would appear that there must be two ways of considering the notion of 'threats or intimidation'. The first is that the threats or intimidation must relate to the procuring only, rather than to the sexual intercourse. The second is that the threat or intimidation must relate to obtaining the woman's consent to sexual intercourse but that the threat or intimidation is less serious than that required for an offence of rape. It is submitted that in an age when the courts, and indeed public opinion, are likely to conclude that any threat or intimidation whatsoever that induces consent to sexual intercourse would constitute rape[1], the former interpretation is preferable.

1 See for example, *Camplin* (1845) 1 Den 89, CCR.

7.14 If one considers a dictionary definition of the word 'procure' (eg 'obtain by care or effort, acquire') then the offence under SOA 1956, s 2(1) must be proven by the defendant obtaining or acquiring the woman by 'threats or intimidation'.

7.15 As the SOA 1956 does not define the terms, recourse should, perhaps, be had to other statutes. For example, in the case of *I v DPP; M v DPP; H v DPP*[1], which was concerned with the Public Order Act 1986, s 3 (affray), it was said that what amounts to a threat is a question of fact, depending on the circumstances of each case. Similarly, the CJPOA 1994, s 51 created the offence of intimidating witnesses, jurors, etc and may be of some help in interpreting the word.

1 [2001] UKHL 10, [2002] 1 AC 285, [2001] 2 All ER 583.

Sexual Intercourse

7.16 For an offence under SOA 1956, s 2(1) to be committed, it must be proved that sexual intercourse took place. This is said because in the case of *Mackenzie and Higginson*[1], when a man procured a woman in Scotland and brought her to England in order to have sexual intercourse with her, it was held that the offence was not complete until sexual intercourse had taken place. Such an interpretation of the offence, however, is at odds with that submitted in paragraph 7.13 above as being the most appropriate interpretation of the offence.

1 (1910) 6 Cr App Rep 64, CCR.

7.17 For issues pertaining to the term 'sexual intercourse' see paragraphs 1.19 to 1.21 above.

7.18 It should be noted that the discussion in paragraphs 1.19 to 1.20 concerns 'sexual intercourse' as it relates to the offence of rape. Those aspects of the notion of 'sexual intercourse' that pertain to this offence must only relate to vaginal intercourse rather than anal intercourse. This is said because if this offence concerned anal intercourse there would be no need to confine it to an offence whereby the victim must be female. If the offence was intended to relate to buggery, then it is reasonable to suggest that Parliament would have amended the provision at the same time the offence of rape was altered to include anal intercourse.

Mens Rea

7.19 All that must be proved for this offence is that when the defendant procured the victim, his intention was to have sexual intercourse with her, or for her to have sexual intercourse with another man.

Sentence

7.20 The maximum sentence for this offence, together with an attempt to commit the full offence, is two years in prison[1]. In addition. If the offence is committed against a child complainant, the offender can be ordered to be disqualified from working with children under CJCSA 2000, ss 26 to 31.

1 SOA 1956, s 37(2) and Sch 2, para 7.

B Procurement of a Woman by False Pretences

7.21 The SOA 1956, s 3(1) reads as follows:

> 3(1) It is an offence for a person to procure a woman, by false pretences or false representations, to have sexual intercourse in any part of the world.

7.22 SOA 1956, s 3(2) was repealed by the CJPOA 1994, s 33(1). CJPOA 1994, s 168(1), (3) and Sch 9, para 2 and Sch 11 amended SOA 1956, s 3(1) to remove the word 'unlawful' before the word 'sexual'.

7.23 The use of the word 'woman' in the section applies just as much to girls. By virtue of the SOA 1956, s 46, the two words are interchangeable.

General Issues

Mode of Trial

7.24 This offence, together with an attempt to commit it, can only be tried on indictment[1]. They are both Class 3 offences and as such can be tried by a High Court judge, a circuit judge or a recorder who has been properly authorised by a presiding judge[2].

1 See the SOA 1956, s 37(2) and Sch 2, para 7.

2 Practice Direction (Crown Court: allocation of business) (No 3) [2000] 1 All ER 380, [2000] 1 WLR 203.

7.25 It should be noted that in certain circumstances the United Kingdom courts do not have jurisdiction to try 'a member of a visiting force or a civilian component of such a force'. Under the VFA 1952, s 3(1) an offence under SOA 1956, s 3(1) may come under this provision.

Parties to the Offence

7.26 By the use of the word 'person' in the provision it is clear that the offence can be committed as a principal, by both males and females. The complainant must of course be a female.

Complainant's Anonymity

7.27 Complainants in an allegation of an offence under SOA 1956, s 3(1) are entitled to comprehensive anonymity[1]. The anonymity of the complainant stretches to cover the publication of any matter relating to her 'if it is likely to lead members of the public to identify that person as the person against whom the offence is alleged to have been committed'[2]. The anonymity in these provisions remains in place throughout the complainant's lifetime. The anonymity provisions can however be over-ridden by an application by the accused to the trial judge to direct that the SO(A)A 1992, s 1 should not apply in relation to the complainant. Under the SO(A)A 1992, s 3(1), in order for such a direction to be made the judge must be satisfied of two things, namely that:

(i) the direction is required for the purpose of inducing persons who are likely to be needed as witnesses at the trial to come forward; and
(ii) the conduct of the applicant's defence at the trial is likely to be substantially prejudiced if the direction is not given.

1 SO(A)A 1992, ss 1-4.

2 See SO(A)A 1992, s 1(1).

7.28 The trial judge can also direct that the SO(A)A 1992, s 1 should not apply if he is satisfied that such anonymity 'imposes a substantial and unreasonable restriction upon the reporting of proceedings at the trial' and 'that it is in the public interest to remove or relax the restriction'[1].

1 See SO(A)A 1992, s 3(2).

Actus Reus

Procure

7.29 For issues pertaining to the definition of 'procure' see paragraphs 4.31 and 7.12 above.

By False Pretences or False Representations

7.30 As with the offence under SOA 1956, s 2(1), it is an arguable point as to whether the 'false pretences or false representations' relate to the procuring or to the sexual intercourse. If a man were to induce a female to have sexual intercourse with him by falsely representing, for example, that he was her husband[1], following the full act he would have committed the offence of rape. Similarly, if a man falsely represents that the sexual intercourse is a form of medical therapy[2] then, again, he has committed rape rather than the offence under SOA 1956, s 3(1).

1 As in *Elbekkay*; see paragraph 1.24 above.

2 As in *Case*; see paragraph 1.23 above.

7.31 While it is difficult to say just what does constitute 'false pretences or false representations', it is a term that is unlikely to be seen as being as wide as that of 'deception' as defined in the Theft Act 1968. The definition given there is 'any deception (whether deliberate or reckless) by words or conduct as to fact or as to law, including a deception as to the present intentions of the person using the deception or any other person'[1]. Having said that, however, it is submitted that, when the above statutory definition is considered, an offence under SOA 1956, s 3(1) should concern the intentions of the person falsely pretending or falsely representing at the time the pretence or representation is being made.

1 See the TA 1968, s 15(4).

Sexual Intercourse

7.32 This issue is fully discussed in paragraphs 1.19 to 1.21 and 7.16 to 7.18 above.

Mens Rea

7.33 All that must be proved for this offence is that when the defendant procured the victim, his intention was to have sexual intercourse with her, or for her to have sexual intercourse with another man.

Sentence

7.34 The maximum sentence for this offence, together with an attempt to commit the full offence, is two years in prison[1]. In addition. If the offence is committed against a child complainant, the offender can be ordered to be disqualified from working with children under CJCSA 2000, ss 26 to 31.

1 SOA 1956, s 37(2) and Sch 2, para 8.

C Procurement of a Girl under 21

7.35 The SOA 1956, s 23(1) reads as follows:

> 23(1) It is an offence for a person to procure a girl under the age of 21 to have unlawful sexual intercourse in any part of the world with a third person.

7.36 SOA 1956, s 23(2) was repealed by the CJPOA 1994, s 33(1). It should be noted that, unlike the offences under SOA 1956, ss 2(1) and 3(1), this provision has retained the word 'unlawful' before the words 'sexual intercourse'.

General Issues

Mode of Trial

7.37 This offence, together with an attempt to commit it, can only be tried on indictment[1]. They are both Class 3 offences and as such can be tried by a High Court judge, a circuit judge or a recorder who has been properly authorised by a presiding judge[2].

1 See the SOA 1956, s 37(2) and Sch 2, para 7.

2 Practice Direction (Crown Court: allocation of business) (No 3) [2000] 1 All ER 380, [2000] 1 WLR 203.

7.38 It should be noted that in certain circumstances the United Kingdom courts do not have jurisdiction to try 'a member of a visiting force or a civilian component of such a force'. Under the VFA 1952, s 3(1) an offence under SOA 1956, s 23(1) may come under this provision.

Parties to the Offence

7.39 By the use of the word 'person' in the provision it is clear that the offence can be committed as a principal, by both males and females. The complainant must of course be a female who must be under the age of 21.

7.40 It should be noted that the procuring of the girl in question must be for her to have unlawful sexual intercourse with a third person. It is not the case that any such third person can be regarded as a party to an offence under SOA 1956, s 23(1), but, so long as all other criteria are satisfied, and assuming that he is known to the prosecution authorities, he may be prosecuted as a conspirator to such an offence.

Alternative Verdicts

7.41 Unlike the offences under SOA 1956, ss 2 and 3, there is nothing that qualifies the word 'procure'. Further, the section does not provide that the procuring is undertaken in any particular way. As a result of the case of *MacKenzie and Higgins*[1] it is submitted that in order for this offence to be complete, sexual intercourse must take place. If the complainant is under 21 and is procured in order to have unlawful sexual intercourse with a third person, but no such intercourse takes place, then it is arguable that the defendant can be convicted of an attempt to commit the offence.

1 See paragraph 7.16 above.

Actus Reus

Procure

7.42 For issues pertaining to the definition of 'procure' see paragraphs 4.31 and 7.12 above.

Under the Age of 21

7.43 As the offence relates directly to females under the age of 21, it is incumbent upon the prosecution to prove that the victim does qualify under that criterion. Reference should be made to paragraph 3.18 above for a discussion of this issue.

Unlawful Sexual Intercourse

7.44 Reference should be made to paragraphs 1.18 to 1.20 and 3.15 to 3.17 above for issues relating to this term.

Mens Rea

7.45 All that must be proved for this offence is that when the defendant procured the victim, his intention was that she would have sexual intercourse with another man.

7.46 It is submitted that if the procuring of the woman was with the intention that she should have 'lawful' sexual intercourse – that is sexual intercourse with a female within the bonds of a legal marriage – then the offence is not made out.

7.47 It is submitted that, as in all other 'age-related' offences, it would have to be proved that the defendant was aware that the complainant was under 21 at the time of the procuring. Reference should be made to paragraphs 6.43 to 6.46 for a full discussion of this issue.

Sentence

7.48 The maximum sentence for this offence, together with an attempt to commit the full the offence, is two years in prison[1]. In addition. If the offence is committed against a child complainant, the offender can be ordered to be disqualified from working with children under CJCSA 2000, ss 26 to 31.

1 SOA 1956, s 37(2) and Sch 2, para 24.

D Administering Drugs to Obtain or Facilitate Sexual Intercourse

7.49 The SOA 1956, s 4 reads as follows:

> 4(1) It is an offence for a person to apply or administer to, or cause to be taken by, a woman any drug, matter or thing with intent to stupefy or overpower her so as thereby to enable any man to have unlawful sexual intercourse with her.

7.50 SOA 1956, s 4(2) was repealed by the CJPOA 1994, s 33(1). It should be noted that, unlike the offences under SOA 1956, ss 2(1) and 3(1), this provision has retained the word 'unlawful' before the words 'sexual intercourse'.

General Issues

Mode of Trial

7.51 This offence, together with an attempt to commit it, can only be tried on indictment[1]. They are both Class 3 offences and as such can be tried by a High Court judge, a circuit judge or a recorder who has been properly authorised by a presiding judge[2].

1 See the SOA 1956, s 37(2) and Sch 2, para 7.

2 Practice Direction (Crown Court: allocation of business) (No 3) [2000] 1 All ER 380, [2000] 1 WLR 203.

7.52 It should be noted that in certain circumstances the United Kingdom courts do not have jurisdiction to try 'a member of a visiting force or a civilian component of such a force'. Under the VFA 1952, s 3(1) an offence under SOA 1956, s 4(1) may come under this provision.

Parties to the Offence

7.53 By the use of the word 'person' in the provision it is clear that the offence can be committed as a principal, by both males and females. The complainant must of course be a female.

Actus Reus

'Apply', 'Administer to' and 'Cause to be Taken'

7.54 This cover-all phrase has been used by the draftsman to incorporate any way in which a drug or stupefying substance can be made to have an effect upon the victim. Although the words and phrases are not defined in any way within the statute, it is likely that any form of administration of the substance will come within the ambit of the provision.

7.55 It is submitted that it must be the case that the woman in question was either unaware of the substance being administered or did not consent to any substance being administered to her. If a woman, for example, shares an illegal drug voluntarily with a man, knowing what it is she is taking, the offence cannot be made out even if the man intends that the drug will lead to her having sexual intercourse with him. Having said that of course, if her mind is so taken over by the intoxicating, or stupefying, substance that she becomes unable to consent to sexual intercourse, and such an act takes place, the man is likely to be charged with the offence of rape.

Drug, Matter or Thing

7.56 This phrase is likely to be regarded as very wide and should incorporate anything that is capable of stupefying or overpowering a person.

Unlawful Sexual Intercourse

7.57 Reference should be made to paragraphs 1.18 to 1.20 and 3.15 to 3.17 above for a discussion of this term.

Mens Rea

7.58 All that need be proved by the prosecution for this aspect of the offence is that, when the substance was administered, the defendant's intention was that she would become stupefied or overpowered and that a man could have unlawful sexual intercourse with her. If the intention was anything other than that then the offence is not committed.

7.59 It is submitted that if the procuring of the woman was with the intention that she should have 'lawful' sexual intercourse – that is sexual intercourse with a female within the bonds of a legal marriage – then the offence is not made out.

Sentence

7.60 The maximum sentence for this offence, together with an attempt to commit the full the offence, is two years in prison[1]. In addition. If the offence is committed against a child complainant, the offender can be ordered to be disqualified from working with children under CJCSA 2000, ss 26 to 31.

1 SOA 1956, s 37(2) and Sch 2, para 9.

E Abduction of a Woman by Force

7.61 The SOA 1956, s 17, as amended by the CLA 1967, reads as follows:

> 17(1) It is an offence for a person to take away or detain a woman against her will with the intention that she shall marry or have unlawful sexual intercourse with that or any other person, if she is so taken away or detained either by force or for the sake of her property or expectations of property.
>
> (2) In the foregoing subsection, the reference to a woman's expectations of property relates only to property of a person to whom she is next of kin or one of the next of kin, and 'property' includes any interest in property.

7.62 The SOA 1956, s 43 grants the courts, in certain circumstances relating to the detention of women, the power to issue a warrant permitting a constable to search for her and to take her to a place of safety.

7.63 The use of the word 'woman' in the section applies just as much to girls. By virtue of the SOA 1956, s 46, the two words are interchangeable.

General Issues

Mode of Trial

7.64 This offence, together with an attempt to commit it, can only be tried on indictment[1]. They are both Class 3 offences and as such can be tried by a High Court judge, a circuit judge or a recorder who has been properly authorised by a presiding judge[2].

1 See the SOA 1956, s 37(2) and Sch 2, para 7.

2 Practice Direction (Crown Court: allocation of business) (No 3) [2000] 1 All ER 380, [2000] 1 WLR 203.

7.65 It should be noted that in certain circumstances the United Kingdom courts do not have jurisdiction to try 'a member of a visiting force or a civilian component of such a force'. Under the VFA 1952, s 3(1) an offence under the SOA 1956, s 17(1) may come under this provision.

Parties to the Offence

7.66 By the use of the word 'person' in the provision it is clear that the offence can be committed as a principal, by both males and females. The complainant must of course be a female.

7.67 It should be noted that the taking away of the female in question must be for her to marry or have unlawful sexual intercourse with the defendant or another person. It is not the case that any such third person can be regarded as a party to an offence under the SOA 1956, s 23(1) but, so long as all other criteria are satisfied, and assuming that he is known to the prosecution authorities, he may be prosecuted as a conspirator to such an offence. In those circumstances, at least one of the people involved must be a male in order for the complainant to 'marry or have unlawful sexual intercourse with'.

Complainant's Anonymity

7.68 Complainants in an allegation of an offence under the SOA 1956, s 17(1) are entitled to comprehensive anonymity[1]. The anonymity of the complainant stretches to cover the publication of any matter relating to her 'if it is likely to lead members of the public to identify that person as the person against whom the offence is alleged to have been committed'[2]. The anonymity in these provisions remains in place throughout the complainant's lifetime. The anonymity provisions can however be over-ridden by an application by the accused to the trial judge to direct that the SO(A)A 1992, s 1 should not apply in relation to the complainant. Under the SO(A)A 1992, s 3(1), in order for such a direction to be made the judge must be satisfied of two things, namely that:

(i) the direction is required for the purpose of inducing persons who are likely to be needed as witnesses at the trial to come forward; and

(ii) the conduct of the applicant's defence at the trial is likely to be substantially prejudiced if the direction is not given.

1 SO(A)A 1992, ss 1-4. These provisions apply to a large number of sexual offences.

2 See SO(A)A 1992, s 1(1).

7.69 The trial judge can also direct that the SO(A)A 1992, s 1 of should not apply if he is satisfied that such anonymity 'imposes a substantial and unreasonable restriction upon the reporting of proceedings at the trial' and 'that it is in the public interest to remove or relax the restriction'[1].

1 See SO(A)A 1992, s 3(2).

Actus Reus

Take Away or Detain

7.70 This phrase is not defined in the statute but it is submitted that, as the two concepts are very different, it must be the case that the offence can be committed in two distinct ways; ie one where the defendant takes the female away from wherever she is, and one where he detains her. Either way, he could also be guilty of other offences, namely kidnap and false imprisonment.

7.71 The question of whether the defendant has taken away or detained the complainant should be left to the jury, taking into consideration all of the surrounding circumstances. As there is no magic formula to defining such words, reference ought to be made to *Brutus v Cozens*[1] for assistance on this point.

1 [1973] AC 854, [1972] 2 All ER 1297, HL.

Against Her Will

7.72 Again, there is no definition in the statute but it must be the case that this phrase merely means without the consent of the female in question. The question of whether the female is consenting must be considered at the time of the 'taking away' or 'detaining'. If it were the case that the female later acquiesces in the detention or taking away, that would not nullify the lack of her consent earlier and the offence would still be committed.

Unlawful Sexual Intercourse

7.73 Reference should be made to paragraphs 1.18 to 1.20 and 3.15 to 3.17 above for issues relating to this term.

By Force

7.74 In order for this offence to be proved, the Crown would have to satisfy the jury that the victim was the subject of force of some kind. It was decided in the case of *R v D*[1] that for the offence of kidnapping, the will of the victim could be overborne by the use of force or fraud. It is submitted that for this case to be proved it must be shown that the victim was subjected to force of some kind, which might include an influence held over her by the defendant that did not amount to physical force, although there have been no reported cases that support that contention.

1 [1984] AC 778, [1984] 1 All ER 574, CA.

For the Sake of Her Property or Expectations of Property

7.75 Reference should be made to SOA 1956, s 17(2) for a full explanation of this term. It is interesting to note that any expectation of an inheritance from somebody who is not the complainant's next of kin is not covered by the provision.

Mens Rea

7.76 The intention that must be proved by the prosecution is set out in the provision and amounts to an intention that the complainant will marry or have unlawful sexual intercourse with the defendant or with any other person. In the light of *Mackenzie and Higginson*[1], it is arguable that in order for the offence to be made out, the prosecution must prove that the complainant did indeed marry or have unlawful sexual intercourse with the defendant or a third person. It must be said however, that this point is far from clear.

1 See paragraph 7.16 above.

7.77 It is submitted that if the procuring of the woman was with the intention that she should have 'lawful' sexual intercourse – that is sexual intercourse with a female within the bonds of a legal marriage – then the offence is not made out.

Sentence

7.78 The maximum sentence for this offence is 14 years in prison[1]. In addition. If the offence is committed against a child complainant, the offender can be ordered to be disqualified from working with children under CJCSA 2000, ss 26 to 31.

1 SOA 1956, s 37(2) and Sch 2, para 4.

F Abduction of an Unmarried Girl under 18 from Her Parent or Guardian

7.79 The SOA 1956, s 19, as amended, reads as follows:

> 19(1) It is an offence, subject to the exception mentioned in this section, for a person to take an unmarried girl under the age of 18 out of the possession of her parent or guardian against his will, if she is taken with the intention that she shall have unlawful sexual intercourse with men or with a particular man.
>
> (2) A person is not guilty of an offence under this section because he takes such a girl out of the possession of her parent or guardian as mentioned above, if he believes her to be of the age of 18 or over and has reasonable cause for the belief.
>
> (3) In this section 'guardian' means any person having the parental responsibility for or care of the girl.

General Issues

Mode of Trial

7.80 This offence, together with an attempt to commit it, can only be tried on indictment[1]. They are both Class 3 offences and as such can be tried by a High Court judge, a circuit judge or a recorder who has been properly authorised by a presiding judge[2].

1 See the SOA 1956, s 37(2) and Sch 2, para 7.

2 *Practice Direction (Crown Court: allocation of business) (No 3)* [2000] 1 All ER 380, [2000] 1 WLR 203.

Parties to the Offence

7.81 By the use of the word 'person' in the provision it is clear that the offence can be committed as a principal, by both males and females. The complainant must of course be a female under the age of 18.

7.82 It should be noted that the taking of the girl in question must be for her to have unlawful sexual intercourse with men or with a particular man. It is not the case that any such person/people can be regarded as parties to an offence under SOA 1956, s 19(1), but, so long as all other criteria are satisfied, and assuming that he/they is/are known to the prosecution authorities, he/they may be prosecuted as (a) conspirator(s) to such an offence.

Actus Reus

An Unmarried Girl under the Age of 18

7.83 For the offence to be committed it must be established by acceptable evidence that the complainant came under these three criteria. The first two issues ought to be comparatively easy. See paragraph 3.18 for a discussion on the acceptable ways of proving a person's age.

Out of the Possession

7.84 The prosecution would have to prove that the complainant was in the possession of her parent or guardian at the time the offence was committed. This would be a matter of fact for the jury to conclude taking into account all of the surrounding circumstances. It has been held in a succession of Victorian cases that, for example, the complainant does not leave the possession of her parents or guardian if she leaves her home simply to meet with the defendant, but that she does once she decides not to return home.

7.85 It is submitted that in an age when consent to sexual acts can be given at age 16, this is an offence that is likely not to be used to charge men because it would be extremely difficult to prove, to the satisfaction of a jury, that the complainant (assuming consent to whatever sexual activity occurred) was taken out of the possession of her parent or guardian.

Against His Will

7.86 See paragraph 7.72 above for a discussion of this phrase.

Unlawful Sexual Intercourse

7.87 Reference should be made to paragraphs 1.18 to 1.20 and 3.15 to 3.17 above for issues relating to this term.

Mens Rea

7.88 As with many of the offences discussed above in this chapter, what must be proved is that the defendant committed the actus reus of the offence with the intention that the complainant have unlawful sexual intercourse with men or with a particular man. In the light of *Mackenzie and Higginson*[1], it is arguable that in order for the offence to be made out, the prosecution must prove that the complainant did indeed have unlawful sexual intercourse with men or with a particular man. It must be said however, that this point is far from clear.

1 See paragraph 7.16 above.

7.89 It is submitted that if the taking of the girl was with the intention that she should have 'lawful' sexual intercourse – that is sexual intercourse with a female within the bonds of a legal marriage – then the offence is not made out.

Statutory Defences

7.90 SOA 1956, s 19(1) provides a statutory defence for a man who takes such a girl out of the possession of her parent or guardian who believes that she is at least 18 years of age or has a reasonable cause for such a belief. By virtue of the SOA 1956, s 47, the burden of establishing that the exception applies to him lies on the man in question.

7.91 Reference should also be made to paragraph 3.20 above with regard to the man's genuine belief that the girl was over the age of 18.

Sentence

7.92 The maximum sentence for this offence is 14 years in prison[1]. In addition. If the offence is committed against a child complainant, the offender can be ordered to be disqualified from working with children under CJCSA 2000, ss 26 to 31.

1 SOA 1956, s 37(2) and Sch 2, para 20.

G Abduction of a Girl under 16 from her Parent or Guardian

7.93 The SOA 1956, s 20, as amended, reads as follows:

> 20(1) It is an offence for a person acting without lawful authority or excuse to take an unmarried girl under the age of 16 out of the possession of her parent or guardian against his will.
>
> (2) In the foregoing subsection 'guardian' means any person having parental responsibility for or care of the girl.

7.94 Although this offence relates purely to the abduction of girls, the Child Abduction Act 1984, s 2 covers the same activity by a defendant and concerns children in general and, it is submitted, is a much more appropriate provision to use in charging people who undertake such a pursuit.

Chapter eight

Prostitution and related offences

8.1 There are a large number of offences relating to prostitution, the exploitation of prostitutes and the use of premises for such purposes. It is important to note that it is not a criminal offence to actually be a prostitute, although various statutes have been introduced over the years in order to suppress such activity, or at least attempt to hide it away. It is also true to say that, on occasion, the higher courts have indulged in a certain amount of conceptual gymnastics in order to bring the marketing activities of prostitutes within the definition of certain offences.

8.2 The offences considered in this chapter pertain primarily – though not exclusively – to those concerning female prostitutes. There are very few statutory offences which directly affect men only on this issue and they will be dealt with in chapter 1 below.

8.3 It is also important to bear in mind that such offences have troubled the criminal courts for a very long time and much of the terminology used in both the various statutes and the case law intermingle. So that, for example, the definition of 'soliciting' in an offence of a male soliciting a woman for immoral purposes is relied on in order to satisfy the offence of soliciting for the purpose of prostitution.

A Loitering or Soliciting for Purposes of Prostitution

8.4 The Street Offences Act 1959, s 1 reads as follows:

> 1(1) It shall be an offence for a common prostitute to loiter or solicit in a street or public place for the purpose of prostitution.
>
> (2) A person guilty of an offence under this section shall be liable on summary conviction to a fine of an amount not exceeding level 2 on the standard scale ... or, for an offence committed after a previous conviction, to a fine of an amount not exceeding level 3 on that scale.
>
> (3) A constable may arrest without warrant anyone he finds in a street or public place and suspects, with reasonable cause, to be committing an offence under this section.

8.5 The provision creates two distinct offences, one of 'loitering in a public street ...' and one of 'soliciting in a public street ...'. The prosecution must decide which of the offences should be charged but it must be able to substantiate that the woman was doing one thing or the other, depending on the charge. Each of these terms is considered below.

General Issues

Mode of Trial

8.6 The SOA 1959, s 1(2)[1] makes it clear that this offence is triable only summarily.

1 As substituted by the CJA 1982, s 71.

Parties to the Offence

8.7 The act concerns only women acting as prostitutes. This may appear surprising when the only term relating to a person in the provision is 'common prostitute'. However, the issue was raised in the case of *DPP v Bull*[1] when the prosecution appealed against the decision of a stipendiary magistrate to dismiss a case against a male prostitute on the grounds that the SOA 1959, s 1(1) related only to females. Mann LJ considered the legislation and, in particular, part of a report produced by the Wolfenden Committee relating to homosexual offences and prostitution. In dismissing the appeal he stated the following:

> The ... [Wolfenden] report confirms my strong impression that, notwithstanding the use of 'person' and 'anyone' in subsections (2) and (3), section 1(1) of the Act of 1959 is confined to women. The term 'common prostitute' is ordinarily regarded as applying to a woman and, importantly, it seems improbable that Parliament intended to create a new male offence which was but subtly different from the extant section 32 of the Sexual Offences Act 1956[2].

1 [1995] 1 Cr App Rep 413.

2 [1995] 1 Cr App Rep 413 at 418F.

Power of Arrest

8.8 Following the Wolfenden Committee's report on prostitution, a system of cautioning first-time offenders for an offence under the SOA 1959, s 1(1) was introduced. This was without statutory force but was endorsed by all chief constables of provincial forces together with the Commissioner of the Metropolitan Police, and was introduced shortly after the SOA 1959 came into force. The rationale behind the cautioning was that it was thought it may deflect away from the industry those young women just setting out on a career of prostitution. The SOA 1959, s 2 allows for the woman in question to apply to the court for the record of her caution, in certain circumstances, to be expunged.

8.9 The SOA 1959, s 1(3) gives a constable power to arrest without warrant any person he finds to be in a street or public place and suspects, with reasonable cause, to be committing an offence under the SOA 1959, s 1(1). This provision does not, however, give a constable the power to detain a suspect for the purpose of cautioning her. This was illustrated in the case of *Collins v Wilcock*[1] in which the appellant was convicted of assaulting a police officer in the course of her duty. She had walked away from a policewoman who suspected her of being a prostitute and who was intent on establishing her identity in order to administer a caution. The policewoman took hold of Ms Collins and restrained her; Ms Collins scratched the policewoman's arm as she tried to escape her clutches. In allowing her appeal it was held that the power in the SOA 1959, s 1(3) did not allow the policewoman to stop and detain the woman in order to ascertain if she had ever been cautioned in the past, merely to arrest her if she fitted the criteria set out in the provision.

1 [1984] 3 All ER 374, [1984] 1 WLR 1172.

Actus Reus

Common Prostitute

8.10 Taking each of the terms in the provision in turn, the first matter to consider is the phrase 'common prostitute'. There is no statutory definition of the term and all legal definitions stem from the case of *De Munck*[1] which concerned a 14-year-old girl who had taken part in certain lewd acts with various men. It was discovered later that she remained a virgin and one of the issues in the case revolved around whether sexual intercourse was an essential ingredient in the offence of prostitution. It was held that it was not. Indeed, in setting out the definition of 'common prostitute', Darling J said

> The court is of opinion that the term 'common prostitute' in the statute is not limited so as to mean only one who permits acts of lewdness with all and sundry, or with such as hire her, when such acts are in the nature of ordinary sexual connection. We are of opinion that prostitution is proved if it be shown that a woman offers her body commonly for lewdness for payment in return[2].

1 [1918] 1 KB 635, 13 Cr App Rep 113, CCA.

2 [1918] 1 KB 635 at 637-638, 13 Cr App Rep 113 at 115, CCA.

8.11 Although the above dictum still stands as an acceptable definition of prostitution, it is sometimes said that it is not necessary for money to change hands between the participants. It was said, somewhat quaintly by Swift J in the case of *Winter v Woolfe*,[1] that:

> ... payment in such a case need not be in money: the consideration may be a motor drive, a tea or a dance ticket.

However, that comment was made during submissions being made on behalf of the appellant and does not form part of the ratio decidendi of the case. The issue is not mentioned in the speeches of either Avory J or Swift J.

1 [1931] 1 KB 549, CCA.

8.12 As a result of the ruling in *De Munck*, any act of lewdness on the part of the woman can meet the criteria for the offence. Thus, it does not matter whether the woman involves herself in active or passive acts of sexual activity, and it may well be the case that even where there is no direct physical contact between the woman and her 'customer' the act is that of a 'prostitute'. In *R v Webb*[1] it was held that prostitution was proved if it was shown that a woman offered herself as a participant in physical acts of indecency for the sexual gratification of men. As was suggested by Lord Parker CJ in the case, it matters not whether the woman whips the man or the man whips the woman for her to be considered a prostitute within the legal definition.

1 [1964] 1 QB 357, [1963] 3 All ER 177, CCA.

8.13 As to the use of the word 'common' in the section, it was held in *Morris-Lowe*[1] that the use of the word in the SOA 1956, s 22(1)(a) was not mere surplusage and that a 'common prostitute' was a woman who offered herself for acts of lewdness for reward 'commonly'. The ruling in the case distinguished between what was called a 'prostitute'; ie a woman who performs a single act of lewdness with a man on one occasion for reward, and a 'common prostitute' who was described thus:

> ... someone who is prepared for reward to engage in acts of lewdness with all and sundry, or with anyone who may hire her for that purpose.

1 (1984) 80 Cr App Rep 114, CA.

8.14 It would appear then that, using the logic of the Lord Chief Justice in *Morris-Lowe*, a woman who has yet to be cautioned for prostitution[1] could not realistically be called a 'common prostitute', but that a woman who has received such a caution would be.

1 See paragraph 8.8 above.

Loiter

8.15 There is no statutory definition of this term and the higher courts have never had to consider such a definition. It is submitted that the starting point must be a dictionary definition such as 'to proceed lingeringly; to dawdle; to linger'. However, merely loitering is not enough to satisfy the provision, and it is for the prosecution to prove that the said loitering was 'for the purpose of prostitution'.

8.16 The concept of 'loitering' is inevitably much greater than that of 'soliciting' and it is likely that, without direct evidence of a woman soliciting men, this offence will be charged. It is likely that evidence that the woman was in fact loitering for the purposes of prostitution save for any admissions by her, could come from witnesses who saw her in a particular spot acting in a particular way, or even dressed in a certain fashion.

Solicit

8.17 As long ago as 1912, the law as to what constitutes 'soliciting' was settled in the case of *Horton v Mead*[1]. In that case Horton was convicted under the Vagrancy Act 1898, in effect, that he had been 'soliciting or importuning for immoral purposes' outside a public toilets in London's Leicester Square. The evidence in the case was that:

> [W]hile in the said lavatories and also while in the street he smiled in the faces of gentlemen, pursed his lips, and wriggled his body. He did not at any time during this period speak to anybody or touch anybody, nor did he attempt to speak to or touch anybody. No complaint was made by anybody as to his conduct.

The man's appeal was dismissed on the grounds that it was irrelevant that he did not succeed in attracting the attention of any of the men towards whom he had been gesturing and smiling. The ruling went onto to say that for solicitation to be proved it is not necessary to show that it 'reached the ears or affected the senses of the person solicited'.

1 [1913] 1 KB 154.

8.18 A case that concerned facts that were at the other end of the spectrum to those of *Horton v Mead* was *Behrendt v Burridge*[1]. In that case the respondent was being watched by police officers while she sat in the bay window of a private house. She was scantily clad and the area she sat in was lit only by a single red light. During the period she was being watched two men entered the premises and one of the men later admitted to having paid money for sexual intercourse. It was said by the prosecution that her intention was to advertise herself for the purposes of prostitution. At trial it was decided that she did not have a case to answer because at no point was she in direct communication with any men, or anyone who was in a public place. The prosecution appealed that decision and the Divisional Court allowed the appeal, holding that her appearance in the window in the way that she did constituted soliciting for the purposes of prostitution. This was said because her sole purpose in sitting in the window was to allure and tempt men into her home for the purposes of sexual activity for reward. It is submitted that this case is an example of the higher courts distorting the English language so as to turn 'private home' into 'street or public place' merely in order to bring the respondent's activity within the Act and to put a stop to such marketing in the future. Having said that, the courts, in attempting to deal with the mischief the provision was enacted to avoid, have certainly taken the view that members of the public are entitled to walk along public thoroughfares without being solicited by prostitutes[2].

1 (1976) 63 Cr App Rep 202, DC.

2 See *Smith v Hughes* for another example of the Divisional Court ruling that soliciting from a room in a private house came within the definition of the offence.

8.19 It is however, essential, that the woman is present when the solicitation is occurring. An advertisement of any kind displayed in a street or public place indicating that a woman is available as a prostitute does not satisfy the criteria for soliciting within the provision[1] – hence the multitude of such advertising in telephone boxes and other public places.

1 See *Weisz v Monahan* [1962] 1 All ER 664,]1962] 1 WLR 262.

Street or Public Place

8.20 The definition of 'street' is given in the Street Offences Act 1959, s 1(4) and includes 'any bridge, road, lane, footway, subway, square, court, alley or passage, whether a thoroughfare or not, which is for the time being open to the public; and the doorways and entrances of premises abutting on a street (as defined above), and any ground adjoining and open to a street.' This extensive list of locations was, of course, added to by the case of *Behrendt v Burridge* to include a window of a house adjoining any street.

8.21 The most significant phrase in the Street Offences Act 1959, s 1(4) is 'open to the public'. The effect of this phrase in the provision is that even private property may come within the ambit of the provision so long as members of the public have access to them. This is said because the section does not contain a specific definition for the term but must be taken to mean 'any place to which the public have access (whether on payment or otherwise)'[1].

1 See for example the Prevention of Crime Act 1953, s 4 and *Collinson* (1931) 23 Cr App Rep 49, CCA.

8.22 The list of places to which the public have access is likely to be regarded quite loosely when considering this aspect of the offence because of the particular mischief the Act is aimed at. Thus public houses, nightclubs and hotels are likely to be considered public places up to the time when their doors are closed and members of the public have actually left the premises.

For the Purposes of Prostitution

8.23 The acts of 'loitering' or 'soliciting' must be done for the purposes of prostitution and if the prosecution cannot prove as much then the woman should be acquitted. However, justices are entitled to infer from the surrounding circumstances that the woman's actions were for that purpose[1].

1 See for example *Knight v Fryer* [1976] Crim LR 322.

Sentence

8.24 The Street Offences Act 1959, s 1(2) makes it clear that a woman convicted of this offence can be sentenced to a fine up to level 2 on the standard scale[1]. In addition, by reason of the Crime and Disorder Act 1998, s 1, the police and/or local authority can apply for an anti-social behaviour order (ASBO).

1 See the MCA 1980, s 32.

B Causing Prostitution of Women

8.25 The SOA 1956, s 22 reads as follows:

> 22(1) It is an offence for a person –
> (a) to procure a woman to become, in any part of the world, a common prostitute; or
> (b) to procure a woman to leave the United Kingdom, intending her to become an inmate of or frequent a brothel elsewhere; or
> (c) to procure a woman to leave her usual place of abode in the United Kingdom, intending her to become an inmate of or frequent a brothel in any part of the world for the purposes of prostitution.

8.26 The section comprises three separate offences and care should be taken to ensure that the correct offence is charged so as to reflect the evidence. By virtue of the Interpretation Act 1978, s 5, and Sch 1, 'United Kingdom' is made up of Great Britain and Northern Ireland.

8.27 It is to be noted that not a few of the statutory provisions of the SOA 1956 relating to prostitution offences are something of a hangover from Victorian legislation which was much concerned with what became known as the 'white slave trade'. It is for that reason that the subsections contain the phrase 'in any part of the world'. The phrase is not likely to play a significant part in any charge that might be brought in this day and age.

8.28 The use of the word 'woman' in the section applies just as much to girls. By virtue of the SOA 1956, s 46, the two words are interchangeable.

General Issues

Mode of Trial

8.29 The offence is one that can only be tried on indictment[1]. It is a Class 3 offence and as such can be tried by a High Court judge, a circuit judge or a recorder who has been properly authorised by a presiding judge[2]. The same factors apply when the charge is one of an attempt to commit the offence.

1 See the SOA 1956, s 37(2) and Sch 2, para 23.

2 Practice Direction (Crown Court: allocation of business) (No 3) [2002] 1 All ER 380, [2000] 1 WLR 203.

8.30 It should be noted that in certain circumstances the United Kingdom courts do not have jurisdiction to try 'a member of a visiting force or a civilian component of such a force'. Under the VFA 1952, s 3(1) an offence under the SOA 1956, s 22 may come under this provision.

Parties to the Offence

8.31 As the section uses the word 'person', it is clear that both males and females can be prosecuted as principals. It is equally clear that the victim of the offence must be a woman. It is important to differentiate this offence, which is aimed at the prevention of the procurement of women for the purposes of prostitution, with that under the SOA 1956, s 23(1)[1], which concerns merely the procuring of a girl under the age of 21 for the purposes of having unlawful sexual intercourse with a third person. The latter offence may not have anything whatsoever to do with prostitution.

1 See Chapter 7(C) above.

Actus Reus

8.32 The definition of the word 'procure' is fully considered in paragraph 4.31 above.

8.33 The offence in SOA 1956, s 22(1)(a) contains the words '... to become ... a common prostitute' and thus if the woman in question was already a prostitute, then the offence is not made out. In the case of *Broadfoot*[1] the trial judge's direction to the jury that '[I]f [the women in question] were prostitutes then he could not commit this offence, but if ... those women were not prostitutes then the attempt to turn them into prostitutes would be the offence alleged', was not criticised. Thus it must be for the prosecution to prove, to the satisfaction of the jury, that the woman was not a prostitute before she came into contact with the defendant.

1 [1976] 3 All ER 753, 64 Cr App Rep 71, CA.

8.34 The definition of the term 'common prostitute' is dealt with in paragraphs 8.10 to 8.14 above.

Mens Rea

8.35 The only issue as to the question of the defendant's mens rea with regard to the offence under SOA 1956, s 22(1)(a) pertains to his belief that the woman was not a prostitute prior to his procuring her to become one. It has already been shown that the offence cannot be committed if the woman is already a common prostitute before she comes into contact with the man[1], so that, if the man's defence is that he believed, on reasonable grounds, her to be one, then it will be for the prosecution to disprove that assertion[2].

1 See paragraph 8.33 above.

2 See *Brown* (1984) 80 Cr App Rep 36, CA for a case in which a conviction was overturned because such a defence was prevented from going before the jury.

8.36 The converse situation to that in the case of *Brown* would be where a defendant thought that the woman was not a prostitute, but in fact she was. If he tried to procure her into becoming a prostitute, he could not commit the offence in question. However, it is possible for him to be convicted of an attempt by reason of the Criminal Attempts Act 1981, s 1(3).

Sentence

8.37 By SOA 1956, s 37(3) and Sch 2, para 23(a) and (b), the maximum sentence for the full offence, as well as an attempt to commit it, is two years in prison.

C Detention of a Woman in a Brothel or Other Premises

8.38 The SOA 1956, s 24 reads as follows:

> 24(1) It is an offence for a person to detain a woman against her will on any premises with the intention that she shall have unlawful sexual intercourse with men or with a particular man, or to detain a woman against her will in a brothel.
>
> (2) Where a woman is on any premises for the purpose of having unlawful sexual intercourse or is in a brothel, a person shall be deemed for the purpose of the foregoing subsection to detain her there if, with the intention of compelling or inducing her to remain there, he either withholds from her her clothes or any other property belonging to her or threatens her with legal proceedings in the event of her taking away clothes provided for her by him or on his directions.
>
> (3) A woman shall not be liable to any legal proceedings, whether civil or criminal, for taking away or being found in possession of any clothes she needed to enable her to leave premises on which she was for the purpose of having unlawful sexual intercourse.

8.39 The SOA 1956, s 43 grants the courts, in certain circumstances relating to the detention of such women, the power to issue a warrant permitting a constable to search for her and to take her to a place of safety.

8.40 The use of the word 'woman' in the section applies just as much to girls. By virtue of the SOA 1956, s 46, the two words are interchangeable.

General Issues

Mode of Trial

8.41 The offence is one that can only be tried on indictment[1]. It is a Class 3 offence and as such can be tried by a High Court judge, a circuit judge or a recorder who has been properly authorised by a presiding judge[2].

1 See the SOA 1956, s 37(2) and Sch 2, para 25.

2 Practice Direction (Crown Court: allocation of business) (No 3) [2002] 1 All ER 380, [2000] 1 WLR 203.

8.42 It should be noted that in certain circumstances the United Kingdom courts do not have jurisdiction to try 'a member of a visiting force or a civilian component of such a force'. Under the VFA 1952, s 3(1) an offence under the SOA 1956, s 24(1) may come under this provision.

Parties to the Offence

8.43 As the section uses the word 'person', it is clear that both males and females can be prosecuted as principals. It is equally clear that the victim of the offence must be a woman.

Actus Reus

8.44 The first element to be considered so far as the actus reus of this offence is concerned is the notion of 'unlawful sexual intercourse'. Definitions of these words are addressed in paragraphs 1.19 to 1.20 and 3.15 to 3.17 above and reference should be made to them.

8.45 The question of whether a premises is a 'brothel' is one for the jury having considered all of the available evidence. In *Stevens and Stevens v Christy*[1] it was said that premises were not precluded from being a brothel by the fact that, on any one day, only one prostitute was there. The case also makes it clear that the word 'premises' does not have to refer to a house but can also relate to 'a house or room, or set of rooms in any house kept for the purpose of prostitution'[2]. The case concerned a team of prostitutes who only ever used the premises one at a time, and it was held that this was enough to constitute a brothel in the minds of the Divisional Court. In the earlier case of *Gorman v Standen; Palace-Clark v Standen*[3] it was held that a premises constituted a brothel if it was resorted to by more than one woman for the purposes of prostitution. The case is also authority for the contention that it matters not that one of the women involved is a legal tenant and occupier of the premises. If a premises of any description is used for purposes of prostitution by only one woman, it cannot be defined as a brothel[4].

1 (1987) 85 Cr App Rep 249.

2 (1987) 85 Cr App Rep 249 at 251.

3 [1964] 1 QB 294, [1963] 3 All ER 627.

4 See *Singleton v Ellison* [1895] 1 QB 607.

8.46 In *Kelly v Purvis*[1] it was reconfirmed that for prostitution to be made out by the prosecution it is not necessary to show that sexual intercourse occurred. In that case it was said that it was sufficient to prove that more than one woman offered herself as a participant in physical acts of indecency for the sexual gratification of men. The case further reiterated that it is not necessary to prove that the lewd behaviour of the women involved payment for services rendered. It was said that a 'brothel is also constituted where the women (for there must be more than one woman) do not charge for sexual intercourse'[2].

1 (1988) 76 Cr App Rep 165, DC.

2 (1988) 76 Cr App R 165, DC at 169.

8.47 It is possible for the prosecution to prove that the premises is being used as a brothel by inferences being drawn from the surrounding evidence[1].

1 See the Crown Court case of *Korie* [1966] 1 All ER 50 and *Roberts v DPP* [1994] Crim LR 926 for examples of cases where the prosecution were allowed to rely on surrounding evidence to prove the existence of brothels.

Mens Rea

8.48 The only element that the prosecution would need to show in order to prove their case is that the defendant had the intention of detaining the woman at the premises (or in the brothel) so that she would have unlawful sexual intercourse with men or with a particular man. Such intention can be properly inferred from the surrounding circumstances of the case and if it can be said that the intended outcome was virtually certain to happen.

Sentence

8.49 By the SOA 1956, s 37(3) and Sch 2, para 25, the maximum sentence for this offence is two years in prison. In addition, if the offence is committed against a child complainant, the offender can be ordered to be disqualified from working with children under CJCSA 2000, ss 26 to 31.

D Causing or Encouraging Prostitution

8.50 The SOA 1956, s 28, as amended by the Children Act 1989, s 108(4) and Sch 12, reads as follows:

> 28(1) It is an offence for a person to cause or encourage the prostitution of, or the commission of unlawful sexual intercourse with, or of an indecent assault on, a girl under the age of 16 for whom he is responsible.
>
> (2) Where a girl has become a prostitute, or has had unlawful sexual intercourse, or has been indecently assaulted, a person shall be deemed for the purposes of this section to have caused or encouraged it, if he knowingly allowed her to consort with, or to enter or continue in the employment of, any prostitute or person of known immoral character.
>
> (3) The persons who are to be treated for the purposes of this section as responsible for a girl are (subject to subsection (4) of this section) –
> (a) her parents; and
> (b) any person who is not a parent of hers but who has parental responsibility for her; and
> (c) any person who has care of her.
>
> (4) An individual falling within subsection 3(a) or (b) of this section is not to be treated as responsible for a girl if –
> (a) a residence order under the Children Act 1989 is in force with respect to her and he is not named in the order as the person with whom she is to live;

(b) a care order under that Act is in force with respect to her.

(5) If, on a charge of an offence against a girl under this section, the girl appears to the court to have been under the age of 16 at the time of the offence charged, she shall be presumed for the purposes of this section to have been so, unless the contrary is proved.

General Issues

8.51 The offence is one that can only be tried on indictment[1]. It is a Class 3 offence and as such can be tried by a High Court judge, a circuit judge or a recorder who has been properly authorised by a presiding judge[2]. The same factors apply when the charge is one of an attempt to commit the offence.

1 See the SOA 1956, s 37(2) and Sch 2, para 28.

2 Practice Direction (Crown Court: allocation of business) (No 3) [2002] 1 All ER 380, [2000] 1 WLR 203.

8.52 In certain circumstances the United Kingdom courts do not have jurisdiction to try 'a member of a visiting force or a civilian component of such a force'. Under the VFA 1952, s 3(1) an offence under the SOA 1956, s 28(1) may come under this provision.

Parties to the Offence

8.53 As is clear from both SOA 1956, s 28(1) and (3), both males and females can commit this offence as principals so long as they come under the criteria set out in sub-s (3). The complainant must be female and must be under the age of 16 at the time of the commission of the offence.

Actus Reus

Cause or Encourage

8.54 It was held in the case of *Ralphs*[1] that it was sufficient to come under the term 'cause or encourage ... the commission of unlawful sexual intercourse' that a defendant does nothing to prevent the act when he is in a position to do so. In that case (which dealt with a precursor to the present provision) the defendant allowed a man to sleep with his two daughters in the same bed. He was the boyfriend of the elder girl, but the younger was only 11 years old and, when he had sexual intercourse with her, the father was convicted of an offence under this provision.

1 (1913) 9 Cr App Rep 86, CCA.

8.55 Similarly, in the case of *Drury*[1] the defendant was convicted of an offence under this section when he allowed a man in his house to ply a 14-year-old baby-sitter with alcohol. The man later went on to indecently assault her. Although Drury had given her a small amount of alcohol during the evening, most of the drink was supplied by the man who assaulted her. It was held by the Court of Appeal that this was sufficient evidence to support the Crown's proposition that the defendant had 'encouraged' the indecent assault. It was further held that the circumstances were sufficient to hold that the girl was properly in the care of the accused. As a result of this case, it is possible to say that whether or not a person has the care of the girl in question is a matter for the jury.

1 (1974) 60 Cr App Rep 195.

Prostitution

8.56 For a discussion of this term, refer to paragraphs 8.10 to 8.14 above.

Unlawful Sexual Intercourse

8.57 For a discussion of this term, refer to paragraphs 3.15 to 3.17 and paragraphs 1.18 to 1.20 above.

8.58 An issue that arose in the case of *Gillick v West Norfolk and Wisbech Area Health Authority*[1] was whether a doctor could be found guilty of an offence under this section if s/he provided contraceptive treatment to a girl under 16 years of age. For a discussion of the point, refer to paragraph 3.9 above.

1 [1986] 1 AC 112, [1985] 3 All ER 402, HL.

Indecent Assault

8.59 For a full discussion of this term, refer to Chapter 6 above.

Under the Age of 16

8.60 For a discussion of this term, refer to paragraph 3.18 above. That paragraph relates to how the prosecution must prove a girl to be under the age of 13. The factors set out there are the same as for this offence except that the age is of course different.

8.61 It should also be noted on this issue that SOA 1956, s 28(5) allows the court to 'presume' that the girl is under 16 at the time of the commission of the offence, unless the defendant can prove otherwise.

Mens Rea

Belief as to the Age of the Complainant

8.62 A crucial aspect of the offence that needs to be proved by the prosecution is that the defendant knew that the girl in question was under the age of 16. It is open to the defendant to assert that s/he had an honest belief the girl was at least 16 years old. For a full discussion of this aspect of the offence, refer to paragraphs 6.43 to 6.46 above.

8.63 This aspect of the defence to an allegation of an offence under this section is particularly important when one considers SOA 1956, s 28(5). It is not difficult to envisage a case in which the defendant asserts that s/he had an honest belief that the girl was at least 16 years of age but that the court presumes otherwise. The defendant may well be convicted not because the court does not believe him/her but because it thinks the girl 'appears' to be under 16. The court would be helped in this presumption, it is to be assumed, by the fact that the girl would inevitably be under

16, otherwise the charge would not have been brought in the first place.

Sentence

8.64 By the SOA 1956, s 37(3) and Sch 2, para 28, the maximum sentence for this offence is two years in prison. In addition, if the offence is committed against a child complainant, the offender can be ordered to be disqualified from working with children under CJCSA 2000, ss 26 to 31.

E Man Living on the Earnings of Prostitution

8.65 The SOA 1956, s 30 reads as follows:-

> 30(1) It is an offence for a man knowingly to live wholly or in part on the earnings of prostitution.
>
> (2) For the purposes of this section a man who lives wholly or is habitually in the company of a prostitute, or who exercises control, direction or influence over a prostitute's movements in a way which shows he is aiding abetting or compelling her prostitution with others, shall be presumed to be knowingly living on the earnings of prostitution, unless he proves the contrary.

8.66 SOA 1956, s 30(1) creates the offence of living on the earnings of prostitution but it is s 30(2) which provides the prosecution with (usually) the necessary evidentiary presumptions to prove that the offence has been committed. Most of the case law pertaining to this section concerns the interpretation of SOA 1956, s 30(2).

8.67 The use of the word 'man' in this provision should be read as referring to both men and boys. By virtue of SOA 1956, s 46 the two terms are interchangeable.

8.68 SOA 1956, s 42 gives power to a magistrates' court to issue a warrant authorising a police officer to enter and search a house in which there is some evidence that a man is residing or frequenting and that he is living wholly or in part on the earnings of a prostitute.

General Issues

Mode of Trial

8.69 An offence under SOA 1956, s 30(1) is triable either way[1]. It is a Class 4 offence and, as such, when committed to the Crown Court may be tried by a High Court judge, a circuit judge or a Recorder[2].

1 MCA 1980, s 17(1) and Sch 1.

2 *Practice Direction (Crown Court: allocation of business) (No 3)* [2002] 1 All ER 380, [2000] 1 WLR 203.

Parties to the Offence

8.70 The offence under SOA 1956, s 30(1) can only be committed by a male as principal. As a result of the case of *Tan*[1] a person who is born a man remains, biologically speaking, a man, even though he has undergone surgical treatment in order to change his apparent sex and hormone treatment in order to become, psychologically, female; he remains a man for all legal reasons. Thus even if a man has undergone such treatment, he is still liable to be charged under this section if there is sufficient evidence to warrant it.

1 [1983] QB 1053, 76 Cr App Rep 300, CA.

8.71 It is highly unlikely that the prostitute upon whose earnings the man lives would be prosecuted as an accomplice to the man. This is said because, in considering SOA 1956, s 30(2), it must be right that the offence was instituted in order to protect women and thus the woman should only be seen as the victim of such an offence.

Actus Reus

8.72 It must be proved that the woman upon whose earnings the man was living was a prostitute. In the case of *Grizzle*[1] the following was contained within the ruling of the Court of Appeal:

> It was not necessary to prove that he was living with or habitually in the company of such a prostitute in a way which showed that he was aiding, abetting or compelling her prostitution with others, but it must be shown that at the time when he was habitually in the woman's company she was in fact a prostitute.

1 [1991] Crim LR 553.

8.73 For a definition of the term 'prostitute', refer to paragraphs 8.10 to 8.14 above.

The Earnings of Prostitution

8.74 The leading case on this issue is that of *Shaw v DPP*[1] in which Viscount Simonds said:

> I think that ... a person may fairly be said to be living in whole or in part on the earnings of prostitution if he is paid by prostitutes for goods or services supplied by him to them for the purpose of their prostitution which he would not supply but for the fact that they were prostitutes. I emphasise the negative part of this proposition, for I wish to distinguish beyond all misconception such a case from that in which the service supplied could be supplied to a woman whether prostitute or not[2].

Viscount Simonds was at pains to differentiate the cases of men such as the appellant (who published, for a fee, a booklet containing telephone numbers of prostitutes) and other regular, and honest, traders such as landlords, tailors, etc.

1 [1962] AC 220, [1961] 2 All ER 446, HL.

2 [1962] AC 220 at 264, HL.

8.75 The question for the court as to whether a man is living wholly or in part on the earnings of prostitution is one of degree and can only really be decided by the tribunal of fact. The section is clearly aimed at pimps who exercise some control over the prostitute and reap the financial rewards of that control. However, in the past men have been held to fall foul of the section when they received money direct from the prostitute's customers[1], even where the prostitutes were unaware of his involvement[2] and landlords who charge higher rents to a woman knowing that she is working as a prostitute[3].

1 *Calvert v Mayes* [1954] 1 QB 342, [1954] 1 All ER 41.

2 *R v Ansell* [1975] QB 215, [1974] 3 All ER 568, CA.

3 *R v Silver* [1956] 1 All ER 716, [1956] 1 WLR 281.

Mens Rea

8.76 The prosecution must prove that the man lived wholly or in part on the earnings of prostitution 'knowingly'. This means that it must be proved first that he knew she was a prostitute and, secondly, that he knew that he was living wholly or partly on her earnings. If the prosecution are not able to establish one or both of those features then he is entitled to be acquitted of the charge.

8.77 The prosecution can of course rely on the presumptions set out in SOA 1956, s 30(2) to prove their case. It was said by Bridge LJ in the case of *Clarke*[1] that:

> What is to be presumed once one of the three alternative legs provided by [SOA 1956,] s 30(2) has been established is that the man accused is 'knowingly living on the earnings of prostitution'. The presumption, on the ordinary meaning of the words, has two facets. It is presumed that he is living on immoral earnings and it is presumed that he is doing so knowingly[2].

1 [1976] 2 All ER 696, CA.

2 [1976] 2 All ER 696 at 699, CA.

8.78 The three alternative legs referred to by Lord Bridge are as follows:

(i) he was living with a prostitute,

(ii) he was habitually in the company of a prostitute,

(iii) he exercised control, direction or influence over the prostitute's movements in a way which showed that he was aiding, abetting or compelling her prostitution.

8.79 So long as the prosecution can satisfy the tribunal of fact of at least one of those three legs, then the presumption will apply unless the defendant can prove otherwise. The most significant aspect of this presumption is that the prosecution do not have to rely on evidence from the prostitute in question but can rely merely on circumstantial evidence, for example of police officers who have been keeping her under surveillance, or even real evidence found at her premises.

8.80 The question of whether or not the evidence adduced is sufficient to bring into play the presumption is a question of fact to be answered by the tribunal of fact. Once the issue has been raised by the prosecution, it is for the defendant, on a balance of probabilities, to prove that he was not, in fact, living on the earnings of a prostitute[1].

1 See for example, *Ptohopoulos* (1967) 52 Cr App Rep 47, CA.

Sentence

8.81 By SOA 1956, s 37(3) and Sch 2, para 30, as amended, the maximum sentence for this offence, when tried on indictment, is seven years in prison. When tried summarily the maximum sentence is six months in prison together with a fine not exceeding £5,000. In addition, if the offence is committed against a child complainant, the offender can be ordered to be disqualified from working with children under CJCSA 2000, ss 26 to 31.

8.82 In the case of *Farrugia*[1] the sentences of four appellants were considered together and certain guidance was given by Lawton LJ with regard to sentences for offences under this provision. He said that a most important consideration in sentencing was whether or not there was any element of coercion of the prostitutes. He went on to say that in cases where there is no evidence of coercion, or of corruption, the old maximum penalty of two years in prison is probably adequate. He continued: '[A]nything exceeding two years should be reserved for a case where there is an element of coercion or there is some strong evidence of corruption'[2]. Other decided cases suggest that a custodial sentence is not wrong in principle for offences under this section.

1 (1979) 69 Cr App Rep 108, CA.

2 (1979) 69 Cr App Rep 108 at 113, CA.

F Living on Earnings of Male Prostitution

8.83 SOA 1967, s 5 reads as follows:

> 5(1) A man or woman who knowingly lives wholly or in part on the earnings of prostitution of another man shall be liable –
> (a) on summary conviction to imprisonment for a term not exceeding six months; or
> (b) on conviction on indictment to imprisonment for a term not exceeding seven years.
>
> (2) *Repealed*
>
> (3) Anyone may arrest without a warrant a person found committing an offence under this section.

8.84 The power of arrest in SOA 1967, s ??(3) has become otiose since the introduction of the powers of arrest in PACE 1984, s 26(1), which are rather more extensive than is allowed for in this provision.

8.85 The use of the words 'man' and 'woman' in this provision should be read as referring to both 'boys' and 'girls'. By virtue of the SOA 1956, s 46 the words are interchangeable. Reference should be made to paragraph 8.70 above with regard to the legal status of a man who has undergone treatment in order to change his apparent sex.

General Issues

Mode of Trial

8.86 An offence under the SOA 1967, s 5(1) is clearly triable either way. It is a Class 4 offence and, as such, when committed to the Crown Court may be tried by a High Court judge, a circuit judge or a Recorder[1].

1 *Practice Direction (Crown Court: allocation of business) (No 3)* [2002] 1 All ER 380, [2000] 1 WLR 203.

Parties to the Offence

8.87 It is equally clear from the wording of the section that both males and females can commit this offence as principals and that the prostitute in question must be a male.

Actus Reus

8.88 The actus reus for this particular offence is identical to that for the offence under the SOA 1956, s 30(1) and reference should be made to paragraphs 8.72 to 8.75 above.

Mens Rea

8.89 The mens rea for this particular offence is identical to that for the offence under the SOA 1956, s 30(1) and reference should be made to paragraphs 8.76 to 8.80 above.

Sentence

8.90 The sentences for this offence are set out in the SOA 1956, s5(1)(a) and (b). In addition, if the offence is committed against a child complainant, the offender can be ordered to be disqualified from working with children under CJCSA 2000, ss 26 to 31.

G Woman Exercising Control Over a Prostitute

8.91 The SOA 1956, s 31 reads as follows:

> 31 It is an offence for a woman for purposes of gain to exercise control, direction or influence over a prostitute's movements in a way which shows she is aiding, abetting or compelling her prostitution.

8.92 The use of the word 'woman' in this provision should be read as referring to both women and girls. By virtue of the SOA 1956, s 46 the two terms are interchangeable.

General Issues

Mode of Trial

8.93 An offence under the SOA 1956, s 31 is triable either way[1]. It is a Class 4 offence and, as such, when committed to the Crown Court, may be tried by a High Court judge, a circuit judge or a Recorder[2].

1 MCA 1980, s 17(1) and Sch 1.

2 *Practice Direction (Crown Court: allocation of business) (No 3)* [2002] 1 All ER 380, [2000] 1 WLR 203.

Parties to the Offence

8.94 It is clear that only a female can commit this offence. It is also clear that the prostitute in question must be a female. If the prostitute is male then only an offence under SOA 1967, s 5(1) should be charged.

Actus Reus

8.95 The actus reus for this particular offence is identical to that for the offence under SOA 1956, s 30(1) and reference should be made to paragraphs 8.72 to 8.75 above.

Mens Rea

8.96 The mens rea for this particular offence is identical to that for the offence under SOA 1956, s 30(1) and reference should be made to paragraphs 8.76 to 8.80 above.

Sentence

8.97 By SOA 1956, s 37(3) and Sch 2, para 31, as amended, the maximum sentence for this offence, when tried on indictment, is seven years in prison. When tried summarily the maximum sentence is six months in prison together with a fine not exceeding £5,000. In addition, if the offence is committed against a child complainant, the offender can be ordered to be disqualified from working with children under CJCSA 2000, ss 26 to 31.

H Brothel-keeping

8.98 SOA 1956, ss 33 to 36 are concerned with the keeping of brothels and the allowing and permitting of premises to be used as brothels or for habitual prostitution. The statutes are very similar and much of the terminology pertaining to those four sections is similar. It is felt appropriate to deal with all four sections here together.

8.99 The four sections considered below have a certain amount of overlap with other offences considered in this chapter and it is not unusual for defendants to be charged with an offence under one of the following sections together with an offence of living off immoral earnings.

8.100 The four sections in question read as follows:

> 33 It is an offence for a person to keep a brothel, or to manage, or act or assist in the management of, a brothel.
>
> 34 It is an offence for the lessor or landlord of any premises or his agent to let the whole or part of the premises with the knowledge that it is to be used, in whole or in part, as a brothel, or, where the whole or part of the premises is used as a brothel, to be wilfully a party to that use continuing.
>
> 35(1) It is an offence for the tenant or occupier, or person in charge, of any premises knowingly to permit the whole or part of the premises to be used as a brothel.

SOA 1956, s 35(2) and (3) relate to the legal powers of a lessor or landlord following the conviction of a person for this offence. They pertain to the assignment and determination of the lease or other contract affecting the property in question and have no significant bearing on the criminal aspects of the offence.

> 36 It is an offence for the tenant or occupier of any premises knowingly to permit the whole or part of the premises to be used for the purposes of habitual prostitution.

8.101 Something of an addendum was added to the above offences by SOA 1967, s 6 which reads as follows:

> 6 Premises shall be treated for the purposes of sections 33 to 35 of the Act of 1956 as a brothel if people resort to it for the purpose of lewd homosexual practices in circumstances in which resort thereto for lewd heterosexual practices would have led to its being treated as a brothel for the purposes of those sections.

General Issues

Mode of Trial

8.102 Offences under all four sections are triable only summarily[1].

1 See SOA 1956, s 37(2) and Sch 2, paras 33 to 36.

Parties to the Offence

8.103 It is clear from each of the provisions that both males and females may be defendants. A prostitute working in a brothel is in a similar position to the prostitute on whose earnings a man may be living, contrary to SOA 1956, s 30(1), and so should not be charged as an accomplice to the person charged with an offence under SOA 1956, s 33.[1]

1 See paragraph 8.71 above.

8.104 A significant feature so far as these sections are concerned is that the first three refer to 'brothels' and SOA 1956, s 36 refers to 'habitual prostitution'. The case of *Stevens and Stevens v Christy*[1] made it apparent that a single woman using premises (whether her own or not) did not make the premises a brothel[2], and so a person acting alone should not be charged under SOA 1956, ss 33, 34 and 35(1). The wording of SOA 1956, s 36 states that the 'tenant or occupier' must 'knowingly ... permit' the premises to be used for habitual prostitution. Thus it is submitted that this must refer to a person other than the tenant or occupier, and so, if a prostitute uses her own home for such purposes, she does not commit an offence under this SOA 1956, s 36.

1 (1987) 85 Cr App Rep 249, DC.

2 See paragraph 8.45 above.

Actus Reus

SOA 1956, s 33

8.105 A section 33 offence can be committed in one of three ways: (a) by keeping a brothel, (b) by managing a brothel, and (c) by acting or assisting in the management of a brothel. As is made clear in paragraph 8.45 to 8.47 above, the question of whether or not a premises constitutes a brothel is one for the tribunal of fact, taking into consideration all of the surrounding circumstances.

8.106 The fact that the first part of the section uses the word 'keep' suggests that a person must have some significant control over the premises. A landlord, for example, who rents out parts of a house but does not retain any part of the house or exercise any control over those parts rented out, is not keeping a brothel. Equally, in managing a brothel, it must be shown that the defendant was able to, and did, exercise some control over the premises. In *Abbott v Smith*[1] it was said that there must be evidence of the defendant taking an 'active part in the running of the business as a business' with something more than simply menial or routine duties being performed.

1 [1965] 2 QB 662n, [1964] 3 All ER 762.

8.107 The question of whether a person acts or assists in the management of a brothel is, again, a matter of fact. As with the term 'managing a brothel' mere menial duties are unlikely to be regarded as being sufficient to bring the accused within the ambit of SOA 1956, s 33. However, actions such as taking advertisements to the post office and paying for them[1], working as a receptionist[2] and negotiating terms[3] have all been held to constitute managing or assisting in the management of a brothel. However, as the provision uses the phrase 'assist *in* the management' it might be said that simply assisting the management would not constitute an offence. If the defendant in *Jones v DPP* only took the advertisements to the post office but had nothing whatsoever to do with paying for them, it is unlikely that an offence under SOA 1956, s 33 would have been committed.

1 *Jones v DPP* (1992) 96 Cr App Rep 130.

2 *Stevens and Stevens v Christy* (1987) 85 Cr App Rep 249.

3 *Elliott v DPP* (1989) Times, 19 January.

SOA 1956, s 34

8.108 The prosecution must first prove that the defendant is a lessor or landlord of the premises said to be a brothel, or that s/he is an agent of either. These factors are again, matters of fact and degree for the tribunal of fact to consider.

SOA 1956, s 35(1)

8.109 The prosecution must first prove that the defendant is a tenant, an occupier or a person in charge of the premises said to be a brothel. As with other aspects of these offences, while the determination of whether a defendant comes within one or other of those three terms is a matter of fact and degree. In the case of *Siviour v Napolitano*[1] it was said that only those with immediate control over the premises were liable under this provision. Thus if a tenant sublets the entire premises that he leases then s/he cannot be said to have any control whatsoever over those premises. Alternatively, if a tenant retains any control, then s/he may well be charged under the section.

1 [1931] 1 KB 636.

Section 36

8.110 See the above paragraphs for issues pertaining to the phrase 'tenant or occupier'.

8.111 Reference should be made to paragraphs 3.78 to 3.79 above for a discussion of the term 'occupier'.

Mens Rea

8.112 SOA 1956, ss 34, 35(1) and 36 use the word 'knowingly' and so it must be proved to the satisfaction of the tribunal of fact that the defendant did indeed know that what they were doing was letting or permitting the premises in question to be used as a brothel or to be used for the purposes of habitual prostitution.

8.113 Similarly, though the word 'knowingly' is not used in SOA 1956, s 33, it must be the case that the prosecution would have to prove that the defendant was keeping, managing or assisting in the management of a brothel. For further consideration of the legal concept of 'knowingly', refer to paragraph 8.76 above.

Sentence

8.114 SOA 1956, s 37 and Sch 2 allows for two distinct sentences for offences committed under all four of these provisions. For a first-time offence the maximum penalty is three months in prison and/or a fine not exceeding level 3 on the standard scale. For any further offences the maximum penalty is six months in prison and/or a fine not exceeding level 4 on the standard scale.

Chapter nine

Solicitation by men

9.1 This chapter deals solely with offences relating to the solicitation of others by men for immoral purposes. It is entitled 'Solicitation by Men' so as to differentiate it from the situation in which a female prostitute is charged with soliciting for the purposes of prostitution contrary to SOA 1959, s 1(1)[1]. In addition to the offence of soliciting for immoral purposes, the chapter also deals with two summary offences commonly referred to as 'kerb crawling' and 'persistent kerb crawling'.

1 See Section A of Chapter 8.

A Solicitation for Immoral Purposes

9.2 SOA 1956, s 32 reads as follows:

> 32 It is an offence for a man persistently to solicit or importune in a public place for immoral purposes.

9.3 The use of the word 'man' in this provision should be read as referring to both men and boys. By virtue of SOA 1956, s 46 the two terms are interchangeable.

9.4 It should be noted that SOA 1956, s 41, as amended by PACE 1984, deals with the power of arrest for an offence under this provision and reads as follows:

41 Anyone may arrest without warrant a person found committing an offence under section 32 of this Act but a constable may only do so in accordance with section 25 of the Police and Criminal Evidence Act 1984.

General Issues

Mode of Trial

9.5 An offence under this section is an offence that is triable either way[1]. It is a Class 4 offence and as such, when committed to the Crown Court may be tried by a High Court judge, a circuit judge or a recorder[2].

1 MCA 1980, s 17(1) and Sch 1.

2 *Practice Direction (Crown Court: allocation of business) (No 3)* [2000] 1 All ER 380, [2000] 1 WLR 203.

Parties to the Offence

9.6 It is clear from the section that only males can be prosecuted for this offence. As will become apparent from the analysis set out below, the sex of the person towards whom the soliciting or importuning is aimed is immaterial.

Actus Reus

9.7 The case of *Goddard*[1] makes it clear that the offence relates to soliciting or importuning for the purposes of heterosexual behaviour just as much as to homosexual behaviour.

1 (1990) 92 Cr App Rep 185, CA.

Persistently

9.8 The first aspect of the offence that the prosecution must prove is that the defendant solicited or importuned 'persistently' which implies at least two approaches towards other people for immoral purposes.

9.9–9.10 In *Dale v Smith*[1] the appellant was charged under this section with persistent importuning on 13 February 1966. The prosecution was allowed to adduce evidence that he had approached two youths on the 12 February on a number of occasions and said 'hello' to them. He had asked one of them if he wanted to see some 'sexy photographs'. On 13 February one of the same youths went into a public lavatory and the appellant was there and again, said 'hello' to him. The two youths watched the man enter a café and soon leave with a boy of 10. They made him then go to the local police station with them where he was arrested and charged. He was convicted and appealed, asserting that there was no evidential basis to warrant a finding of persistent importuning on 13 February. In dismissing the appeal Lord Parker CJ stated that:

> 'persistently' means ... a degree of repetition of either more than one invitation to one person or a series of invitations to different people[2].

1 [1967] 2 All ER 1133, [1967] 1 WLR 700.

2 [1967] 1 WLR 700 at 704G.

9.11 Similarly, in *Goddard*[1] the defendant approached two different women on the same day and importuned them to go with him in order to have sexual intercourse. He was charged and convicted under this section.

1 (1990) 92 Cr App Rep 185, CA.

9.12 While the repetition of an act may bring that act within the ambit of SOA 1956, s 32, it is less clear that a single act that lasts a length of time also qualifies. In *Tuck*[1], the defendant asserted that masturbating in a public toilet while other men came and went did not come under the term 'persistent'. The Court of Appeal however, held that it did. In *Burge*[2] an advertisement left in a shop window for an unspecified time was held, at first instance, also to amount to 'persistently' within the section. Although the defendant in *Burge* appealed his conviction, the Divisional Court, presided over by Lord Parker CJ, while allowing the appeal on other grounds, unfortunately did not address this particular issue.

The only interpretation to be taken from these two cases is that persistence in a course of conduct, as well as persistently repeating the same act, in the opinion of the higher courts comes within the ambit of the provision.

1 [1994] Crim LR 375.

2 [1961] Crim LR 412.

Solicit or Importune

9.13 For a full discussion of the term 'solicit' refer to paragraphs 8.17 to 8.19 above.

9.14 Although the case was decided before the introduction of the SOA 1956, it was made clear in *Field v Chapman*[1] that the words 'solicit' and 'importune' have identical meanings. The reasoning from that case must mean that the section creates only one offence, ie an offence of 'soliciting or importuning', rather than two distinct offences.

1 [1953] CLY 787.

In a Public Place

9.15 For a discussion of this phrase, refer to paragraphs 8.21 and 8.22 above.

For Immoral Purposes

9.16 Nowhere does the SOA 1956 define this term and it has been left to the courts to decide its legal meaning. In *Crook v Edmondson*[1] the issue arose as to the meaning of the phrase within the context of SOA 1956, s 32. Winn LJ giving a categorical opinion on the issue stated the following:

> I am convinced at least of this: Parliament cannot be supposed to have used those words in their general sense, as comprising all wrong conduct, in a statute relating solely to sexual offences ... It seems to me to follow that the 'immoral purposes' here in question must be immoral in respect of sexual conduct.[2]

1 [1966] 2 QB 81, [1966] 1 All ER 833.

2 [1966] 2 QB 81 at 90 and 91.

9.17 In practice then, it is a question of law for the judge or magistrates to decide as to whether or not an act comes within the section in terms of it being capable of consideration as 'sexual conduct', and if it is so considered, it then becomes a question of fact as to whether, applying contemporary standards of right-thinking people, the suggested act for which the person is being solicited or importuned, is immoral.

9.18 In *Ford*[1] it was decided that importuning a man to come home in order to indulge in homosexual acts was for an 'immoral purpose' even though the men in question were over the age of consent. While it was accepted by Lord Widgery CJ that the SOA 1967 had de-criminalised consensual homosexual acts between adult males in private, his opinion was that 'the fact that the conduct contemplated by the accused has now itself ceased to have the stamp of a criminal offence does not ... make the slightest difference'[2]. It is submitted that it is only a matter of time before this issue is reconsidered on the grounds that, in such circumstances, the commission of perfectly legal acts can form the basis of a criminal offence. If an adult male invites another adult male back to his home for consensual sexual intercourse, and that invitation is overheard by another person, should it really be the case that the first man is committing a criminal act?

1 [1978] 1 All ER 1129, [1977] 1 WLR 1083, CA.

2 [1978] 1 All ER 1129 at 1131f, CA.

9.19 It might be thought that as the standards of right-thinking people change over time, a jury may one day conclude that the factual situation in *Ford*, were they to occur again, would not come under the term 'for immoral purposes'.[1] Such an event was presaged somewhat by the dissenting opinion of Sachs J in *Crook v Edmondson*[2] when he said that in his view:

> The decision as to what is an immoral purpose should be the responsibility of the jury of the day or of whoever is entrusted with that decision in lieu of a jury[3].

While this goes some way to supporting the contention that an invitation to perform perfectly legal acts should not be a crime, it is surely not for juries to decide what is and what is not a criminal offence. The job of a jury should be simply to decide whether the evidence supports a conviction for an offence that has been constructed by Parliament.

1 See *Gray* (1981) 74 Cr App Rep 324, CA for a case in which the trial judge was criticised for preventing defence counsel from addressing the jury on the question of whether activity similar to that in *Ford* could constitute 'for immoral purposes'. See also *Kirkup* (1993) 96 Cr App Rep 352, CA on the same topic.

2 See paragraph 9.16 above.

3 [1966] 2 QB 81 at 96.

Mens Rea

9.20 All that can realistically be said about the mental element necessary to commit an offence under SOA 1956, s 32 is that the man or boy in question must clearly be aware of what he is doing. When one considers the wording of the section it is difficult to imagine any defence that is specific to the offence.

Sentence

9.21 When an offence under this section is dealt with on indictment the maximum penalty is two years in prison. When dealt with summarily the maximum penalty is six months in prison and/or a fine not exceeding the statutory maximum[1].

1 The SOA 1956, s 37 and Sch 2, para 32 and the MCA 1980, s 32 and Sch 1.

B 'Kerb Crawling'

9.22 SOA 1985, s 1 reads as follows:

> 1(1) A man commits an offence if he solicits a woman (or different women) for the purposes of prostitution –
> (a) from a motor vehicle while it is in a street or public place; or
> (b) in a street or public place while in the immediate vicinity of a motor vehicle that he has just got out of or off,
> persistently or, subject to section 5(6) below, in such manner or in such circumstances as to be likely to cause annoyance to

the woman (or any of the women) solicited, or nuisance to other persons in the neighbourhood.

(2) A person guilty of an offence under this section shall be liable on summary conviction to a fine not exceeding level 3 on the standard scale (as defined in section 75 of the Criminal Justice act 1982).

(3) In this section 'motor vehicle' has the same meaning as in Road Traffic Act 1988.

9.23 The use of the word 'man' in this provision should be read as referring to both men and boys. By virtue of SOA 1985, s 4(2), the two terms are interchangeable. The same situation applies to the words 'woman' and 'girl'.

General Issues

Mode of Trial

9.24 SOA 1959, s 1(2) makes it clear that an offence under this provision can only be tried summarily.

Parties to the Offence

9.25 Again, it is clear from SOA 1959, s 1(1) that the offence can only be committed by a man, and the person he solicits for the purposes of prostitution must be a woman. This latter point may or may not have been an oversight by the Act's draftsman, but if there is evidence that a man has been soliciting another man for the purposes of prostitution, a charge under SOA 1956, s 32 (solicitation for immoral purposes) should be laid[1].

1 See section A above.

Actus Reus

Soliciting

9.26 SOA 1985, s 4(1) states that references in the Act to a man 'soliciting a woman for the purpose of prostitution are references to his soliciting her for the purposes of obtaining her services as a prostitute'. This is not to say that the woman approached need be a prostitute. Indeed, when one considers that SOA 1959, s 1(1) refers to '... likely to cause annoyance to the woman ...' it is apparent that the aim of the provision was to prevent such approaches being made to women who are not prostitutes.

Nuisance

9.27 It is not necessary for the prosecution to prove that any actual nuisance had been caused to other persons in the neighbourhood. In the case of *Paul v DPP*[1] it was held that magistrates are entitled to apply their local knowledge of the area where the offence occurred and conclude that the defendant's activities would have been likely to cause a nuisance to other persons in the neighbourhood. It was also held that, by using the word 'likely' in the section, it was not envisaged by Parliament that evidence that a specific member of the public had in fact been caused annoyance or nuisance would be required[2].

1 (1989) 90 Cr App Rep 173.

2 See also *Cheeseman v DPP* (1991) 93 Cr App Rep 145.

Persistently

9.28 For a full discussion of this term refer to paragraphs 9.8 to 9.11 above.

Street or Public Place

9.29 SOA 1985, s 4(4) reads as follows:

> For the purposes of this Act 'street' includes any bridge, road, lane, footway, subway, square, court, alley or passage, whether a thoroughfare or not, which is for the time being open to the public; and the doorways and entrances or premises abutting on a street (as hereinbefore defined), and any ground adjoining and open to a street, shall be treated as forming part of the street.

9.30 Reference should also be made to paragraphs 8.20 to 8.22 above.

Motor Vehicle

9.31 SOA 1985, s 1(3) states that 'motor vehicle' has the same meaning as that given in the RTA 1988 which defines a 'motor vehicle' as 'a mechanically propelled vehicle intended or adapted for use on roads'[1].

1 Road Traffic Act 1988, s 185(1).

9.32 SOA 1959, s 1(1)(b) refers to the man being 'in the immediate vicinity of a motor vehicle that he has just got out of or off' and so it must be a matter of fact for the magistrates to consider whether he is indeed in the vehicle's 'immediate vicinity'.

Mens Rea

9.33 All that can realistically be said about the mental element necessary to commit an offence under this section is that the man or boy in question must clearly be aware of what he is doing. When one considers the wording of the section it is difficult to imagine any defence that is specific to the offence.

Sentence

9.34 SOA 1959, s 1(2) sets out the sentence for an offence under this provision.

C Persistent 'Kerb Crawling'

9.35 SOA 1985, s 2 reads as follows:

> 2(1) A man commits an offence if in a street or public place he persistently solicits a woman (or different women) for the purposes of prostitution.

(2) A person guilty of an offence under this section shall be liable on summary conviction to a fine not exceeding level 3 on the standard scale (as defined in section 75 of the (Criminal Justice Act 1982).

9.36 The only difference between this section and SOA 1985, s 1 is that there is no requirement that the man be in or near a motor vehicle. Thus, if the evidence is that the man did indeed get out of a motor vehicle but when he persistently solicited a woman (or women) he was not in the vehicle's 'immediate vicinity' a charge should be laid under this provision rather than under s 1.

9.37 All other aspects of the offence are identical to those of an offence coming under SOA 1985, s 1 and reference should be made to the analysis set out in section B above.

Chapter ten

Indecent photographs of children

10.1 There are two statutory provisions that create offences concerning the possession of indecent photographs of children. The Protection of Children Act 1978, s 1(1) created a number of offences that are triable either way and relate to the taking, distribution, possession in order to distribute of such photographs and publishing of advertisements relating to those photographs. By the time that the Criminal Justice Act 1988 was under discussion, it had been recognised that the PCA 1978 contained something of a lacuna in that it did not contain an offence of simple possession of the photographs for a person's own personal use. Section 160 was added to the CJA 1988 to create such an offence. When this latter offence was introduced it could only be tried summarily but that situation was changed by the CJCSA 2000, s 41(3) and it is an offence that is now triable either way.

A Protection of Children Act 1978

10.2 The PCA 1978, s 1, as amended by the CJPOA 1994, reads as follows:

> 1(1) It is an offence for a person –
> (a) to take, or permit to be taken or to make any indecent

photograph or pseudo-photograph of a child (meaning in this Act a person under the age of 16); or

(b) to distribute or show such indecent photographs or pseudo-photographs; or

(c) to have in his possession such indecent photographs or pseudo-photographs, with a view to their being distributed or shown by himself or others; or

(d) to publish or cause to be published any advertisement likely to be understood as conveying that the advertiser distributes or shows such indecent photographs or pseudo-photographs, or intends to do so.

(2) For purposes of this Act, a person is to be regarded as distributing an indecent photograph or pseudo-photograph if he parts with possession of it to, or exposes or offers it for acquisition by, another person.

(3) Proceedings for an offence under this Act shall not be instituted except by, or with the consent of the Director of Public Prosecutions.

(4) Where a person is charged with an offence under subsection 1(1)(b) or (c), it shall be a defence for him to prove –

(a) that he had a legitimate reasons for distributing or showing the photographs or pseudo-photographs or (as the case may be) having them in his possession; or

(b) that he had not himself seen the photographs or pseudo-photographs and did not know, nor had any cause to suspect, them to be indecent.

Subsections (5) and (6) to section 1 relate to insertions into other provisions and are not relevant to the criminal nature of this offence.

10.3 PCA 1978, s 4 allows for the entry, search and seizure by a constable following the laying before a magistrate of information that there is reasonable grounds for suspecting that, in certain premises, there is an indecent photograph or pseudo-photograph of a child. PCA 1978, s 5 makes provision for the summons before a magistrates' court of the occupier of certain premises, to show cause why such articles should not be forfeited.

General Issues

Mode of Trial

10.4 Offences under this provision are triable either way[1]. They are Class 4 offences and as such, when committed to the Crown Court, may be tried by a High Court judge, a circuit judge or a recorder[2].

1 See the PCA 1978, s 6(1).

2 Practice Direction (Crown Court: allocation of business) (No 3) [2000] 1 All ER 380, [2000] 1 WLR 203.

10.5 In certain circumstances the United Kingdom courts do not have jurisdiction to try 'a member of a visiting force or a civilian component of such a force'. Under the VFA 1952, s 3(1) an offence under PCA 1978, s 1(1) may come under this provision.

10.6 As will be seen from PCA 1978, s 1(3), proceedings for an offence under this provision can only be brought by or with the consent of the DPP.

Parties to the Offence

10.7 As the crux of the offence is the possession and/or distribution of indecent photographs, it is an offence that can be committed by males, females and corporations. PCA 1978, s 3 reads as follows:

> 3(1) Where a body corporate is guilty of an offence under this Act and it is proved that the offence occurred with the consent or connivance of, or was attributable to any neglect on the part of, any director, manager, secretary or other officer of the body, or any person who was purporting to act in any such capacity he, as well as the body corporate, shall be deemed to be guilty of that offence and shall be liable to be proceeded against and punished accordingly.
>
> (2) Where the affairs of the body corporate are managed by its members, subsection (1) shall apply in relation to acts

and defaults of a member in connection with his functions of management as if he were a director of the body corporate.

10.8 It is to be presumed that, in using the terms 'neglect', the aim of this section is to put a real responsibility on the officers of a body corporate to ensure that no such material is kept in the possession of that corporation, especially in electronic format. In addition, it is clear that, in referring to the senior officers of the body corporate, the focus would be placed on someone who holds a managerial position within the body corporate rather than a mere employee[1].

1 See *Boal* (1992) 95 Cr App Rep 272, CA for a legal definition of company decision-makers, etc.

Actus Reus

Photograph or Pseudo-Photograph

10.9 PCA 1978, s 7 sets out the definitions of what constitutes an indecent photograph or pseudo-photograph for the purposes of the Act and defines those terms in the following ways:

- an indecent film, a copy of an indecent photograph or film, and an indecent photograph comprised in a film (PCA 1978, s 7(2))
- the negative version as well as the positive version and data stored on a computer disc or by other electronic means which is capable of conversion into a photograph (PCA 1978, s 7(4))
- 'film' includes any form of video-recording (PCA 1978, s 7(5))
- 'pseudo-photograph' means an image, whether made by computer graphics or otherwise howsoever, which appears to be a photograph (PCA 1978, s 7(7))
- a copy of a 'pseudo-photograph' and data stored on a computer disc or by other electronic means which is capable of conversion into a 'pseudo-photograph' (PCA 1978, s 7(9)).

10.10 It should also be noted that, by virtue of PCA 1978, s 7(3), photographs (including those comprised in a film) shall, if they show children and are indecent, be treated as indecent photographs of children.

10.11 In the case of *Fellows and Arnold*[1] the two defendants pleaded guilty after the trial judge ruled that images kept as computer data did not comprise a photograph (the case was heard before the amendments made by the CJPOA 1994) within the meaning of PCA 1978, s 1(1). On appeal Evans LJ concluded that, though the computer disc itself was not a photograph it was a 'copy of an indecent photograph'. He went on to say that

> the disk contained data, not visible to the eye, which could be converted by appropriate technical means into a screen image and into a print which exactly reproduced the original photograph from which it was derived. It was a form of copy which made the original photograph, or a copy of it, available for viewing by a person with access to the disk ... The definitions in sections 1 and 7(2) were wide enough to include later as well as contemporary forms of copies of photographs.

1 [1997] Crim LR 524, CA.

10.12 The reference to 'pseudo-photograph' in PCA 1978, s 7(7) means that if the image in question, even one created by means of computer graphics rather than a photograph of actual people, gives the impression that the person shown is a child then it will be treated for all purposes of the Act as showing a child. This is the case even if some of the physical characteristics of the person in the pseudo-photograph appear to be those of an adult.

Indecent

10.13 The question of whether or not a photograph is indecent is one for the tribunal of fact alone. In *Stamford*[1] it was held that such a question was solely for the jury to answer and that evidence from persons who may have a view on the matter was not admissible. In the earlier case of *Stanley*[2] it was said that the words 'indecent and obscene convey one idea, namely offending against the recognised standards of propriety[3]'.

1 [1972] 2 QB 398, [1972] 2 All ER 427, CA.

2 [1965] 2 QB 327, [1965] 1 All ER 1035, CCA.

3 [1965] 2 QB 327 at 333, CCA.

10.14 In the case of *Owen*[1] a photographer was asked by a 14-year-old girl who wanted to become a model to take some photographs of her scantily clad and with her breasts showing. He was prosecuted under PCA 1978, s 1(1) and, following his conviction, appealed contending that the jury should have been directed to decide whether or not the photographs were indecent per se. In dismissing his appeal, the Court ruled that the word 'indecent' qualifies 'photograph of a child' and not the words 'to take or permit to take'. Professor Smith disagreed with this finding in his commentary to the case (in the CLR). He opens his commentary to the case with the following:

> It is an offence under the Act to take an indecent photograph of a child, not 'indecently photograph a child'.

He continues:

> The ruling seems to envisage that, if there were two photographs, exactly similar in all material respects, one of an 18-year-old girl and one of a well-developed 14-year-old, the jury might, on being informed of the 14-year-old's age, properly consider the latter photograph to be indecent even though they would not so regard the former.

It is submitted that this is a very valid point. In such circumstances it should be incumbent on the trial judge to direct the jury that they must decide whether the photograph is an indecent photograph of a child (as opposed to merely an indecent photograph), rather than whether the defendant has indecently photographed a child.

1 [1988] 1 WLR 134, [1988] Crim LR 120, CA.

10.15 In *Graham-Kerr*[1] it was held that the jury must be directed to ask themselves two questions; first whether the defendant took the photographs intentionally and deliberately and, secondly, whether the photographs were indecent, by applying the recognised standards of propriety. It was said that the motivation of the taker was entirely irrelevant. This case was decided a little over three months before *Owen*, but does not seem to have been considered in that case. It is submitted that, on the logic of Professor Smith's argument, the conclusion in *Graham-Kerr* is to be preferred.

1 [1988] 1 WLR 1098, 88 Cr App Rep 302, CA.

Child

10.16 By PCA 1978, s 7(6) a 'child' means a person under the age of 16 years. By virtue of the FLRA 1969, s 9(1), a person reaches the age of 16 at the commencement of the anniversary of his or her birth. In the light of the ruling in *Owen*[1] the age of the child is a material consideration. However, in the vast majority of cases it is likely to be the case that the age of the child(ren) in the photograph(s) will be unknown. In such circumstances the prosecution can rely on CYPA 1933, s 99(2), which allows for the court to draw a rebuttable presumption from the person's appearance that he or she was under the age of 16 at the time the photograph was taken.

1 See paragraph 10.14 above.

10.17 In addition, and with just such a situation in mind, PCA 1978, s 2(3) states that '[I]n proceedings under this Act a person is to be taken as having been a child at any material time if it appears from the evidence as a whole that he was then under the age of 16.'

Permit

10.18 It is submitted that the only way a defendant could possibly come under the ambit of this word is that if it can be proven that s/he was in a position to prevent the photograph being taken in the first place. If that is the case and s/he allows the photograph to be taken then, s/he would be giving permission, either tacit or implied, for the offence to be committed.

To Make

10.19 It was decided in *Bowden*[1] that by the action of downloading an image onto a computer and by printing that image, the offence under PCA 1978, s 1(1)(a) was committed. In saying that the words 'to make' should be given their ordinary, dictionary meaning, Otton LJ said:

> [P]hotographs or pseudo-photographs found on the Internet might have originated from outside the United Kingdom but to download or print within the jurisdiction was to create new material which hitherto might not have existed therein.

1 [2001] QB 88, [2000] 2 All ER 418, CA.

10.20 This ruling was followed in the cases of *Smith and Jayson*[1] in which defendants who opened emails and downloaded images from the Internet onto their computer screens constituted acts of 'making an indecent photograph'.

1 [2002] EWCA Crim 683, [2002] All ER (D) 71 (Mar).

To Distribute or Show

10.21 In the case of photographs or pseudo-photographs physically in the possession of the defendant, it will be a matter of evidence as to whether s/he distributed or showed them to another person. However, the question of whether or not such artefacts kept on a computer and merely made available to people via the internet were thereby distributed or shown arose in the case of *Fellows and Arnold*[1]. It was decided that, in such circumstances, the images were distributed. Evans LJ said that:

> [T]he fact that the recipient obtained an exact reproduction of the photograph contained in the archive in digital form did not mean that the copy photographs in the archive were not held in the first appellant's possession with a view to their being shown to others.

1 See paragraph 10.11 above.

Mens Rea

10.22 Any discussion of the question of mens rea in relation to an offence under PCA 1978, s 1(1) must leave out issues as to whether or not the defendant thought that the photograph in question was not indecent. It has already been noted that such a question is purely for the jury to decide and such issues relate purely to the question of the offence's actus reus. It might even be said that a defendant cannot contend that s/he thought that the subject of the photograph was over the age of 16. To that extent that aspect of the offence might be said to be one of strict liability.

Deliberate and Intentional

10.23 It was said in the appeals of *Smith and Jayson*[1] that 'the mens rea was that the act of making should be a deliberate and intentional act with knowledge that the image made was, or was likely to be an indecent photograph or pseudo-photograph of a child. It is submitted that such a standard must equally apply to all aspects of the offences covered by PCA 1978, s 1(1). It has already been noted that one of the questions a jury must ask themselves is; was the photograph taken, or made, deliberately and intentionally[2]? Thus the prosecution must prove first that the defendant did indeed take, or make, the photograph in question deliberately and intentionally.

1 See paragraph 10.20 above.

2 See paragraph 10.14 above.

Permitting

10.24 If a person is charged under PCA 1978, s 1(1)(a) with permitting a photograph to be taken then s/he can only be liable if it is proved to the satisfaction of the tribunal of fact that s/he knew that such a photograph was being taken.

Possession

10.25 Possession is a word that is likely to be considered in the same way that it is defined in other areas of English law, especially in respect to drugs offences. That is to say that there must be both a physical and a mental element to the act of possession. It should be noted that a person remains in possession of something even though s/he may have claimed to forgotten about it[1] or that s/he thought it had been destroyed.

1 See for example, *Martindale* [1986] 3 All ER 25, [1986] 1 WLR 1042, CA.

10.26 The words 'with a view to their being distributed or shown' in PCA 1978, s 1(1)(c) imports a further requirement of intention into the mere act of possession. It is not the case that an offence is committed under the PCA 1978 by merely having such photographs or pseudo-photographs in one's possession[1]. Under PCA 1978, s 1(1)(c) the offence is only committed if they are in the defendant's possession with a view to them being distributed or shown. Thus an offence under this provision is one of specific intent.

1 Though it is an offence under the CJA 1988, s 160, see section B below.

Defences

10.27 The statutory defences to an offence under this provision are set out in PCA 1978, s 1(4) and are comparatively straightforward. In *Smith and Jayson*[1] Dyson LJ accepted that a person was not guilty of an offence of making photographs or being in possession if he had not known the attachment contained indecent photographs of a child, which accords with the defence set out in PCA 1978, s 1(4)(b). The case concerned the opening of attachments to e-mails which was comprised of images of a naked girl. Had it transpired that the defendant had not opened the attachments to the e-mail then he could not have been guilty of the offence. Similarly, if a person opens such an attachment innocently, and then discovers that it comprises of an indecent photograph of a child, no offence is committed under the PCA 1978, but one under the CJA 1988, s 160 may be.

1 See paragraph 10.20 above.

Sentence

10.28 PCA 1978, s 6, as amended by the CJCSA 2000, s 41(1), reads as follows:

> 6(1) Offences under this Act shall be punishable either on conviction on indictment or on summary conviction.
>
> (2) A person convicted on indictment of any offence under this Act shall be liable to imprisonment for a term of not more than ten years, or to a fine or both.

(3) A person convicted summarily of any offence under this Act shall be liable –

(a) to imprisonment for a term not exceeding six months; or

(b) to a fine not exceeding the prescribed sum for the purposes of section 32 of the MCA 1980 (punishment on summary conviction of offences triable either way: £1,000 or other sum substituted by order under that Act), or to both.

10.29 The CJCSA 2000 amended PCA 1978, s 6 so as to increase the maximum penalty, following conviction on indictment, from three years to 10 years. The increase applies to offences committed after 11 October 2001 and so care should be taken when considering sentences for offences committed prior to that date. Having said that, it was decided in the case of *Bolingbroke*[1] that offences of this sort created problems for the courts in relation to sentencing and that it had to be made clear that, even if they were committed by people of previous good character, a very firm line would be taken.

1 [2001] 1 Cr App Rep (S) 80.

10.30 In *Toomer*[1] it was held that the authorities relating to such offences produced the following principles:

(i) Sentences up to the statutory maximum should be imposed where there was a contested case and there was evidence of commercial or large scale exploitation and the amount of the material was significant, especially if the offender had previous convictions.

(ii) Non-custodial sentences should normally be reserved for isolated offences where the amount of material was very small, and it was for personal use, or use within a very restricted circle, when there was no commercial aspect to the case and the defendant had pleaded guilty and was a first-time offender.

(iii) Where a case falls between those two extremes, all of the circumstances of the case must be considered, and in particular the following:

  (a) the quantity, quality and nature of the material,

  (b) whether there was any element of exploitation of the subject, or commercial gain,

  (c) whether the offence was one of simply making; ie merely downloading and saving such photographs or pseudo-photographs,

(d) if the offence involves distribution whether that distribution was to a single specified recipient or if it was aimed at a more widespread distribution,
(e) the character of the defendant and the effect such a conviction will have upon him/her,
(f) whether there has been a plea of guilty, coupled with co-operation with the prosecuting authorities.

1 [2001] 2 Cr App Rep (S) 30, CA.

10.31 Offences under this provision seem to generate an inordinate amount of publicity and, if one believes the mass media, the general public take a great interest in sentences for such offences. Such a claim ought to be taken with a pinch of salt. However, the Court of Appeal was so concerned with what the appropriate sentences should be for such offences that in 2002 it approached the independent Sentencing Advisory Panel (SAP) for guidance. Following extensive consultation and in particular with an organisation called the Combined Paedophile Information Networks in Europe (COPINE) it identified five levels of material according to the degree of harm to the victims. These levels are as follows:
(1) images depicting nudity or erotic posing, with no sexual activity
(2) sexual activity between children, or solo masturbation by a child
(3) non-penetrative sexual activity between adult(s) and child(ren)
(4) penetrative sexual activity between child(ren) and adult(s)
(5) sadism or bestiality.

10.32 The recommendation from the SAP was that sentencers should always see the photographs or pseudo-photographs and consider them in the light of the above table.

10.33 The SAP further recommended that the following appropriate sentences should be considered by sentencing courts:
(i) a community sentence where the offender as in possession of a large amount of material at level 1 and/or no more than a small number of images at level 2, but where the material had not been distributed to others;
(ii) the custody threshold is passed in a case where any of the material has been shown or distributed to others, or in cases of

possession where there is a moderate or large amount of material at level 2 or abovc;

(iii) a prison sentence of up to six months where:
- (a) the offender was in possession of a large amount of material at level 2 or a small amount at level 3, or
- (b) the offender had shown or distributed material at level 1 or 2, or
- (c) there had been some exchange of material with other 'collectors' without any financial gain.

(iv) a prison sentence of between six months and 12 months where:
- (a) a large quantity of material at level 3 was found in the defendant's possession but there was no distribution or showing, or
- (b) the offender was in possession of a small number of images at levels 4 or 5, or
- (c) a large number of images at level 2 had been shown or distributed, or
- (d) a small quantity of material at level 3 had been shown or distributed.

(v) a prison sentence of between 12 months and three years where:
- (a) the offender was in possession of a large quantity of the most pornographic material (levels 4-5), even if there was no showing or distribution to others, or
- (b) a large number of images at level 3 was shown or distributed, or
- (c) the offender had been involved with the production of, or traded in, material at levels 1-3.

(vi) prison sentences longer than three years should be reserved for case where:
- (a) images at levels 4 or 5 have been shown or distributed, or
- (b) the offender was actively involved in the production of highly pornographic images of children (levels 4-5), especially where this involves a breach of trust on the part of someone responsible for the care of the child(ren) whether or not there was an element of commercial gain, or
- (c) the offender had commissioned or encouraged the production of such images.

(vii) Sentences close to the 10-year maximum should be reserved for very serious examples of the offences[1].

1 The full text of the advice to the Court of Appeal is available at www.sentencing-advisory-panel.gov.uk.

10.34 Following a conviction for an offence under PCA 1978, s 1(1) the offender is also liable to the following:

- registration under the SOA 1997, Part 1
- disqualification from working with children under the CJCSA 2000, ss 26–31.

B The Criminal Justice Act 1988, s 160

10.35 The CJA 1988, s 160 reads as follows:

> 160(1) It is an offence for a person to have an indecent photograph or pseudo-photograph of a child in his possession.
>
> (2) Where a person is charged with an offence under subsection (1) above, it shall be a defence for him to prove –
> (a) that he had a legitimate reason for having the photograph or pseudo-photograph in his possession, or
> (b) that he had not himself seen the photograph or pseudo-photograph and did not know, nor had any cause to suspect, it to be indecent, or
> (c) that the photograph or pseudo-photograph was sent to him without any prior request made by him or on his behalf and he did not keep it for an unreasonable time.
>
> (2A) A person shall be liable on conviction on indictment of an offence under this section to imprisonment for a term not exceeding five years or a fine, or both.
>
> (3) A person shall be liable on summary conviction of an offence under this section to imprisonment for a term not exceeding six months or a fine not exceeding level 5 on the standard scale, or both.
>
> (4) Sections 1(3), 2(3), 3 and 7 of the Protection of Children Act 1978 shall have effect as if any reference in them to that Act included a reference to this section.

10.36 The CJA 1988, s 160(4) means that proceedings under this provision can only be instituted by or with the permission of the DPP, that if the subject of the photograph(s) or pseudo-photograph(s) is taken to be a child if he, she or they appear(s), from the evidence as a whole, to be under the age of 16, that corporations can be convicted of an offence under this provision and that the definitions of certain terms set out in the PCA 1978, s 7 apply equally to this provision.

General Issues

Mode of Trial

10.37 Offences under this provision are triable either way[1]. They are Class 4 offences and as such, when committed to the Crown Court may be tried by a High Court judge, a circuit judge or a recorder[2].

1 See the CJA 1988, s 160(2A) and (3).

2 *Practice Direction (Crown Court: allocation of business) (No 3)* [2000] 1 All ER 380, [2000] 1 WLR 203.

Parties to the Offence

10.38 As the only difference between this offence and the offences under the PCA 1978, s 1(1) is that only possession is required, issues under this heading are identical and reference should be made to paragraphs 10.7 and 10.8 above.

Actus Reus

10.39 As has already been noted, this provision was introduced so as to close the lacuna that existed in the PCA 1978, s 1(1). All that is required for this offence to be committed is mere possession of indecent photographs or pseudo-photographs of children. Reference should be made to the paragraphs above dealing with the actus reus for offences under the earlier provision.

Mens Rea

10.40 Similarly, reference should be made to the above paragraphs on this topic, especially paragraphs 10.25 and 10.26.

10.41 It should be noted that, in addition to the two statutory defences that apply to the offences under the PCA 1978, s 1(1), CJA 1988, s 160(2)(c) allows for a further defence. This further defence would apply to a person who opened an unsolicited e-mail only to discover that it contained an indecent photograph or pseudo-photograph of a child and that it was disposed of in a reasonable period of time.

Sentence

10.42 It should be noted that the maximum sentence on indictment for this offence is five years in prison. Other than that, all of the factors set out in paragraphs 10.28 to 10.34 above should be considered as applying equally to an offence under this provision.

Chapter eleven

Witness competence and sexual history evidence

A Competence of Witnesses

11.1 The YJCEA 1999, Chapter V, which comprises ss 53 to 57, deals with the competence of witnesses and their capacity to be sworn so as to give truthful evidence. Throughout the discussion of those sections below it should be borne in mind that the overall thrust of Chapter V is that too many trials were either not being proceeded with, or were aborted due to witnesses not being able to give evidence effectively. The tenor of the sections is that more witnesses should be deemed competent to give their evidence and should thus be allowed to do so. For example, until the introduction of the YJCEA 1999, s 53, evidence given by children was governed by the CJA 1988, s 33A (as amended) and was dependent upon the judge's view of the child's ability to give 'intelligible testimony'. Over the years the judiciary have shaped this test so as to consider the child's ability to, first, understand the questions being put and, secondly, to give a comprehensible and coherent account of the salient events. As was said in *Hampshire*[1] 'it is a matter of [the judge's] perception of the child's understanding demonstrated in the course of ordinary discourse'.

1 [1995] 2 All ER 1019 at 1026, CA.

11.2 Attitudes such as that stated in *Hampshire* have clearly been taken on board in the drafting of the YJCEA 1999, Chapter V and the question of a witness's competence to give coherent evidence is now governed by those provisions. Indeed, as will be seen below, all witnesses are to be presumed competent to give evidence under the YJCEA 1999 and the situations where a witness is to be deemed not competent are severely constrained. The greatest beneficiaries of this new attitude are likely to be adults with learning disabilities and those suffering from some form of mental illness; both groups having been shown to be particularly susceptible to sexual (and violent) crime[1].

1 Report of the Advisory Group on Video-Recorded Evidence (London: HMSO, 1989). This report is better known as 'The Pigot Report'.

11.3 It should also be noted that, by virtue of the YJCEA 1999, s 55, more witnesses are now allowed to give unsworn testimony than were under the old regime. Prior to the YJCEA 1999 it was only children who were allowed to give such evidence but the new provisions apply equally to adults who the court deems ought to be allowed to give their evidence without having sworn to tell the truth first.

11.4 The YJCEA 1999, s 53 considerably altered the picture with regard to the issue of a witness's competence to give evidence. It reads as follows:

> **53 Competence of witnesses to give evidence**
>
> (1) At every stage in criminal proceedings all persons are (whatever their age) competent to give evidence.
>
> (2) Subsection (1) has effect subject to subsections (3) and (4).
>
> (3) A person is not competent to give evidence in criminal proceedings if it appears to the court that he is not a person who is able to –
> (a) understand questions put to him as a witness, and
> (b) give answers to them which can be understood.
>
> (4) A person charged in criminal proceedings is not competent to give evidence in the proceedings for the prosecution (whether he is the only person, or is one of two or more persons, charged in the proceedings).

(5) In subsection (4) the reference to a person charged in criminal proceedings does not include a person who is not, or is no longer, liable to be convicted of any offence in the proceedings (whether as a result of pleading guilty or for any other reason).

11.5 The starting point of this provision is that people of all ages are competent to give evidence in criminal proceedings. The only people who are not so competent are those who the trial judge rules are unable to understand questions put to them and give understandable answers to those questions. Both the YJCEA 1999, s 53(1)(a) and (b) must be taken into account. If, for example, the court is of the opinion that a witness can understand a question put, but is unable to give a coherent answer to that question then the witness ought to be considered not competent to give evidence[1].

1 In determining this question, courts are likely to refer back to cases decided under the old rules which applied to children only. Reference should be made to *DPP v M* [1997] 2 Cr App Rep 70 and *G v DPP* [1997] 2 Cr App Rep 78.

11.6 While the YJCEA 1999, s 53 applies equally to both prosecution and defence witnesses, the only person who is categorically not competent to give evidence for the prosecution is, of course, the accused (or any of them) and the section merely puts into statutory form the common law rules relating to such matters. The situation alters once that person ceases to be liable to be convicted of any offence in those proceedings. This latter situation has not changed from the old regime pertaining to such individuals.

11.7 Determining whether a witness is competent to give evidence is governed by YJCEA 1999, s 54. It is an issue that can be raised by any party to the proceedings or by the court of its own motion[1]. In deciding on the point, the onus is on the party calling the witness to satisfy the court, on a balance of probabilities, that the witness is competent to give evidence[2]. The court must take into account any special measures that may be available to the witness under a SMD[3].

1 YJCEA 1999, s 54(1).

2 YJCEA 1999, s 54 (2).

3 YJCEA 1999, s 54(3) and Chapter 12 below.

11.8 Proceedings to determine whether the witness is competent to give evidence must be held in the absence of the jury (if there is one)[1], with the benefit of expert evidence if required[2] and with all parties present[3].

1 YJCEA 1999, s 54(4).

2 YJCEA 1999, s 54(5).

3 YJCEA 1999, s 54(6).

11.9 It remains the case that children under the age of 14 may not be sworn for the purpose of giving evidence under oath. However, when the witness is at least 14 years of age, it is for the court to determine, either when the issue is raised by any party to the proceedings or on its own motion, whether the witness in question 'has a sufficient appreciation of the solemnity of the occasion and of the particular responsibility to tell the truth which is involved in taking the oath'[1]. If s/he is able to give intelligible testimony and no evidence is adduced (by any party) that tends to show the contrary, then it is to be presumed that s/he does have a sufficient appreciation of the solemnity of the occasion and the responsibility to tell the truth[2].

1 YJCEA 1999, s 55(2)(b).

2 YJCEA 1999, s 55(3).

11.10 As with the determination of the witness's competence to give evidence in the first place, in determining whether the witness should give sworn evidence or not, the onus of showing that the witness should give sworn evidence is on the party seeking to have him/her sworn. This means that that party must show, on the balance of probabilities, that the witness has attained 14 years of age 'and has a sufficient appreciation of the matters mentioned in YJCEA 1999, s 54(2)(b)'[1]. Expert evidence is permissible and the determination should take place in the absence of the jury (if there is one)[2].

1 YJCEA 1999, s 55(4).

2 YJCEA 1999, ss 55(6) and (7).

11.11 A person is able to give intelligible testimony for the purposes of the section if s/he is able to understand questions put and to give understandable answers to those questions[1].

1 See paragraph 11.5 above.

11.12 YJCEA 1999, s 56 allows for the reception of unsworn evidence (including a written deposition) in criminal proceedings making that evidence admissible. Section 56(5) prevents an appeal against conviction being successful solely on the ground that the Court of Appeal deems that the witness did fall under the YJCEA 1999, s 55(2) and should accordingly have given sworn evidence. This provision takes away the right of a convicted person to appeal against their conviction simply on the basis that the unsworn evidence (that, in the normal course of events, should have been sworn) was inadmissible against him/her. Such a situation could only ever be due to an oversight by the determining judge and it is tempting to suggest that the subsection was inserted into the Act on the assumption that, taking into account the complexities of the rules pertaining to such matters, mistakes are bound to occur as to when a witness should give sworn or unsworn evidence.

11.13 The YJCEA 1999, s 57 creates a summary offence of giving unsworn evidence. The offence is set out in similar terms to the offence of perjury and only applies when the evidence given by the witness was given unsworn and the witness wilfully gave false evidence in the criminal proceedings.

B Sexual History Evidence

11.14 Until the introduction of Chapter III of the YJCEA 1999, the only offence that attracted parliamentary attention with regard to issues of the complainant's previous sexual experiences was that of rape. When a defendant was charged with such an offence, the SO(A)A 1976, s 2 prohibited the admission of evidential material relating to the complainant's sexual history without the leave of the court. That situation changed with the YJCEA 1999, which states that a complainant to *any* sexual offence must receive the same protection. The YJCEA 1999, ss 41 and 42 are the relevant provisions and these will be considered in detail below. As with most other parts of the Act, they are extremely complicated. References will be made to case law that has grown up in relation to the common law rules that prevailed prior to the SO(A)A 1976 and since then, but care should be taken when considering them as the Government's clear intention in drafting these provisions was to get away from, what it saw to be, the idea that the pendulum had swung too far in favour of the defendant.

11.15 The YJCEA 1999, s 41 reads as follows:

41 Restriction on evidence or questions about complainant's sexual history

(1) If at a trial a person is charged with any sexual offence, then, except with the leave of the court –
(a) no evidence may be adduced, and
(b) no question may be asked in cross-examination,
by or on behalf of any accused at the trial, about any sexual behaviour of the complainant.

(2) The court may give leave in relation to any evidence or question only on an application made by or on behalf of an accused, and may not give such leave unless it is satisfied –
(a) that subsection (3) or (5) applies, and
(b) that a refusal of leave might have the result of rendering unsafe a conclusion of the jury or (as the case may be) the court on any relevant issue in the case.
(3) This subsection applies if the evidence or question relates to a relevant issue in the case and either –
(a) that issue is not an issue of consent; or
(b) it is an issue of consent and the sexual behaviour of the complainant to which the evidence or question relates is alleged to have taken place at or about the same time as the event which is the subject matter of the charge against the accused; or
(c) it is an issue of consent and the sexual behaviour of the complainant to which the evidence or question relates is alleged to have been, in any respect, so similar –
 (i) to any sexual behaviour of the complainant which (according to evidence adduced or to be adduced by or on behalf of the accused) took place as part of the event which is the subject matter of the charge against the accused, or
 (ii) to any other sexual behaviour of the complainant which (according to such evidence) took place at or about the same time as that event,
that the similarity cannot reasonably be explained as a coincidence.

(4) For the purposes of subsection (3) no evidence or question shall be regarded as relating to a relevant issue in

the case if it appears to the court to be reasonable to assume that the purpose (or main purpose) for which it would be adduced or asked is to establish or elicit material for impugning the credibility of the complainant as a witness.

(5) This subsection applies if the evidence or question –
(a) relates to any evidence adduced by the prosecution about any sexual behaviour of the complainant; and
(b) in the opinion of the court, would go no further than is necessary to enable the evidence adduced by the prosecution to be rebutted or explained by or on behalf of the accused.

(6) For the purposes of subsections (3) and (5) the evidence or question must relate to a specific instance (or specific instances) of alleged sexual behaviour on the part of the complainant (and accordingly nothing in those subsections is capable of applying in relation to the evidence or question to the extent that it does not so relate).

(7) Where this section applies in relation to a trial by virtue of the fact that one or more of a number of persons charged in the proceedings is or are charged with a sexual offence –
(a) it shall cease to apply in relation to the trial if the prosecutor decides not to proceed with the case against that person or those persons in respect of that charge; but
(b) it shall not cease to do so in the event of that person or those persons pleading guilty to, or being convicted of, that charge.

(8) Nothing in this section authorises any evidence to be adduced or any question to be asked which cannot be adduced or asked apart from this section.

11.16 The YJCEA 1999, s 42 reads as follows:

42 Interpretation and application of section 41

(1) In section 41 –
(a) 'relevant issue in the case' means any issue falling to be proved by the prosecution or defence in the trial of the accused;

(b) 'issue of consent' means any issue whether the complainant in fact consented to the conduct constituting the offence with which the accused is charged (and accordingly does not include any issue as to belief of the accused that the complainant so consented);

(c) 'sexual behaviour' means any sexual behaviour or other sexual experience, whether or not involving any accused or other person, but excluding except in section 41(3)(c)(i) and (5)(a) anything alleged to have taken place as part of the event which is the subject matter of the charge against the accused; and

(d) subject to any order made under subsection (2), 'sexual offence' shall be construed in accordance with section 62.

(2) The Secretary of State may by order make such provisions as he considers appropriate for adding or removing, for the purposes of section 41, any offence to or from the offences which are sexual offences for the purposes of this Act by virtue of section 62.

(3) Section 41 applies in relation to the following proceedings as it applies to a trial, namely –

(a) proceedings before a magistrates' court inquiring into an offence as examining justices,

(b) the hearing of an application under paragraph 5(1) of Schedule 6 to the Criminal Justice Act 1991 (application to dismiss charge following notice of transfer of case to Crown Court),

(c) the hearing of an application under paragraph 2(1) of Schedule 3 to the Crime and Disorder Act 1998 (application to dismiss charge by person sent for trial under section 51 of that Act),

(d) any hearing held, between conviction and sentencing, for the purpose of determining matters relevant to the court's decision as to how the accused is to be dealt with, and

(e) the hearing of an appeal,

and references (in section 41 or this section) to a person charged with an offence accordingly include a person convicted of an offence.

11.17 The term 'sexual offence' in the context of this provision is defined as being, subject to any order made by the Secretary of State altering the list in any way, any of the offences set out in the YJCEA 1999, s 62[1]. Thus, it is no longer merely an allegation of rape that attracts protection for the complainant.

1 See paragraph 12.45 below.

11.18 The term 'sexual behaviour' is defined as being 'any sexual behaviour or other sexual experience, whether or not involving any accused or other person, but excluding (except in the YJCEA 1999, s 41(3)(c)(i) and (5)(a)) anything alleged to have taken place as part of the event which is the subject matter of the charge against the accused'[1]. As there is no further assistance from the Act as to what this term means, it is likely that courts will look to earlier guidance from the higher courts to interpret the phrase, though it should be remembered that the SO(A)A 1976, which governed this topic referred to a complainant's 'sexual experience' rather than 'sexual behaviour'. It is expected that the courts will see this latter phrase as having a somewhat wider ambit than the former.

1 YJCEA 1999, s 42(1)(c).

11.19 The first step for the court, on an application to adduce evidence or allow cross-examination, will be to make a decision as to whether or not the alleged activity of the complainant constitutes 'sexual behaviour'. Thus evidence of sexual promiscuity on the part of the complainant is likely to come under the provision, but what of, for example, evidence of games such as strip poker or postman's knock that may have been played by him/her? If it is known that a complainant has had a pregnancy terminated, it might be said that evidence of the medical operation itself does not refer to 'sexual behaviour', and is therefore admissible (depending on its relevance) but the fact that she was pregnant clearly does, and would be likely to lead to a ruling that such evidence be excluded.

11.20 The primary effect of the YJCEA 1999, s 41(1) is that, in a case involving any of the qualifying sexual offences against any defendant, leave should always be sought before attempting to adduce evidence or asking a question in cross-examination about any sexual behaviour of the complainant.

11.21 Once it is established that the evidence sought to be adduced or the questions in cross-examination relates to 'sexual behaviour' of the complainant, the court has to decide whether leave should be granted. This question is governed by the YJCEA 1999, s 41(2). It is important to note that the subsection does not give the court a discretion to allow such evidence or questions. The judge or magistrates may not give leave unless they are satisfied that certain criteria have been fulfilled. The first question to be asked is whether the evidence comes under sub-s (3) or (5)[1]. If the court is satisfied that any of the criteria in those two subsections are fulfilled, then the second question to be considered is whether or not a refusal of leave might have the result of rendering unsafe a conclusion of the jury or the court on any issue in the case.

1 See paragraph 11.24 below.

11.22 In considering whether the YJCEA 1999, s 41(3) applies – which is essential before leave to adduce evidence or cross-examine can be granted – two findings must be made. The first is that the evidence or question must be relevant to an issue in the case. This aspect itself has two limbs to it. The YJCEA 1999, s 42(1)(a) states that a 'relevant issue in the case' means any issue falling to be proved by the prosecution or defence in the trial, whereas the YJCEA 1999, s 41(4) states that no evidence or question shall be regarded as relating to a 'relevant issue in the case' if it appears to the court to be reasonable to assume that the purpose (or main purpose) for which it would be adduced or asked is to establish or elicit material for impugning the credibility of the complainant as a witness. In the first instance, the court must decide that the evidence or question relates to a relevant issue in the case, but if it decides that the purpose (or main purpose) for adducing the evidence or asking the question is to impugn the credibility of the complainant then it should not be allowed, as not being an issue relevant in the case. Thus even if it is proposed to introduce evidence, or to ask any witness questions that might be seen as being aimed at impugning the credibility of the complainant to the offence, it must be disallowed.

11.23 In untangling the rather tortuous structure of the YJCEA 1999, s 41, sub-s (4) should realistically be considered first so far as whether or not the evidence or question is a 'relevant issue in the case' because if it is deemed that its purpose (or main purpose) is to impugn the credibility of the complainant then it cannot, under any circumstances, be considered a 'relevant issue in the case'. Having said that, if the court concludes that the evidence or question is a 'relevant issue in the case' then it must move on to the second question which relates to the nature of the evidence or question.

11.24 The second issue for the court is to decide whether or not the evidence or question comes under any of the three categories set out in the YJCEA 1999, s 41(3). These are dealt with in turn below.

Issue not Consent

11.25 This means that whatever it is that the evidence or question relates to does not have anything to do with the accused claiming that the alleged criminal act was undertaken with the complainant's consent. Examples of situations that might arise under this heading would be where the defendant asserts either that no offence occurred or that if it did it was not committed by him/her.

11.26 Perhaps perversely, another situation that could arise under this heading is when the accused's defence is that the act in question took place but that s/he honestly thought the complainant was consenting[1]. This is said because the YJCEA 1999, s 42(1)(b) specifically states that 'issue of consent' does not include any issue as to the belief of the accused that the complainant so consented. Thus whenever the *Morgan* defence is put forward, such matters pertaining to that defence cannot be regarded as being an 'issue of consent' and therefore the YJCEA 1999, s 41(3)(b) and 41 (3)(c) do not apply.

1 Often termed the *Morgan* defence after the case of *DPP v Morgan* [1976] AC 182, [1975] 1 All ER 8, CA.

Issue is Consent and Relates to Behaviour at or About the Same Time as the Offence

11.27 This means that the defence to the charge is consent and the evidence or question relates to alleged sexual behaviour on the part of the complainant undertaken by him/her in close proximity to the offence charged[1]. It is important to note that this must refer to the consent being given to a specific person rather than to any person. This aspect of the section is likely to cause difficulties for courts. It is submitted that the aim of this part of the provision is to prevent a defendant claiming that because the complainant consented to sexual behaviour with other people at an earlier time s/he therefore also consented with him/her at the time of the alleged offence.

1 YJCEA 1999, s 41(3)(b).

11.28 A case that gives a good illustration of such difficulty is that of *Viola*[1]. In that case the complainant, who was 22 at the time, was visited shortly before midnight by the defendant whom she knew slightly. He asked if she could help him find his car keys which were apparently near to her doorway. She helped him and then invited him into her home for an innocent purpose. Her evidence was that he went on to to rape her. He contended that the intercourse was entirely consensual. The trial judge ruled that the defence could not cross-examine the complainant as to her previous sexual experiences with persons other than the defendant. The questioning that was disallowed related to the complainant making sexual advances to two men who visited her flat, to her having sexual intercourse with her ex-boyfriend the afternoon after the alleged rape and that in the morning immediately after the alleged rape a man was seen sleeping on the complainant's sofa wearing nothing but a pair of slippers. Mr Viola's appeal was allowed on the ground that, had the jury been made aware of those incidents, in particular the sexual advances and the naked man on her sofa, they may well have concluded that his defence had some substance. Although the case was considered with regard to the earlier situation pertaining to rape under the SO(A)A 1976, s 2, it is interesting to note that the then Lord Chief Justice made the following remark:

> ... evidence of sexual promiscuity may be so strong or so closely contemporaneous in time to the event in issue as to come near to, or indeed reach, the border between mere credit and an issue in the case.[2]

1 [1982] 1 WLR 1138, 75 Cr App Rep 125, CA.

2 (1982) 75 Cr App Rep 125 at 130, CA.

11.29 Although an old case now, *Viola* may well be one that courts consider in trying to decide what amounts to 'sexual behaviour of the complainant which ... took place at or about the same time as that event'. There is no further help from the statute itself although, as the tenor of YJCEA 1999, s 41 is to protect the complainant from such questioning, courts may take a somewhat more strict line than that taken in *Viola*.

Issue is Consent and Relates to Similar Behaviour

11.30 Reference should be made to the YJCEA 1999, s 41(3)(c) throughout the discussion of this issue. The aim of this provision is to prevent any reference to sexual behaviour of the complainant unless it can be shown to amount to so-called 'similar fact evidence'.

11.31 There is a significant problem that arises in discussing the issue of similar fact evidence and YJCEA 1999, s 41(3)(c) that is, how will the courts approach the question of what constitutes similar fact evidence? The leading case in relation to similar fact evidence is that of *DPP v P*[1] which considerably broadened the approach that courts were allowed to take in considering such evidence. Prior to that case, the topic was governed by the earlier case of *DPP v Boardman*[2] which allowed for a much more constrained view of similar fact evidence. *DPP v P* was a quite revolutionary decision in that it immediately made the introduction of similar fact evidence a much more regular occurrence in criminal trials because it made the qualifying hurdle for such evidence much lower than it had been. The problem faced by the government in drafting YJCEA 1999, s 41(3)(c) was that it wanted a much narrower definition of similar fact evidence so that it would be that much harder for defendants to adduce it at trial.

1 [1991] 2 AC 447, 93 Cr App Rep 267, HL.

2 [1975] AC 421, [1974] 2 All ER 958, CA.

11.32 When the wording of the provision is considered, it seems that the parliamentary draftsman went back to the case of *DPP v Boardman* for his template in creating a situation where, for the evidence to be admitted, or question allowed, the sexual behaviour of the complainant in question would have to be akin to the similar evidence that was allowable against a defendant up until the case of *DPP v P.* In considering the topic in *DPP v Boardman* Lord Salmon said the following:

> ... if the crime charged is committed in a uniquely or strikingly similar manner to other crimes committed by the accused the manner in which the other crimes committed may be evidence upon which a jury could reasonably conclude that the accused was guilty of the crime charged. *The similarity would have to be so unique or striking that common sense makes it inexplicable on the basis of coincidence.* [Emphasis added][1]

1 [1975] AC 421 at 462C, HL.

11.33 Thus, for the question or evidence to be allowed under this limb, it is likely that courts will take on board the intention of Parliament in referring to the state of the law prior to *DPP v P* and be slow to allow such evidence or questions unless it can be shown that the sexual behaviour of the complainant does qualify under this more restricted interpretation of similar fact evidence.

Prosecution Evidence

11.34 It will be remembered that for the court to give leave for any evidence to be adduced or question to be asked, it must be satisfied that YJCEA 1999, s 41(3) or (5) applies. YJCEA 1999, s 41(3) has been fully dealt with above and sub-s (5) allows for leave to be given when the accused merely wishes to introduce evidence or ask questions in order to rebut evidence that has already been adduced by the prosecution of the complainant's sexual behaviour. An example of such a situation might be where the prosecution is put on the basis that the complainant was sexually inexperienced and was only able to explain the facts of the alleged offence because of those events. In such circumstances the defence might wish to adduce evidence of previous sexual behaviour of the complainant which rebuts the prosecution contention[1].

1 See *Funderburk* [1990] 1 WLR 587, 90 Cr App Rep 466, CA, for an example of a case in which such an application might have been successful.

11.35 It should be noted that the power of the court under this subsection is in addition to that under YJCEA 1999, s 41(2)(b) which allows for the court to consider whether or not a refusal to allow such evidence or question might render unsafe a conclusion of the jury or the court.

Procedure

11.36 The procedure for making an application under YJCEA 1999, s 41 is set out in YJCEA 1999, s 43. Section 43(1) states that the application must be made in private and in the absence of the complainant. It is submitted that the prohibition on the complainant being present during such an application is merely to protect his/her sensibilities. The thrust of the legislation is to encourage more complainants to come forward and give evidence at trial. It may have been considered that, even in the absence of the jury, complainants to sexual offences should still be protected from investigations into their past sexual behaviour.

R v A

11.37 The first case to be considered by the Court of Appeal and the House of Lords on this topic following the introduction of these provisions was that of *R v A (No 2)*[1] which had a very unusual, and rapid, journey from the Crown Court to the Court of Appeal, by way of an interlocutory application, and then to the House of Lords – even before trial! The defendant was charged with rape and his defence was that the complainant consented to the sexual intercourse, and possibly that he thought she was consenting. At a preparatory hearing prior to the trial the judge ruled that the defendant would not be allowed to ask questions about a consensual sexual relationship he had had with the complainant during the three-week period prior to the alleged offence and that he would be able to ask her questions about her having sexual intercourse with a friend of his during the evening before the alleged rape. The trial judge allowed the questioning in relation to the sexual intercourse with the defendant's friend because it was deemed to be 'at or about the same time as the event which is the subject matter of the charge' within the meaning of YJCEA 1999, s 41(3)(b) whereas the evidence of the previous sexual relationship with the defendant would not be admissible under YJCEA 1999, s 41. In giving leave to appeal his decision, the judge opined that his ruling, though made under the constraints of YJCEA 1999, s 41, might breach the defendant's right to a fair trial under Article 6 of the Convention for the Protection of Human Rights and Fundamental Freedoms and the Human Rights Act 1998.

1 [2001] UKHL 25, [2002] 1 AC 45, [2001] 3 All ER 1.

11.38 The Court of Appeal[1] reversed the judge's ruling in relation to the friend's sexual intercourse with the complainant and ruled that evidence and questioning as to the defendant's previous sexual relationship with the complainant could be relevant to his belief in her consent and could therefore properly be admitted under YJCEA 1999, s 41(3)(a), but that such material was inadmissible on the issue of consent. Thus, the evidence was ruled to be inadmissible if the defence was consent, but admissible if the *Morgan* defence was advanced. This was said of course because of YJCEA 1999, s 42(1)(b).

1 Reported as R v Y (sexual offence: complainant's sexual history) (2001) Times, 13 February.

11.39 This latter point was conceded by the Crown at the Court of Appeal and led the Court of Appeal to note that a summing-up in such circumstances must direct the jury to consider the evidence only when considering the state of mind of the defendant, but to disregard it when considering the state of mind of the complainant. That interpretation of the legislation led to the Vice President to state that:

> If, and it appears to be so, that is the consequence of this legislation, it might be thought that a summing-up in such terms would owe more to Lewis Carroll than to sensible jurisprudence.

The Court went onto rule that the evidence of sexual behaviour of the complainant weeks, or even days, prior to the alleged offence cannot be admitted under YJCEA 1999, s 41(3)(b) or (c), but such evidence would be admissible under YJCEA 1999, s 41(3)(a).

11.40 Up to that point, although the Court of Appeal did not express any final and conclusive view on the issue (because at that stage it was not asked to) it was clear that, on the basis of their ruling, a defendant charged with a sexual offence would be best advised to claim that the complainant was consenting, or that s/he honestly thought the complainant was consenting.

11.41 The Court of Appeal recognised that the case raised an issue of general public importance and allowed an appeal to the House of Lords. It also recognised that, as the defence would be inviting the House of Lords to read down YJCEA 1999, s 41 in accordance with the HRA 1998, s 3 so that YJCEA 1999, s 41 could be given effect that would be compatible with the defendant's Convention rights and, if that was not possible, to invite the House to make a declaration of incompatibility, the Secretary of State should be represented at the appeal before the House of Lords. This meant that when their Lordships considered the issues pertaining to YJCEA 1999, s 41, they would have the benefit of full argument from the Director of Public Prosecutions, the defence and the Secretary of State.

11.42 As a result of the arguments put forward before their Lordships, it is interesting to note that the Secretary of State argued, on the Article 6 question, that 'unfairness to an accused will rarely arise because evidence of sexual experience between a complainant and an accused will almost always be admissible on the basis of the defence that the accused thought that the complainant consented'[1]. This appears to have been a tacit acceptance that the two defences go hand in hand, which suggests that the Vice President, in the Court of Appeal, was correct in his view of how a summing-up should be approached.

1 Paragraph 35 at 1559.

11.43 Following a comprehensive review of the relevant case law and academic literature, Lord Steyn concluded that the prohibition on potentially relevant evidence and questioning was far too restrictive to be compatible with a fair trial under Article 6 of the Convention. In his words:

> ... ordinary methods of purposive construction of [YJCEA 1999,] s 41(3)(c) cannot cure the problem of the excessive breadth of s 41, read as a whole, so far as it relates to previous sexual experience between a complainant and the accused. While the statute pursued desirable goals, the methods adopted amounted to legislative overkill'[1].

1 Paragraph 43 at 1562.

11.44 For the House of Lords, YJCEA 1999, s 41 is concerned with two distinct evidential issues. First, whether evidence of a sexual relationship between the accused and the complainant is entirely irrelevant to the offence charged and, therefore, should always be excluded; and, secondly, whether evidence of sexual behaviour between the complainant and a third party can ever be relevant to the issue of consent on the part of the complainant to a sexual act by the accused. Following a full analysis of the state of the case law and a purposive interpretation of YJCEA 1999, s 41 it was held that the temporal restriction in YJCEA 1999, s 41(3)(b) could not be construed as permitting evidence or questioning other than in respect of acts which were really contemporaneous with the incident charged and that it cannot be said that evidence of previous sexual history between the accused and the complainant should always be excluded.

11.45 In concluding his decision, Lord Steyn said the following:

> The effect of the decision today is that under [YJCEA 1999,] s 41(3)(c), construed where necessary by applying the interpretative obligation under [HRA 1998,] s 3, and due regard always being paid to the importance of seeking to protect the complainant from indignity and from humiliating questions, the test of admissibility is whether the evidence (and questioning in relation to it) is nevertheless so relevant to the issue of consent that to exclude it would endanger the fairness of the trial under Article 6 of the Convention. If this test is satisfied the evidence should not be excluded[1].

1 Paragraph 46 at 1564.

11.46 Following the ruling in *R v A* where the defence is consent, the situation with regard to the strictures set out in YJCEA 1999, s 41 can be said to be as follows:

(i) In order for evidence or questions to be admissible with regard to an issue under YJCEA 1999, s 41(3)(b), the sexual behaviour of the complainant in question would have to be contemporaneous to the alleged offence. An example might be where the accused asserts that sexual intercourse occurred twice while the two parties remained in bed together and the allegation of rape related to one of those incidents of sexual intercourse.

(ii) Evidence of a previous sexual relationship between the parties that is logically relevant may be admitted under YJCEA 1999, s 41(3)(c).

(iii) Evidence of sexual behaviour between the complainant and a third party is never likely to be admissible.

11.47 *R v A* is an extremely important decision in the context of interpreting YJCEA 1999, s 41 and it is important to note that the case relates to an allegation of rape and all of the discussions in the Court of Appeal and the House of Lords concern that offence. It should, however be remembered that YJCEA 1999, s 41 applies when the defendant faces an allegation of 'a sexual offence'[1] and the analysis set out by their Lordships applies equally to any qualifying offence.

1 See paragraph 11.17 above.

Chapter twelve

'Special measures' and prohibition on the cross-examination of witnesses

12.1 On 27 July 1999 the Youth Justice and Criminal Evidence Act 1999 received Royal Assent. Part I of the Act deals with the tackling of youth crime and the reform of youth justice procedures. Part II however, deals with a number of issues that have a bearing on the way trials involving sexual offences are carried out. The provisions set out in Chapter 1 of Part II of the YJCEA 1999 were brought into force on 24 July 2002 and the Government produced detailed rules relating to that part of the Act[1]. This Chapter will consider the provisions in Part II of the YJCEA 1999 that relate to so-called 'vulnerable witnesses' and how the Act is aimed at ensuring that the quality of the evidence of such witnesses is not diminished in any way.

1 The Crown Court (Special Measures Directions and Directions Prohibiting Cross-examination) Rules 2002, SI 2002/1688 and the Magistrates' Courts (Special Measures Directions) Rules 2002, SI 2002/1687.

12.2 The YJCEA 1999, Part II is broken up into a number of Chapters with Chapter 1, comprising ss 16 to 33, concerning itself with the issue of vulnerable witnesses and how their evidence should be given to the court. The provisions concerning this topic are quite extensive and complicated and it is not proposed to set them out here in any great detail but only to refer to the salient parts as they arise.

12.3 It is important to bear in mind that the sections of the YJCEA 1999 considered in this chapter relate to the witness rather than to the offence(s) charged. Thus it is not only with regard to sexual offences that the provisions apply. It is also important to note that the various qualification criteria for the use of special measures in a trial are somewhat different depending on whether the witness is a child or an adult. It is for that reason that each type of witness will be considered separately below.

12.4 A final point that should be noted is that the YJCEA 1999, ss 16 and 17 (which set out the eligibility criteria for witnesses) make it absolutely clear that an accused is not to be considered as a vulnerable witness, apparently under any circumstances, although defence witnesses can qualify. Thus, throughout the discussion of Chapter 1 of Part II of the Act, at no point is the defendant considered as qualifying for special measures of any kind when s/he gives evidence. A number of academic commentators have already opined that this aspect of the legislation is unlikely to survive an application under the HRA 1998.

12.5 In addition to the YJCEA 1999, Chapter 1, this Chapter also considers the YJCEA 1999, s 34 which is concerned with the prohibition on cross-examination of witnesses by the accused when s/he is charged with a sexual offence.

A Child Witnesses

Witness Eligibility

12.6 As indicated above, the rules pertaining to the eligibility of witnesses for special measures are extremely complex. However, the first point to consider, in relation to child witnesses, concerns their age at the time of the application or when a video was made of their testimony. The YJCEA 1999, s 16(1)(a) reads as follows:

> **16 Witnesses eligible for assistance on grounds of age or incapacity**
>
> (1) For the purposes of this Chapter a witness in criminal proceedings (other than the accused) is eligible for assistance by virtue of this section –
> (a) if under the age of 17 at the time of the hearing;

The YJCEA 1999, 16(3) makes it clear that the phrase 'at the time of the hearing' means the time when the court makes a determination as to the witness's eligibility for assistance. Thus if the witness in question is under the age of 17 at the time of the application for special measures in relation to him/her, then the direction must be made automatically.

The 'Primary Rule'

12.7 The YJCEA 1999, s 21 provides that a witness who qualifies for assistance under the YJCEA 1999, 16(1)(a) is to be referred to as a 'child witness' and that such a witness is in need of special protection if the offence, or any of the offences, involves sex, neglect, cruelty, violence or kidnapping[1]. Such a determination then leads on to what is called the 'primary rule' as set out in s 21(3). That subsection reads as follows:

> **21 Special provisions relating to child witnesses**
>
> (3) The primary rule in the case of a child witness is that the court must give a special measures direction in relation to the witness which complies with the following requirements–
> (a) it must provide for any relevant recording to be admitted under section 27 (video recorded evidence in chief); and
> (b) it must provide for any evidence given by the witness in the proceedings which is not given by means of a video recording (whether in chief or otherwise) to be given by means of a live link in accordance with section 24.

1 See YJCEA 1999, s 35(3).

12.8 The effect of this subsection is that once it is shown that the witness is under 17 years of age and therefore qualifies as an eligible witness under the YJCEA 1999, s 16(1)(a), the court has no discretion to refuse to make a direction with regard to a 'special measure'. Thus, under this provision there is no scope for the judge to consider the wishes of the witness, whether that particular special measure will improve the quality of the evidence or even to consider any possible prejudice to the defendant.

12.9 The primary rule is subject to limitations only to the extent that:

(i) the facilities to put the special measures in place must be available[1] (YJCEA 1999, s 21(4)(a));

(ii) the video recording, or part of it, may be excluded if the court is of the opinion, having regard to all the circumstances of the case, that in the interests of justice the recording, or that part of it, should not be admitted (YJCEA 1999, s 21(4)(b));

(iii) if compliance with it would not maximise the quality of the witness's evidence (YJCEA 1999, s 21(4)(c)).

However, the limitation in (iii) above does not apply if the witness is in need of special protection[2].

1 It should be noted that if a magistrates' court lacks the appropriate facilities, it is entitled to sit at any location that does have them.

2 See YJCEA 1999, s 21(5).

12.10 Finally, in relation to the eligibility criteria for the videoing of a witness's examination in chief, the YJCEA 1999, s 21(9) allows for the special measures direction to remain in place with regard to the child witness even though the witness reaches the age of 17 either before the evidence is given or before it is concluded.

Videotaped and Assisted Evidence

12.11 The result of all the above is that once a special measures direction is made in relation to a child witness, the admission of his/her evidence in chief by way of a video recording is mandatory so long as the facilities are available and subject to any necessary editing of the video evidence. Following the admission of the evidence in chief by video tape, the witness should then be cross-examined by way of a live television link[1]. It should also be noted that no further evidence in chief is to be adduced from the witness without the leave of the court and in very constrained circumstances[2].

1 See YJCEA 1999, s 24.

2 See YJCEA 1999, s 27(5) and (7).

12.12 The use of videotaped evidence in chief for children is nothing new. However, the YJCEA 1999, s 28 introduces the possibility for cross-examination and re-examination of vulnerable witnesses on video tape. This is a highly controversial innovation and it is difficult to say how it will eventually work in practice, or even if it will work at all[1]. The YJCEA 1999, s 28 allows that where a special measures direction provides for a video recording to be admitted under the YJCEA 1999, s 27 (evidence in chief), the direction may also provide for any cross-examination and any re-examination to be recorded on video tape. It further provides for the cross examination and re-examination to be made in the absence of the accused, but in such circumstances whereby the accused is able to see and hear the examination and to be able to communicate with his/her legal representatives. It is submitted that the only circumstances that would allow such a situation is where the accused watches events behind a two-way mirror, which may make the provision fall foul of the YJCEA 1999, s 21(4)(a), which relates to the availability of the special measure facilities.

1 So controversial in fact that YJCEA 1999, s 28, and also s 29 (the use of an intermediary), was not brought into force at the same time as the rest of Chapter 1. It remains the situation that it has yet to be brought into force.

12.13 The YJCEA 1999, s 29 allows for the witness to have the benefit of an intermediary, ie an interpreter or other person approved by the court for the purposes of the section[1]. The YJCEA 1999, s 30 allows for the witness, while giving evidence, to have use of any aids to communication that the court is satisfied s/he might need. This refers to the court ensuring that the witness can understand what is being asked and is able to properly communicate his/her answers.

1 See note 1 to paragraph 12.12 above.

Special Measures Direction

12.14 Once it has been decided that the witness is under 17 years of age and therefore qualifies as a 'child witness' under the YJCEA 1999, s 16(1)(a), and is 'in need of special protection' under the YJCEA 1999, s 21(1)(b), it must be decided in what form the special measures direction (SMD) should be made. The court must 'determine whether any of the special measures available in relation to the witness (or any combination of them) would, in its opinion, be likely to improve the quality of evidence given by the witness'[1].

B Adult Witnesses

Witness Eligibility

12.21 A 'child witness', as has been seen, is eligible for special measures automatically under YJCEA 1999, s 16(1)(a). The situation with regard to adult witnesses is somewhat different. For witnesses who are aged 17 or over, there are three qualifying criteria. The first appears at YJCEA 1999, s 16(1)(b) and renders a witness eligible for a SMD:

> If the court considers that the quality of evidence given by the witness is likely to be diminished by reason of any circumstances falling within [YJCEA 1999, s 16](2).

YJCEA 1999, s 16(2) reads as follows:

> (2) The circumstances falling within this subsection are –
> (a) that the witness –
>   (i) suffers from mental disorder within the meaning of the Mental Health Act 1983, or
>   (ii) otherwise has a significant impairment of intelligence and social functioning;
> (b) that the witness has a physical disability or is suffering from a physical disorder.

In such circumstances it would be necessary for the party applying for the SMD to satisfy the court that the witness did qualify under this provision and the application allows for the disclosure of expert evidence[1].

1 See Rule 9 at paragraph 12.38 below.

12.22 The other two criteria for eligibility for a SMD are set out in YJCEA 1999, s 17. The first is that the witness becomes eligible on the ground that the quality of their evidence is likely to be diminished due to fear or distress on their part. In determining whether or not the witness satisfies this criterion, the court must take into consideration the following points:

(i) the nature and alleged circumstances of the offence,
(ii) the age of the witness,
(iii) the social and cultural background and ethnic origins of the witness,

(iv) the domestic and employment circumstances of the witness,
(v) any religious beliefs or political opinions of the witness
(vi) any behaviour towards the witness by the accused,
(vii) any behaviour towards the witness by members of the family or associates of the accused,
(viii) any behaviour towards the witness by any other person who is likely to be an accused or a witness in the proceedings,
(ix) the views of the witness.

12.23 It should be remembered that this power is in addition to that under the CJA 1988, s 23(3)(b) which allows for the statement of a witness to be read to the court when the person does not give oral evidence 'through fear or because he is kept out of the way'. It is submitted that the question as to whether a witness is fearful of giving evidence must be considered at the time s/he is due to give that evidence rather than at any earlier stage[1]. If this were not the case then any number of circumstances might change between the videotaped interview being undertaken and the trial itself, that may make the witness less fearful of giving live evidence.

1 See for example *R v H, W and M* [2001] Crim LR 815, CA.

12.24 The final criterion as to eligibility for a SMD appears in YJCEA 1999, s 17(4) and applies when the witness is a complainant to a sexual offence. Such a person becomes eligible automatically unless they inform the court that s/he does not wish to be the recipient of any SMD.

Special Measures Direction

12.25 Once the decision on the eligibility of the witness has been made, all of the other aspects of Chapter 1 of the Act come into play and reference should be made to paragraphs 12.7 to 12.16 above with regard to this.

C Making the Application

12.26 On 24 July 2002 Parliament also brought into force the rules pertaining to the application for a SMD. Although there are two distinct sets of rules for cases that come before the Crown Court and those before the magistrates' court, they are generally set out in similar terms. The discussion below will normally refer to applications to the Crown Court and, where there are differences in the application, this will be made clear. The Schedules to both the Rules set out the format for such applications and prints model application forms. It should be pointed out that whoever was responsible for drafting the notes to the application form was ignorant of the fact that notification of a defendant's alibi is now covered by the CPIA 1996, s 5 and not the CJA 1967, s 11.

Rules 2 to 6

12.27 Rule 2 states that the application must be made in writing in the form prescribed in the Schedule to the Rules, or in a form similar to that set out in the Schedule. It is important to note that the forms in the Schedule appear in three parts (A, B and C). Part A must be completed in all applications whereas Parts B and C apply depending upon whether the application is for evidence to be given by live television link or by video tape, respectively.

12.28 With regard to cases before the Crown Court the application must be sent to all parties in the proceedings and to the relevant officer of the court. The application must be received by the appropriate court officer within 28 days of:

(i) the committal of the defendant; or
(ii) the consent to the preferment of a bill of indictment in relation to the case; or
(iii) the service of a notice of transfer under the CJA 1991, s 53; or
(iv) where a person is sent for trial under the CDA 1998, s 51, the service of copies of the documents containing the evidence on which the charge or charges are based under the CDA 1998, Sch 3, para 1; or
(v) the service of a notice of appeal from a decision of a youth court or a magistrates' court.

12.29 So far as applications made to the magistrates' court are concerned, the rules are slightly different. The application must be sent to all parties to the proceedings and to the justices' chief executive as follows:

(i) in the case of an application to a youth court, within 28 days of the date on which the defendant first appears or is brought before the court in connection with the offence; or
(ii) in any other case, within 14 days of the defendant indicating his intention to plead not guilty to any charge brought against him and in relation to which a special measures direction may be sought.

12.30 Rule 2(5) allows for any party to the proceedings to oppose the application and Rule 2(6) states that if the application is to be opposed then within 14 days of service upon the party opposing, s/he must inform, in writing, the applicant and the appropriate officer of the court of his/her opposition, giving reasons for the opposition. Rule 2(7) states that the person opposing the application must notify the court and the applicant.

12.31 Rule 2(8) states that if no opposition is received by the court, it may determine the application in favour of the applicant without a hearing or direct that a hearing to consider the application take place. If there is to be any opposition to the application then a hearing must take place, at which the defendant, or any defendants, are entitled to be present.

12.32 Rule 3 allows for an application to be made to extend the 28-day (or 14-day) period. The application can be made either before or after the period has expired and must be made in writing setting out the reasons why the applicant was unable to meet the prescribed timetable. The application and the reasons must be served on all parties to the proceedings.

12.33 Rule 4 allows for an oral application to be made even as late as the start of the trial, and for the court of its own motion to raise the issue of whether a SMD should be made. In such circumstances the court must consider whether it is right that any party to the proceedings should be allowed to make representations on the question and, if so, the time allowed for making such representations.

12.34 Rule 5 allows for the discharge or varying of any SMD that has been made. The application must be made in writing and must set out each and every material change of circumstance that the applicant alleges has occurred since the SMD was made. Again, all parties must be informed of the application and opposition may be made by a party in writing and with reasons for the opposition.

12.35 Rule 6 relates to the situation where a SMD has been refused and it is suggested that there has been a material change of circumstance with regard to the witness. Again, the application must be made in writing informing all parties to the proceedings of the renewed application. Any opposition to the renewed application must be made in writing, setting out all reasons for the opposition.

Rules 7, 8 and 9

12.36 Where an application is made to allow the evidence of a witness to be given by way of a live television link, Rule 7(2) states that if a party opposes that application, s/he must state 'why in his view the giving of a [SMD] would not be likely to maximise the quality of the witness's evidence'. However, Rule 7(3) states also that Rule 7(2) does not apply in relation to a child witness in need of special protection within the meaning of the YJCEA 1999, s 21(1)(b).

12.37 Rule 8 relates to the situation where the application is made for the witness to give evidence in chief by way of a videotaped interview. It sets out the detailed information that must be given to both the court and to all parties to the proceedings when the application is made.

12.38 Rule 9 allows for the introduction of expert evidence in support of the application. This might be necessary for example when the application relates to a witness who it is said is suffering from a mental disorder within the meaning of the Mental Health Act 1983, or has a significant impairment of intelligence and social functioning[1].

1 See paragraph 12.21 above.

D Defence Witnesses

12.39 It seems clear from a close reading of the statute and the rules that they were prepared primarily with prosecution witnesses in mind. The only concession to the possibility of an application for a SMD being made on behalf of a defence witness is in the notes to Part A of the Rules, in which it is said that an application for evidence to be given through a live television link or by means of a video tape 'need not disclose who that witness is, except to the extent that the disclosure is required [with regard to alibi evidence]'.

12.40 The provisions in the YJCEA 1999 dealt with in this chapter do, though, apply equally to defence witnesses who may need a SMD prior to them giving evidence. The criteria set out above apply equally to defence as to prosecution witnesses.

12.41 The first matter to be considered by a defendant's solicitor when thought is given to making an application for a SMD, for example in relation to the videotaped examination in chief of the witness, is to the circumstances of that video tape being made. In order for the court to make a SMD in those circumstances, it would have to be satisfied that the evidence on the video tape was given in the appropriate circumstances.

12.42 Perhaps the most significant factors to consider when dealing with an application for a SMD with regard to a defence witness are the extremely detailed provisions that are set out in Rule 8. This rule sets out what information must accompany the application and deals with the time the recording was made, where it was made, and in what circumstances it was made. This is all very well when the application is made by the prosecution whose investigating officers will, hopefully, be fully trained in interviewing child and vulnerable witnesses, will have access to dedicated suites for interviewing witnesses and for videotaping their evidence in appropriate surroundings, but will be rather more difficult for a legally-aided defendant to arrange and justify. In addition to which, as the defence do not need to disclose the existence of any witnesses on their behalf (save for alibi witnesses)[1], the use of a police suite for the videotaping of a defence witness's testimony would inevitably put the prosecution on notice that such a witness exists.

1 See paragraph 12.43 below.

12.43 A further difficulty that may arise for the court is that, save for alibi witnesses, it is not necessary for the defence to notify either the court or any other party to the proceedings of the existence either of the witness or of the intention to apply for a SMD until the close of the prosecution case. Is it to be envisaged that if such witnesses exist, the trial will be held up while the various applications are dealt with?

E Prohibition of Cross-Examination by the Accused

12.44 The YJCEA 1999, s 34 reads as follows:

> **34 Complainants in proceedings for sexual offences**
>
> No person charged with a sexual offence may in any criminal proceedings cross-examine in person a witness who is the complainant, either –
> (a) in connection with that offence, or
> (b) in connection with any other offence (of whatever nature) with which that person is charged in the proceedings.

12.45 The YJCEA 1999, s 62 sets out that the term 'sexual offence' means as follows:

(i) rape or burglary with intent to rape,
(ii) an offence under any of the SOA 1956, ss 2 to 12 and 14 to 17 (unlawful sexual intercourse, indecent assault, forcible abduction, etc).
(iii) an offence under the MHA 1959, s 128 (unlawful sexual intercourse with a person receiving treatment for a mental disorder by a member of hospital staff, etc),
(iv) an offence under the ICA 1960, s 1 (indecent conduct towards a child under 14),
(v) an offence under the CLA 1977, s 54 (incitement of a child under 16 to commit incest).

The YJCEA 1999, s 62(2) makes it clear that a reference to a 'sexual offence' also includes any reference to an attempt to commit the full offence and any offence of conspiracy to commit the substantive offence.

12.46 It is important to note that one of the effects of this provision is that if a defendant faces an indictment with at least one sexual offence on it, then s/he is not allowed to cross-examine the complainant to that sexual offence on any of the matters s/he faces. Thus, if a defendant is charged with kidnapping two people and with raping one of them then s/he would not be allowed to cross-examine the complainant to the rape charge even on the kidnapping charge. This situation is the same with regard to the YJCEA 1999, s 35 which is dealt with below.

12.47 In addition to the protection for complainants to sexual offences set out in the YJCEA 1999, s 34, s 35 also gives extensive protection to what are termed 'protected witnesses'. It reads as follows:

> **35 Child complainants and other child witnesses**
>
> (1) No person charged with an offence to which this section applies may in any criminal proceedings cross-examine in person a protected witness, either –
> (a) in connection with that offence, or
> (b) in connection with any offence (of whatever nature) with which that person is charged in the proceedings.
>
> (2) For the purposes of subsection (1) a 'protected witness' is a witness who –
> (a) either is a complainant or is alleged to have been a witness to the commission of the offence to which this section applies, and
> (b) either is a child or falls to be cross-examined after giving evidence in chief (whether wholly or in part) –
> (i) by means of a video recording made (for the purposes of section 27) at a time when the witness was a child, or
> (ii) in any other way at any such time.
>
> (3) The offences to which this section applies are –
> (a) any offence under –

(i) the Sexual Offences Act 1956,
(ii) the Indecency with Children Act 1960,
(iii) the Sexual Offences Act 1967,
(iv) section 54 of the Criminal Law Act 1977, or
(v) the Protection of Children Act 1978;

(b) kidnapping, false imprisonment or an offence under section 1 or 2 of the Child Abduction Act 1984;

(c) any offence under section 1 of the Children and Young Persons Act 1933;

(d) any offence (not within any of the preceding paragraphs) which involves an assault on, or injury or a threat of injury to, any person.

(4) In this section 'child' means –

(a) where the offence falls within subsection (3)(a), a person under the age of 17; or

(b) where the offence falls within subsection (3)(b), (c) or (d), a person under the age of 14.

(5) For the purposes of this section 'witness' includes a witness who is charged with an offence in the proceedings.

12.48 The YJCEA 1999, ss 34 and 35 were enacted in order to prevent a complainant to a sexual offence or children who are complainants or witnesses to sexual offences having to go through the trauma of answering questions put to him/her by the person alleged to have committed the offence in the first place[1].

1 But see, for example, *Lee* [1996] 2 Cr App Rep 266 a case that came before the Court of Appeal prior to the introduction of the YJCEA 1999 and where the witness was a young boy who watched as his father set fire to a wardrobe belonging to his ex-partner. The Court concluded that under earlier legislation the trial judge was correct to allow his evidence to be given by way of a videotaped interview and to giving the word 'threat' a very wide and purposive interpretation. See also *McAndrew-Bingham* [1999] 1 WLR 1897, [1999] 2 Cr App Rep 293, CA.

12.49 There is a certain amount of overlap in the two provisions and this emphasises Parliament's desire to protect witnesses who might appear to be vulnerable in any sense of the word. Thus, for example, complainants to sexual offences obtain protection from cross-examination by the accused under both provisions.

12.50 It should also be noted that under the YJCEA 1999, s 35(2)(b), where the evidence in chief of a child witness has been adduced by way of a videotaped interview and before his/her cross-examination s/he attains the age of 17, s/he remains a 'protected witness' for the purposes of those proceedings.

12.51 Even though Parliament appeared to envisage every possible scenario involving a vulnerable witness and sought to prevent the cross-examination of witnesses by the accused, just in case any situation was overlooked, it enacted the YJCEA 1999, ss 36 and 37. The former provision allows either the prosecutor to apply to the court, or the court of its own motion, to direct that the accused not be allowed to cross-examine a witness in person. The YJCEA 1999, s 36(2) sets out the criteria that the court must consider before making such an order. The criteria are the same as in relation to the question of whether a SMD should be made[1] and amount to considering whether the quality of the evidence is likely to be diminished by such cross-examination or improved by preventing it.

1 See sections A and B above.

12.52 There are two supplementary sections to the YJCEA 1999 that are of importance with regard to ss 34 and 35. The first is found in s 38 which concerns the situation where a person accused of a sexual offence represents him/herself. Where it appears to the court that ss 34 or 35 will apply it must take the following steps:

(i) invite the accused to arrange for a legal representative to act for him/her for the purpose of cross-examining the witness;
(ii) require the accused to notify it by the end of a specified period whether a legal representative is to act for him for that purpose;
(iii) if, by the end of that period the court is either, informed that no legal representative has been appointed, or not informed at all, it must consider whether it is necessary in the interests of justice for the witness to be cross-examined by a legal representative appointed to represent the interests of the accused;
(iv) if it concludes that, in the interests of justice, the witness should be so cross-examined, it must appoint a qualified legal representative to cross-examine the witness on behalf of the accused.

12.53 The YJCEA 1999, s 38 makes it clear that any person appointed by the court to cross-examine the witness in the interests of the accused shall not be responsible to the accused and will be entitled to be provided with evidence or other material relating to the proceedings. It is not clear from the provision whether the legal representative is entitled, or obliged, to take instructions from the accused before cross-examining the witness or will merely have to rely on papers and information provided by the court.

12.54 The second supplementary provision is the YJCEA 1999, s 39 which provides that the trial judge must give a warning to the jury so as to ensure that the accused is not prejudiced:

(i) by any inferences that might be drawn from the fact that the accused has been prevented from cross-examining the witness in person;

(ii) by the fact that the witness was cross-examined by a legal representative and not by a person acting as the accused's own legal representative.

12.55 While these provisions are of importance, it should be noted that it is extremely rare for a defendant to represent him/herself and one cannot help but remember the old saw that a person who represents himself has a fool for a client.

Chapter thirteen

Disclosure

13.1 This chapter concerns the disclosure of relevant material in the possession, in the first instance, of parties to the criminal process, and in the second, of third parties who play no part in the particular proceedings. It will concern itself primarily with disclosure by the prosecuting authorities followed by that of such third parties.

13.2 For the most part, disclosure of relevant material by the prosecuting authority is governed by the Criminal Procedure and Investigations Act 1996. That Act altered completely the disclosure regime that had built up over many years by way of case law and it specifically decrees that such common law rules shall have no effect following its introduction[1]. Thus while references may be made to earlier authorities in the discussion below, such authorities should be approached with some caution.

1 CPIA 1996, s 21(1) but s 21(2) states that s 21(1) does not affect the rules of common law as to whether disclosure is in the public interest.

13.3 As the rules set out in the CPIA 1996 have now been used by the courts since its inception, it is not proposed to elaborate on them overmuch. It is important to note that they relate to all criminal prosecutions and not just those concerning sexual offences. Unless it is specified in the discussion below, the regulations relating to disclosure of relevant material apply equally to all criminal offences.

13.4 In March 1997, the Sexual Offences (Protected Material) Act 1997 received Royal Assent. Its preamble announces it to be 'an Act to make provision for regulating access by defendants and others to certain categories of material disclosed by the prosecution or by the Criminal Cases Review Commission in connection with proceedings relating to certain sexual offences'. It has not yet been brought into force, but is included in this chapter because, if it is ever made law, it will have a significant impact on the way in which relevant material is disclosed to the defence.

13.5 An area of the law of disclosure that sometimes causes some difficulty and which arises more in relation to sexual offences than other offences is that pertaining to the disclosure of potentially relevant material in the possession of third parties. Such material might be held by schools, local authorities, caring organisations or charities. It is perfectly understandable that such organisations might be wary of disclosing confidential material held by them without a direct order from a court of law. This aspect of the law is dealt with in the third section below.

A Criminal Procedure and Investigations Act 1996

13.6 When a person is charged with a criminal offence in circumstances set out in the CPIA 1996, s 1 – which is intended to affect all possible scenarios concerning the charging of defendants – the part of the Act dealing with disclosure applies. Thus, in any case in which any investigation has taken place since the introduction of the Act (April 1998), CPIA 1996, ss 1 to 21 apply. The rules affecting the provision of a defence statement by the defendant are slightly different depending on whether a magistrates' court proceeds to summary trial or commits or transfers the matter to the Crown Court. In essence, if the trial is to take place at a magistrates' court then the provision of a defence statement by the defendant is voluntary whereas when the matter is dealt with in the Crown Court such provision is compulsory, if 'secondary disclosure' is sought.

13.7 The CPIA 1996, s 3 introduced the concept of 'primary disclosure' which places a duty on the prosecutor. The CPIA 1996, s 3, as amended, reads as follows:

3 Primary disclosure by prosecutor

(1) The prosecutor must –
(a) disclose to the accused any prosecution material which has not previously been disclosed to the accused and which in the prosecutor's opinion might undermine the case for the prosecution against the accused, or
(b) give to the accused a written statement that there is no material of a description mentioned in paragraph (a).

(2) For the purposes of this section prosecution material is material –
(a) which is in the prosecutor's possession, and came into his possession in connection with the case for the prosecution against the accused, or
(b) which, in pursuance of a code operative under Part II, he has inspected in connection with the case for the prosecution against the accused.

(3) Where material consists of information which has been recorded in any form the prosecutor discloses it for the purposes of this section –
(a) by securing that a copy is made of it and that the copy is given to the accused, or
(b) if in the prosecutor's opinion that is not practicable or not desirable, by allowing the accused to inspect it at a reasonable time and a reasonable place or by taking steps to secure that he is allowed to do so;

and a copy may be in such form as the prosecutor thinks fit and need not be in the same form as that in which the information has already been recorded.

(4) Where material consists of information which has not been recorded the prosecutor discloses it for the purposes of this section by securing that it is recorded in such form as he thinks fit and –
(a) by securing that a copy is made of it and that the copy is given to the accused, or
(b) if in the prosecutor's opinion that is not practicable or not desirable, by allowing the accused to inspect it at a reasonable time and a reasonable place or by taking steps to secure that he is allowed to do so.

(5) Where material does not consist of information the prosecutor discloses it for the purposes of this section by

> allowing the accused to inspect it at a reasonable time and a reasonable place or by taking steps to secure that he is allowed to do so.
>
> (6) Material must not be disclosed under this section to the extent that the court, on an application by the prosecutor, concludes it is not in the public interest to disclose it and orders accordingly.
>
> (7) Material must not be disclosed under this section to the extent that it is material the disclosure of which is prohibited by section 17 of the Regulation of Investigatory Powers Act 2000.
>
> (8) The prosecutor must act under this section during the period which, by virtue of section 12, is the relevant period for this section.

13.8 Once the prosecutor has complied with, or purports to have complied with, the 'primary disclosure' provision in the CPIA 1996, s 3, in order for any further disclosure to take place, the defendant must provide to the prosecutor and to the court a defence statement in accordance with the CPIA 1996, s 5. This section contains a number of technical provisions, but the most significant part, so far as the accused is concerned, are sub-ss (6) and (7) which read as follows:

> (6) For the purposes of this section a defence statement is a written statement –
> (a) setting out in general terms the nature of the accused's defence,
> (b) indicating the matters on which he takes issue with the prosecution, and
> (c) setting out, in the case of each matter, the reason why he takes issue with the prosecution.
>
> (7) If the defence statement discloses an alibi the accused must give particulars of the alibi in the statement, including–
> (a) the name and address of any witness the accused believes is able to give evidence in support of the alibi, if the name and address are known to the accused when the statement is given;
> (b) any information in the accused's possession which might be of material assistance in finding any such witness, if

his name or address is not known to the accused when the statement is given.

13.9 While it is allowable for any party at trial to comment on the failure of a defendant to provide a defence statement, the primary reason for producing such a document is to trigger 'secondary disclosure' by the prosecutor. Once a defence statement is provided to the prosecution within the relevant timescale, the onus falls on the prosecution to provide the defendant with 'secondary disclosure'. The provision of such information is governed by CPIA 1996, s 7.

13.10 The CPIA 1996, s 7 reads as follows:

> **7 Secondary Disclosure by Prosecutor**
>
> (1) This section applies where the accused gives a defence statement under section 5 or 6.
>
> (2) The prosecutor must –
> (a) disclose to the accused any prosecution material which has not previously been disclosed to the accused and which might be reasonably expected to assist the accused's defence as disclosed by the defence statement given under section 5 or 6, or
> (b) give to the accused a written statement that there is no material of a description mentioned in paragraph (a).
>
> (3) For the purposes of this section prosecution material is material –
> (a) which is in the prosecutor's possession, and came into his possession in connection with the case for the prosecution against the accused, or
> (b) which, in pursuance of a code operative under Part II, he has inspected in connection with the case for the prosecution against the accused.
>
> (4) Subsections (3) to (5) of section 3 (method by which prosecutor discloses) apply for the purposes of this section as they apply for the purposes of that.
>
> (5) Material must not be disclosed under this section to the extent that the court, on an application by the prosecutor,

concludes it is not in the public interest to disclose it and orders accordingly.

(6) Material must not be disclosed under this section to the extent that it is material the disclosure of which is prohibited by section 17 of the Regulation of Investigatory Powers Act 2000.

(7) The prosecutor must act under this section during the period which, by virtue of section 12, is the relevant period for this section.

13.11 It is CPIA 1996, s 7 that governs the issue of what else the prosecution must disclose to the accused in that the question only arises once a defence statement has been served upon them. Prior to the introduction of the CPIA 1996 the common law rules insisted that the prosecutor was under a duty to disclose everything in its possession that was relevant to the issue(s) at trial. The CPIA 1996, s 7 only authorises the disclosure of material that 'might reasonably be expected to assist the accused's defence *as disclosed by the defence statement*'. It is a provision that has been criticised as it puts the responsibility of concluding what disclosure might assist the defendant on the prosecution. That being said, the effect of the provision is that defence statements should be carefully framed in order to lead to the fullest possible disclosure on the part of the prosecutor.

13.12 The CPIA 1996, s 8 allows for application to be made to the court by the accused if s/he has reasonable cause to believe that the prosecution is in possession of material that might reasonably be expected to assist the accused's defence as disclosed by the defence statement which they are declining to disclose.

13.13 In practice, the prosecution will produce a list of non-sensitive unused material that has been decreed not to be likely to assist the defence as disclosed. It is then for the defendant to consider that list and decide what, if anything, they would like disclosed. If the prosecutor then refuses to disclose it, CPIA 1996, s 8 can come to the aid of the defendant in assisting the court to order disclosure if it thinks it necessary.

13.14 CPIA 1996, s 9 imposes a continuing duty on the prosecution to disclose relevant material that comes into its possession throughout the proceedings in question. It is important to note that the duty imposed on the prosecution by the CPIA 1996, s 9 relates to primary disclosure rather than secondary and thus the criterion to be used by the prosecution is whether or not the material 'might undermine the case for the prosecution' rather than assist the defence as disclosed[1].

1 See CPIA 1996, s 9(2)(a).

13.15 The CPIA 1996, s 10 sets out the sanctions available if the prosecution does not act within the relevant time limits and, in effect, prevents such failure, on its own, constituting grounds for staying the proceedings for abuse of process.

13.16 The CPIA 1996, s 11 sets out the sanctions available for the defendant either failing to provide a defence statement, providing a defence statement beyond the time limit, putting forward inconsistent defences, putting forward a different defence to that set out in his/her defence statement or for not giving details of an alibi put forward at trial. Those sanctions amount to any party, with the leave of the court, making such comment as appears appropriate, and for the court or jury to draw such inferences as appear proper in deciding whether the accused is guilty of the offence concerned[1].

1 See CPIA 1996, s 11(3).

13.17 The CPIA 1996, s 12 provides for the Secretary of State to prescribe the relevant time limits for the provision of defence statements. In accordance with the CPIA 1996, s 12, Parliament introduced the Criminal Procedure and Investigations Act 1996 (Defence Disclosure Time Limits) Regulations 1997, SI 1997/684. In practice, primary disclosure is usually undertaken at the committal or transfer proceedings. If that is not the case then it is normal for the prosecution to make that plain and, in due course, comply with the primary disclosure provisions by way of correspondence. Once that has been complied with the 1997 Regulations allow for the defendant to provide a defence statement within 14 days of the prosecution complying with CPIA 1996, s 3[1]. The court may, on application by the defendant before the expiration of the 14 days, extend that time period[2].

1 Regulation 2.

2 Regulation 3.

13.18 The CPIA 1996, ss 14, 15 and 16 relate to issues of non-disclosure by the prosecution on the grounds that it would be against the public interest. It will be noted that the prosecution can apply to the court not to disclose material on this ground under the CPIA 1996, s 3(6), 7(5), 8(5) and 9(8) which are set out in identical terms. The CPIA 1996, ss 14 and 15 (which relate to matters being dealt with in the magistrates' court and the Crown Court respectively) impose a duty on the court to keep the issue of non-disclosure on grounds of public interest under constant review and, if necessary, order disclosure by the prosecution.

13.19 The CPIA 1996, s 16 allows for an interested party to be heard before the court makes any decision as to the non-disclosure of material under this ground. If a party is able to show that it has an interest in the material or was involved in bringing the prosecutor's attention to the material, then the court must hear from that party before making such an order. This is a provision that is sometimes invoked when defendants are charged with sexual offences[1]. If, for example, material that is claimed to be of a sensitive nature is held by a local authority social services department, then that department should be heard by the court before deciding on the issue of whether to disclose it or not to on the ground that it would not be in the public interest to do so[2].

1 See section C below on the issue of third party disclosure.

2 These provisions should be seen in the light of the case of *Keane* (1994) 99 Cr App Rep 1, CA in which it was said that in deciding whether material held by the prosecution should be disclosed in the interests of justice, the trial judge should rule in favour of disclosure if the material might prove the defendant's innocence or avoid a miscarriage of justice.

13.20 The CPIA 1996, ss 17 and 18 concern the confidentiality of disclosed information. Although these are important provisions when any criminal offence is concerned, they are particularly significant when the accused is charged with a sexual offence. The provisions make it clear that the material disclosed can only be used for the preparation of his/her defence to that charge or for the preparation of an appeal. Any other use of the material is expressly forbidden without the permission of the court. Contravention of the strictures under the CPIA 1996, s 17 is to be treated as a contempt of court carrying with it maximum penalties of six months in prison plus a fine of £5,000 if the court dealing with the matter is a magistrates' court and two years in prison plus a fine if it is dealt with by a Crown Court.

13.21 The CPIA 1996, ss 19 and 20 deal solely with specific rules of court pertaining to disclosure of relevant material and the CPIA 1996, s 21(1) expressly disapplies any common law rules relating to disclosure that existed prior to the introduction of the Act. However, the CPIA 1996, s 21(2) states that s 21(1) does not affect the rules of common law as to whether disclosure is in the public interest.

B The Sexual Offences (Protected Material) Act 1997

13.22 As indicated above, the Sexual Offences (Protected Material) Act 1997 is not yet in force but, if it is ever introduced to the statutory canon, it will have a very significant effect on the disclosure regime as it pertains to sexual offences. The genesis of the SO(PM)A 1997 seems to have been the belief that material that was relevant in the case of sexual offences would inevitably come into the hands of offenders and would later be used, in the cases of convicted people at least, in prisons for nefarious purposes.

13.23 SO(PM)A 1997, s 1 sets out what is described as 'protected material' in relation to any qualifying sexual offence for the purposes of the SO(PM)A 1997. This means a copy (in whatever form) given by the prosecutor to any person under the SO(PM)A 1997, of any of the following material:

(a) a statement relating to that or any other sexual offence made by any victim of the offence (whether recorded in writing or any other form),

(b) a photograph or pseudo-photograph of any such victim, or

(c) a report of a medical examination of the physical condition of any such victim.

13.24 A 'victim of that offence' is defined as being any person who is named in the charge, summons or indictment as being the person against whom that offence was committed. Alternatively it can be a person in relation to whom, in the opinion of the prosecutor, the offence can be reasonably regarded as having been committed.

13.25 SO(PM)A 1997, s 1(3) states that the Act applies equally to any part of the protected material and to copies or part of a copy of such protected material. SO(PM)A 1997, s 1(4) disapplies the Act to any material that has been made by the defendant, that material being a copy of any protected material which is a manuscript copy which is not a whole copy of the protected material.

13.26 SO(PM)A 1997, s 2 concerns definitions of certain terms used in the Act, including 'defendant', 'legal representative' and 'sexual offence'. The relevant sexual offences to which the Act applies are set out in the Schedule to the Act and amount to the following offences:

(i) rape,
(ii) procurement of a woman by threats,
(iii) procurement of a woman by false pretences,
(iv) administering drugs to obtain intercourse with a woman,
(v) intercourse with a girl under 13,
(vi) intercourse with a girl between the ages of 13 and 16,
(vii) intercourse with a mentally handicapped person (although the schedule uses this more acceptable term, the offence still stands in the SOA 1956 as 'sexual intercourse with a defective'),
(viii) procurement of a mentally handicapped person,
(ix) incest by a man,
(x) incest by a woman,
(xi) buggery,
(xii) indecent assault on a woman,
(xiii) indecent assault on a man,
(xiv) assault with intent to commit buggery,
(xv) intercourse with a mentally handicapped person by hospital staff, etc,
(xvi) indecent conduct with young children,
(xvii) incitement of a girl under the age of 16 to commit incest by a man,
(xviii) possession of indecent photographs of children,
(xix) conspiracy to commit any of the above offences,
(xx) attempting to commit any of the above offences,
(xxi) inciting another to commit any of the above offences.

13.27 SO(PM)A 1997, s 2 also states that the term 'proceedings for a sexual offence' in the Act applies equally to any appeal or application for leave to appeal brought or made by the defendant and any application made to the Criminal Cases Review Commission by the defendant.

13.28 SO(PM)A 1997, s 3 is the most important provision in the Act and is therefore set out below in full. It reads as follows:

> **3 Regulation of Disclosure by Prosecutor**
>
> (1) Where, in connection with any proceedings for a sexual offence, any statement or other material falling within any of the paragraphs (a) to (c) of section 1(1) would (apart from this section) fall to be disclosed by the prosecutor to the defendant –
> (a) the prosecutor shall not disclose that material to the defendant; and;
> (b) it shall instead be disclosed under this Act in accordance with whichever of subsections (2) and (3) below is applicable.
>
> (2) If –
> (a) the defendant has a legal representative, and
> (b) the defendant's legal representative gives the prosecutor the undertaking required by section 4 (disclosure to defendant's legal representative),
> the prosecutor shall disclose the material in question by giving a copy of it to the defendant's legal representative.
>
> (3) If subsection (2) is not applicable, the prosecutor shall disclose the material in question by giving a copy of it to the appropriate person for the purposes of section 5 (disclosure to unrepresented defendant) in order for that person to show that copy to the defendant under that section.
>
> (4) Where under this Act a copy of any material falls to be given to any person by the prosecutor, any such copy –
> (a) may be in such form as the prosecutor thinks fit, and
> (b) where the material consists of information which has been recorded in any form, need not be in the same form as that in which the information has already been recorded.

(5) Once a copy of any material is given to any person under this Act by the prosecutor, the copy shall (in accordance with section 1(1)) be protected material for the purposes of this Act.

13.29 Thus, under SO(PM)A 1997, s 3, protected material must not be disclosed directly to the defendant by the prosecution under any circumstances. If the defendant is legally represented then the protected material must only be disclosed to that representative, having obtained an undertaking from him/her that s/he will comply with the obligations set out in SO(PM)A 1997, s 4. These undertakings amount to the following:

(i) S/he must take reasonable steps to ensure that:
  (a) the protected material, or a copy of it, is only shown to the defendant under circumstances of adequate supervision to prevent the defendant making a copy of it, and
  (b) the protected material is not shown to, and no copy is given to, any person other than the defendant. It is permissible to show the protected material to another person if it appears necessary to do so:
    (i) in connection with any relevant proceedings, or
    (ii) for the purposes of any assessment or treatment of the defendant (whether before or after conviction).

(ii) S/he must inform the defendant of the following:
  (a) that the material is protected under the Act,
  (b) that it can only be inspected in circumstances as set out in (i)(a) above, and
  (c) that the defendant would be committing an offence if the material were to be inspected in any other circumstances or if the defendant were to copy the material or otherwise reveal its contents to any other person.

(iii) S/he must inform any person to whom the protected material has been disclosed in accordance with (i)(b) above that no copies must be made of the protected material or its contents otherwise revealed, to any person other than the defendant and to the defendant otherwise than in the circumstances set out in (i)(a) above. S/he must also inform that person that an offence would be committed if the protected material is copied or its contents otherwise revealed in any other circumstances.

(iv) S/he must inform the prosecutor if s/he ceases to be the defendant's legal representative and give to the defendant's new legal representative (who has given the necessary undertakings) the protected material.

(v) S/he must inform the new legal representative, at the time of giving the material over, that it is protected material for the purposes of the Act and inform the new representative of the extent to which the material has been shown to the defendant, whether copies have been given to him/her and whether any copies have been given to any other person.

(vi) S/he must keep a record of every occasion on which the protected material has been shown to either the defendant or another person, or copies (if any) have been given out.

13.30 If the defendant is not legally represented then a different regime obviously applies. By SO(PM)A 1997, s 3(3), the protected material must be given to the 'appropriate person for the purposes of SO(PM)A 1997, s 5'. The appropriate persons under SO(PM)A 1997, s 5 are, if the defendant is remanded in custody, the governor of the prison or any person nominated by the governor for the purposes of this section (SO(PM)A 1997, s 5(2)(a)) or, if the person is not in custody, 'the officer in charge of such police station as appears to the prosecutor to be suitable for enabling the defendant to have access to the material' (SO(PM)A 1997, s 5(2)(b)).

13.31 The appropriate person in either circumstance must then take reasonable steps to ensure that the defendant has access to the material in accordance with SO(PM)A 1997, s 4[1]. SO(PM)A 1997, s 5 also gives the responsibility of informing an unrepresented person that the material is protected and will be passed to whichever person is appropriate on the prosecutor.

1 See paragraph 13.29 above.

13.32 SO(PM)A 1997, s 8 sets out that the offence of having possession of protected material, or a copy of it, of giving that material, or a copy of it to another person, or of otherwise revealing its contents to another person, carries maximum penalties of six months in prison plus a fine if dealt with by a magistrates' court or of two years plus a fine if dealt with in the Crown Court.

13.33 It will be seen then that if SO(PM)A 1997 ever becomes law it will no longer be possible for defendants charged with sexual offences to be in possession of witness statements, exhibits, etc, that formulates the case against him/her, other than in highly constrained circumstances. Apart from any other consideration, SO(PM)A 1997 would make it a very daring defendant who declines to obtain legal representation and who takes on the responsibility of running their own defence.

C Third Party Disclosure

13.34 Unlike parties to criminal proceedings, there is no duty upon anyone who is not a party to the proceedings to disclose any information or document whatsoever. Again it should be stressed that the rules governing the disclosure of relevant material in the possession of people or organisations who are not parties to criminal proceedings apply to trials of all criminal offences. However, they are rules that are often invoked by parties to trials involving sexual offences, primarily because many victims of such offences are vulnerable in one sense or another and have been the recipients of treatment or care of institutions or organisations.

13.35 If it is thought by a party to criminal proceedings that there is in the possession of a third party information or documentation that may be relevant material to the criminal proceedings, the starting point for obtaining access to that material is to attempt to obtain a witness summons. Such matters in the magistrates' court are governed by the Magistrates' Courts Act 1980, s 97 and in the Crown Court by the Criminal Procedure (Attendance of Witnesses) Act 1965, as amended by the CPIA 1996, s 66. The relevant parts of both provisions will be set out below but the discussion that follows will concentrate on applications being made to the Crown Court. The issues remain the same for applications before either court.

13.36 The relevant parts of the MCA 1980, s 97 read as follows:

> 97(1) Where a justice of the peace ... is satisfied that any person in England or Wales is likely to be able to give material evidence, or produce any document or thing likely to be material evidence, at an enquiry into an indictable offence by a magistrates' court ... or at the summary trial of an

information or hearing of a complaint by such a court and that that person will not voluntarily attend as a witness or will not voluntarily produce the document or thing, the justice shall issue a summons directed to that person requiring him to attend before the court ... to give evidence or to produce the document or thing.

(3) On the failure of any person to attend before any magistrates' court in answer to a summons under this section, if – (a) the court is satisfied by evidence on oath that he is likely to be able to give material evidence in the proceedings; and (b) it is proved on oath, or in such other manner as may be prescribed, that he has been duly served with the summons ... and (c) it appears to the court that there is no just excuse for the failure, the court may issue a warrant to arrest him and bring him before the court.

(4) If any person attending or brought before a magistrates' court refuses without just excuse to be sworn or give evidence, or to produce any document or thing, the court may commit him to custody until the expiration of such period not exceeding one month as may be specified in the warrant or until he sooner gives evidence or produces the document or thing or impose on him a fine not exceeding £2,500, or both.

13.37 The CPIA 1996, s 66 made extensive amendments to the CP(AW)A 1965, s 2. With regard to the issue of obtaining disclosure of relevant material in the possession of third parties the provision is comprehensive and of enormous importance and for that reason it is set out in full below. It now reads as follows:

2 Issue of witness summons on application to Crown Court

(1) This section applies where the Crown Court is satisfied that –

(a) a person is likely to be able to give evidence likely to be material evidence, or produce any document or thing likely to be material evidence, for the purpose of any criminal proceedings before the Crown Court, and

(b) the person will not voluntarily attend as a witness or will not voluntarily produce the document or thing.

(2) In such a case the Crown Court shall, subject to the following provisions of this section, issue a summons (a witness summons) directed to the person concerned requiring him to –

(a) attend before the Crown Court at the time and place stated in the summons, and
(b) give the evidence or produce the document or thing.

(3) A witness summons may only be issued under this section on an application; and the Crown Court may refuse to issue the summons if any requirement relating to the application is not fulfilled.

(4) Where a person has been committed for trial for any offence to which the proceedings relate, an application must be made as soon as is reasonably practicable after the committal.

(5) Where the proceedings concerned have been transferred to the Crown Court, an application must be made as soon as is reasonably practicable after the transfer.

(6) Where the proceedings concerned relate to an offence in relation to which a bill of indictment has been preferred under the authority of section 2(2)(b) of the Administration of Justice (Miscellaneous Provisions) Act 1933 (bill preferred by direction of Court of Appeal, or by direction or with consent of judge) an application must be made as soon as is reasonably practicable after the bill was preferred.

(7) An application must be made in accordance with Crown Court rules; and different provision may be made for different cases or descriptions of case.

(8) Crown Court rules –

(a) may, in such cases as the rules may specify, require an application to be made by a party to the case;
(b) may, in such cases as the rules may specify, require the service of notice of an application on the person to whom the witness summons is proposed to be directed;
(c) may, in such cases as the rules may specify, require an application to be supported by an affidavit containing such matters as the rules may stipulate;

(d) may, in such cases as the rules may specify, make provision for enabling the person to whom the witness summons is proposed to be directed to be present or represented at the hearing of the application for the witness summons.

(9) Provision contained in the Crown Court rules by virtue of subsection (8)(c) above may in particular require an affidavit to –
(a) set out any charge on which the proceedings concerned are based;
(b) specify any stipulated evidence, document or thing in such a way as to enable the directed person to identify it;
(c) specify grounds for believing that the directed person is likely to be able to give any stipulated evidence or produce any stipulated document or thing;
(d) specify grounds for believing that any stipulated evidence is likely to be material evidence;
(e) specify grounds for believing that any stipulated document or thing is likely to be material evidence.

(10) In subsection (9) above –
(a) references to any stipulated evidence, document or thing are to any evidence, document or thing whose giving or production is proposed to be required by the witness summons;
(b) references to the directed person are to the person to whom the witness summons is proposed to be directed.

2A Power to require advance production

A witness summons which is issued under section 2 above and which requires a person to produce a document or thing as mentioned in section 2(2) above may also require him to produce the document or thing –
(a) at a place stated in the summons, and
(b) at a time which is so stated and precedes that stated under section 2(2) above,
for inspection by the person applying for the summons.

2B Summons no longer needed

(1) If –

(a) a document or thing is produced in pursuance of a requirement imposed by a witness summons under section 2A above,
(b) the person applying for the summons concludes that a requirement imposed by the summons under section 2(2) above is no longer needed, and
(c) he accordingly applies to the Crown Court for a direction that the summons shall be of no further effect,

the court may direct accordingly.

(2) An application under this section must be made in accordance with Crown Court rules; and different provision may be made for different cases or descriptions of case.

(3) Crown Court rules may, in such cases as the rules may specify, require the effect of a direction under this section to be notified to the person to whom the summons is directed.

2C Application to make summons ineffective

(1) If a witness summons issued under section 2 is directed to a person who –
(a) applies to the Crown Court,
(b) satisfies the court that he was not served with notice of the application to issue the summons and that he was neither present nor represented at the hearing of the application, and
(c) satisfies the court that he cannot give any evidence likely to be material evidence or, as the case may be, produce any document or think likely to be material evidence,

the court may direct that the summons shall be of no effect.

(2) For the purposes of subsection (1) above it is immaterial–
(a) whether or not Crown Court rules require the person to be served with notice of the application to issue the summons;
(b) whether or not Crown Court rules enable the person to be present or represented at the hearing of the application.

(3) In subsection (1)(b) above 'served' means –
(a) served in accordance with Crown Court rules, in a case where such rules require the person to be served with notice of the application to issue the summons;

(b) served in such way as appears reasonable to the court to which the application is made under this section, in any other case.

(4) The Crown Court may refuse to make a direction under this section if any requirement relating to the application under this section is not fulfilled.

(5) An application under this section must be made in accordance with Crown Court rules; and different provision may be made for different cases or descriptions of case.

(6) Crown Court rules may, in such cases as the rules may specify, require the service of notice of an application under this section on the person on whose application the witness summons was issued.

(7) Crown Court rules may, in such cases as the rules may specify, require that where –
(a) a person applying under this section can produce a particular document or thing, but
(b) he seeks to satisfy the court that the document or thing is not likely to be material evidence,
he must arrange for the document or thing to be available at the hearing of the application.

(8) Where a direction is made under this section that a witness summons shall be of no effect, the person on whose application the summons was issued may be ordered to pay the whole or any part of the costs of the application under this section.

(9) Any costs payable under an order made under subsection (8) above shall be taxed by the proper officer of the court, and payment of those costs shall be enforceable in the same manner as an order for payment of costs made by the High Court in a civil case or as a sum adjudged summarily to be paid as a civil debt.

13.38 The CP(AW)A 1965, ss 2D and 2E relate to the issue of witness summons following a motion from the court rather than on an application by a party to the proceedings, the minutiae of which is similar to the details set out above.

13.39 The criteria for deciding whether a witness summons should be issued in circumstances where it is submitted by the applicant that the third party is in possession of relevant material was considered in *R v Derby Magistrates' Court, ex p B*[1]. It was made clear in that case that the procedure under MCA 1980, s 97 could not be used to obtain discovery of documents for use in cross-examination. Lord Taylor of Gosforth CJ, in giving his ruling, referred approvingly to the case of *R v Reading Justices, ex p Berkshire County Council* [1996] 1 Cr App Rep 239, in which Simon Brown LJ said:

> The central principles to be derived from [the] authorities are as follows: (i) to be material evidence documents must be not only relevant to the issues arising in the criminal proceedings, but also documents admissible as such in evidence; (ii) documents which are desired merely for the purpose of possible cross-examination are not admissible in evidence and, thus, are not material for the purposes of [MCA 1980, s] 97 ... [Counsel] contends ... that the jurisprudence under s 97 should be re-examined in the light of the general law governing disclosure in criminal cases, and that a less exacting test of material should be applied in future[2]. That is not a submission that I can accept. It seems to me that quite different considerations arise with regard to the production of documents by third parties ... I regard the principles established under s 97 as untouched by other developments in the criminal law[3].

1 [1995] 4 All ER 526. [1996] AC 487, HL

2 It should be noted that this case was decided before the introduction of the CPIA 1996.

3 [1995] 4 All ER 526 at 535.

13.40 Similarly, in *R v Clowes*[1] with regard to an application under the CP(AW)A 1965, s 2 it was said that a witness summons had to relate to evidence that was not only material but also admissible.

1 [1992] 3 All ER 440, 95 Cr App Rep 440.

13.41 Thus, in deciding whether or not a witness summons should be issued in such circumstances, assuming that the procedural details are satisfied, the court must be sure: first, that the application is not being made in order to obtain discovery of documents or material that it is intended should be used when cross-examining a witness to be called by another party to the proceedings; and, secondly, that the material in question is both relevant to the issues arising in the proceedings and admissible in those proceedings.

13.42 The Crown Court rules referred to in the CP(AW)A 1965, s 2 were produced by Parliament as the Crown Court (Miscellaneous Amendments) Rules 1999, SI 1999/598. They stipulate that the application shall be made in writing to the appropriate officer of the Crown Court and to the directed person and shall:

(a) contain a brief description of the stipulated evidence, document or thing;
(b) set out reasons why it is said the evidence, document or thing is likely to be material evidence;
(c) set out why it is thought the directed person will not voluntarily attend court or produce the document or thing;
(d) if the witness summons is proposed to require the production of a document or thing:
    (i) inform the directed person of their right to make representations at the hearing; and
    (ii) state whether the applicant seeks a requirement also to be imposed under the CP(AW)A 1965, s 2A and, if so, specify the place and time at which the applicant wishes the document or thing to be produced.

13.43 In addition, the application should be supported by an affidavit:

(a) setting out any charge on which the proceedings are based;
(b) specify the stipulated evidence, document or thing in such a way as to enable the directed person to identify it;
(c) specify the grounds for believing that the directed person is likely to be able to give the stipulated evidence or to produce the stipulated evidence or thing;
(d) specify the grounds for believing that the stipulated evidence is likely to be material evidence or, as the case may be, that the stipulated document or thing is likely to be material evidence.

13.44 Within seven days of receipt of the application the directed person is entitled to inform the appropriate court officer whether or not s/he wishes to make representations to the court with regard to the application.

13.45 Third parties who may be in possession of documentation that may be the subject of such an application can realistically make representations that the evidence, document or thing should not be disclosed under three headings: (i) that the evidence sought is not material to any issues in the case, (ii) that the evidence sought is not admissible in the proceedings, and (iii) that the evidence sought is protected under the rules governing public interest immunity. A good example of the procedure that should be followed when such an application is made was given in the case of *R v Higgins*[1] in which an application was made by the defendant for a local authority to disclose all of its records in relation to the complainant in charges of indecent assault (a seven-year-old boy). The local authority contended that the documentation should not be disclosed on the grounds of irrelevance and public interest immunity. The trial judge obtained the entire local authority file and, having read through it, ordered that three reports should be disclosed to the defence as being relevant to the defence. The Court of Appeal supported the way in which the trial judge approached the issue saying:

> ... the judge did the exercise of balancing which is required. He produced three documents which, having regard to the issue he knew to be a live one in this case, he considered to be relevant ...[2].

1 [1996] 1 FLR 137n.

2 [1996] 1 FLR 137n at 140.

13.46 It should be noted that, while an application can be made on behalf of the defendant for disclosure of documents or information in the possession of third parties, there is a sting in the tail of the legislation. The CP(AW)A 1965, s 2C(8) makes it clear that if the third party successfully obtains an order that the witness summons should be of no effect, the party applying for the disclosure could become liable for the third party's costs in opposing the application. This sanction might be enough for defence representatives to think long and hard as to whether such an application should be made in the first place.

13.47 A final point that should be made with regard to evidence, documents or things in the possession of non-parties to the proceedings is that if the prosecuting authorities decide to make an application for such disclosure of such evidence, perhaps in order to further their investigation, once that evidence comes into its possession, it may become disclosable under the provisions of the CPIA 1996, either as primary or secondary disclosure, depending on the circumstances.

Index